LITTERE BARONUM
THE EARLIEST CARTULARY OF THE COUNTS OF CHAMPAGNE

The cartulary of 1211 is the oldest surviving register produced by the chancery of the counts of Champagne. This first edition of the cartulary contains 121 letters received from the barons and prelates of the county during the rule of Count Thibaut III (1198–1201) and the first decade of the regency of his widow, Countess Blanche (1201–22). They deal primarily with feudal matters – homage, tenure, the construction and rendering of castles – and lordship over property and rural communities. Since only one-third of the original letters survive, the cartulary copies are particularly valuable in capturing the range of written records entering the chancery of a major French principality around 1200.

The introduction to the volume traces the evolution of aristocratic letters patent from the 1140s and argues that they were far more important in the twelfth century, both for transactions between laymen and for transactions with religious houses, than historians of medieval diplomacy have allowed. The introduction goes on to discuss the evolution of the chancery in the twelfth century, the creation of a formal chancery archive in the 1190s, and the organization and contents of the cartulary compiled in 1211.

THEODORE EVERGATES is a professor of history at McDaniel College.

Medieval Academy Books, No. 107

Littere Baronum

The Earliest Cartulary of the Counts of Champagne

Edited by Theodore Evergates

Published for the Medieval Academy of America by
University of Toronto Press

University of Toronto Press Incorporated
Toronto Buffalo London
Printed in Canada
Reprinted in paperback 2014
ISBN 978-0-8020-8762-1 (cloth)
ISBN 978-1-4426-5765-6 (paper)

Printed on acid-free paper

National Library of Canada Cataloguing in Publication

Littere baronum : the earliest cartulary of the counts of Champagne / edited by Theodore Evergates.

(Medieval Academy books ; 107)
Includes bibliographical references and index.
ISBN 978-0-8020-8762-1 (bound) ISBN 978-1-4426-5765-6 (pbk.)

1. Champagne-Ardenne (France) – Charters, grants, privileges. 2. Champagne, Counts of – Archives. 3. Champagne-Ardenne (France) – Politics and government – Sources. 4. Champagne-Ardenne (France) – History – Sources. 5. France – Politics and government – 987–1328 – Sources. 6. France – History – Medieval period, 987–1515 – Sources. 7. Nobility – France – Champagne-Ardenne – History – Sources. I. Evergates, Theodore II. Medieval Academy of America III. Series.

DC611.C446L58 2003 944′.3021 C2003-901475-4

University of Toronto Press acknowledges the financial assistance to its publishing program of the Canada Council for the Arts and the Ontario Arts Council.

University of Toronto Press acknowledges the financial support for its publishing activities of the Government of Canada through the Book Publishing Industry Development Program (BPIDP).

CONTENTS

ILLUSTRATIONS

Figures

Tables

Cartulary-Register 1: The *Littere Baronum*
Archives Nationales, KK 1064, fol. 238r

PREFACE

In 1976 I encountered a large volume in the Archives Nationales (Paris) described simply as an 'autre cartulaire' of the counts of Champagne of circa 1230 and 'formé de plusieurs parties reliées ensemble au XVe siècle.'[1] Little did I suspect that the 393-folio volume, KK 1064, was not in fact a single volume of several parts but rather an assemblage of the earliest cartularies of the counts. It was a thrilling discovery, for although that volume is listed in the standard bibliographies on medieval Champagne, it had never been subjected to analysis, not even by Henri d'Arbois de Jubainville, who calendared the other comital cartularies. Within that volume are the surviving folios of the Cartulary of 1211, a copy of letters from the barons and prelates of Champagne stored in the chancery archive. It is today the oldest extant comital register from Champagne and the earliest princely cartulary from northern France.

Although the importance of the cartulary was apparent when I first saw it, teaching responsibilities and other research interests left little time for a close study of the manuscript. In 1999 a meeting of the Commission Internationale de Diplomatique offered me the opportunity to revisit the cartulary, now with the benefit of two decades of research on the medieval county and a resurgent interest in medieval diplomatics and the publishing of cartularies. It became clear that the Cartulary of 1211 deserved a modern edition.

I thank Giles Constable and Kimberly A. LoPrete for a critical reading of earlier versions of this edition, and I am grateful to All Souls College (Oxford) for a most congenial setting in which to explore the wider world of letters patent.

1 Henri Stein, *Bibliographie générale des cartulaires français* (Paris, 1907), 120, no. 858.

LITTERE BARONUM
THE EARLIEST CARTULARY OF THE COUNTS OF CHAMPAGNE

The County of Champagne

INTRODUCTION

The chancery of the counts of Champagne produced eight cartularies in the course of the thirteenth century.[1] Seven survive and the eighth is fully recoverable through modern copies, making them the largest collection of princely cartularies from medieval France. In the strictest sense, the cartularies are codex copies of incoming documents stored in the chancery's archive. When the first volume was produced in 1211, the archive held perhaps two hundred sealed letters (letters patent) from the barons and prelates of Champagne dealing in some respect with comital governance. By 1271, when the last two massive cartularies were compiled, there were well over several thousand letters in the archive. But after the county ceased to exist as an independent entity (1285), its archive was transferred to Paris (ca 1325) and many of the original documents disappeared, leaving the cartulary copies as the only source for many of the letters. It is no wonder that the early historians of medieval institutions regarded the comital cartularies as a storehouse of information on feudal practices and the governance of a medieval state. Louis Chantereau-Lefebvre (1662) and Nicholas Brussel (1727), in particular, borrowed extensively from the cartularies in their influential treatises on feudal institutions.[2] Henri d'Arbois de Jubainville (1859–69) calendared the letters in the cartularies to establish a chronology for his history of the counts, a narrative that has framed our understanding of the county ever since.[3] But neither he nor Auguste Longnon, who edited the feudal, financial, and domanial registers of the counts, explored the creation or significance of the cartularies themselves.[4] Today the cartularies remain unpublished and are rarely consulted.

The Cartulary of 1211 edited here is at once the earliest cartulary produced by the chancery and its oldest surviving register.[5] It belongs to the first generation of princely cartularies in western Europe that includes, notably, the cartularies of the Trencavel of Béziers and the Guilhem of Montpellier, each with

Table 1
The Counts and Countesses of Champagne

Hugh, 1093–1125
Thibaut II, 1125–52
Henry I, 1152–81
Marie, 1181–7 (regent)
Henry II, 1187–90
Marie, 1190–8 (regent)
Thibaut III, 1198–1201
Blanche, 1201–22 (regent)
Thibaut IV, 1222–53
Margaret, 1253–6 (regent)
Thibaut V, 1256–70
Henry III, 1271–4
Blanche of Artois, 1274–84 (regent)
Jeanne, countess and queen, 1285–1305

more than five hundred texts from the eleventh and twelfth centuries, and the *Liber feodorum maior* from Barcelona, which contains more than nine hundred acts from the same period.[6] Compared to those collections, the comital Cartulary of 1211, with about two hundred letters, was a modest achievement. Yet it was the earliest princely cartulary from northern France, predating by more than half a century the comparable volumes from the duchy of Burgundy and the counties of Blois and Bar-le-Duc (ca 1272).[7] And unlike the southern cartularies, the Cartulary of 1211 consists largely of author-sealed letters patent, a type of document that emerged in northern France with the adoption of personal seals by the barons in the middle decades of the twelfth century. What makes the Cartulary of 1211 particularly important in the history of medieval state-building is that it captures the moment when the counts of Champagne first collected sealed instruments from their barons and prelates. In exploiting the capacity of the barons to seal letters for their private affairs, the counts made letters patent, in effect, a tool of governance.

LETTERS OF BARONS

A chancery scribe described the lay letters copied into the Cartulary of 1211 as 'letters of barons' (*littere baronum*).[8] The scribes of the letters themselves also preferred *littere* to its synonyms *carta*, *pagina*, and *scriptum*.[9] Most of the letters refer to the *sigillum*, the pendent seal of authentication that allowed the recipient to read the letter without breaking the seal; four letters in the cartulary cite that very characteristic in referring to 'letters patent' and 'letters pendant.'[10] Unlike 'missive letters,' which simply report or request, letters patent are constitutive in that they convey or confirm something on the authority of the author's seal.[11]

Aristocratic Seals

In Champagne as elsewhere in northern France, it was only from the 1130s that castle lords below the royal, comital, and ducal level first acquired personal seals that enabled them to validate the instruments written in their names.[12] There are several reasons why they did so. In part it may have been a symbolic affirmation of lordly authority at the local level, perhaps in imitation of the king following Louis VI's adoption of a pendant seal in 1134.[13] But the general use of seals also reflected the need to validate written instruments in a period that saw an explosive increase in written records.[14] Monastic communities, too, encouraged the use of self-sealed documents by eliciting them directly from donors instead of seeking episcopal confirmations of oral acts, as had been customary. Simon of Broyes, lord of Beaufort, explained in 1155 that the Cistercian monks of Boulancourt asked him to confirm the gift his father and grandfather had made forty years earlier because, he said, 'at the time the gift was made, it was not customary to seal charters of donation.' Simon gave the monks his sealed letter of confirmation and, for even greater security, asked the bishop of Troyes to add his own seal to the document.[15] The seneschal Geoffroy III of Joinville responded to a similar request in 1157 by sealing a confirmation of his father's donations to the Premonstratensian brothers at La Chapelle-aux-Planches.[16] Related anecdotes described in the letters suggest that sealing by castle lords was still a novelty in the 1150s. Bartholomew of Vignory recounted how, at Clairvaux, he made peace with the monks over their acquisitions from his men and then, at Vignory, with his wife's consent, he sealed a document of confirmation drawn up in his very presence.[17] About the same time the Cistercian abbot of La Crête presented Bartholomew II of Nogent-en-Bassigny a seal matrix made by the monastery's own engraver; Bartholomew used it to seal a document ending his dispute with the monks.[18] By the 1160s most of the barons of Champagne had acquired personal seals.[19] Soon they were reconfirming the sealed letters, as well as the donations, of their ancestors.[20] Contributing to the increased use of sealed instruments in the following decades was Pope Alexander III's decretal, *De fide instrumentorum*, which declared that only documents validated by authentic seals retained their probative value after the deaths of the witnesses.[21] As if responding to that admonition, the letters in this collection consistently refer to the authenticating role of their seals.

Aristocratic women also began to acquire seals in those decades.[22] Ade, viscountess of Meaux, had a seal in 1165, and Agathe, heiress of Pierrefonds, had one in 1180.[23] Agnes of Brienne, on the other hand, one of the most prominent widows in the county, asked her brother to seal her letter of donation to the Premonstratensians at La Chapelle-aux-Planches, while Elizabeth of Pougy, widow of the marshal, used her deceased husband's seal, 'which is mine,' she said, to validate her grant to the Benedictines of Montier-en-Der.[24] But by the end of the century most well-born women were sealing letters patent, both alone and jointly with their husbands or minor sons.[25] Hermsend of Bar-sur-Seine was typical of that first generation of women who acquired personal seals. She lacked a seal during her twenty-five-year marriage (1159–84) to Anselm II of Traînel, the count's butler, and her four years as a widow and seven years as a remarried countess of Bar-le-Duc (1189–96). But after being divorced by her second husband and returning to her dower lands at Traînel, Hermesend acquired a seal. She first used it when asked to arbitrate an intractable dispute between the nuns of the Paraclete and the Cistercian monks of Vauluisant, two nearby communities she had known during her first marriage. Hermesend conducted an inquest, consulted with local wise men, then decided in favor of the nuns and gave them her sealed letter describing her decision.[26] Nine years later, in 1205, Hermesend gave Countess Blanche a sealed letter attesting to the homage she had done for her fortified dower residence; it is the earliest extant letter from a woman in the chancery archive.[27] Hermesend's sealed letters of 1196 and 1205 bracket a turning point in the use of aristocratic letters patent in Champagne. Before the 1190s they were used for private transactions between laymen and between laymen and religious institutions; a decade later self-sealed letters were being submitted to the count or countess of Champagne in recognition of a feudal relationship or other obligation.

Aristocratic Letters Patent

Letters patent are characterized by more than the presence of a personal seal.[28] They begin invariably with *Ego* and the name of the author, without an invocation. Addressed to all (*omnibus*, *universis*), present and future, they state that the author wishes to make known (*notum volo/facio quod*) some matter. The earliest letters often include the names of witnesses to a prior oral act, but soon the letters themselves with their validating seals became constitutive in their own right, without witnesses.[29] The letters are dated, usually to the month, and in some cases they name the place of sealing.[30] They conclude with a prominent corroborative clause, 'in testimony ... I have had this letter sealed by my seal.' The exact phrase varied, as scribes sought to individualize their letters, but in emphasizing the seal as validating the act, they established the probative value of the letter itself.[31] The letters of the barons appear to have been deposited or delivered without ceremony, unlike the letters of the counts, which were formally presented to the beneficiary by the chancellor who often noted in his own hand the place of presentation.[32]

The earliest baronial letters patent, like those cited above, were personal conveyances and confirmations of familial donations to religious institutions. The barons also sealed third-party letters, confirming the actions of their fiefholders and reporting arbitrations and judicial determinations in cases involving religious institutions. Bartholomew of Vignory, for example, sealed a letter for the monks of Clairvaux confirming the resolution of their dispute with his knight, Bertrand of Provenchères.[33] By the end of the twelfth century those various aristocratic letters patent took their place in monastic archives beside the more numerous royal and princely instruments, episcopal confirmations, and the internally produced notices of oral transactions.[34]

Letters patent dealing with transactions between laymen also found their way into the archives of religious institutions. In some cases, as with dower letters, the documents were surrendered as title deeds with the subsequent transfer of the dower property.[35] In other cases, lay letters were deposited in religious archives for safekeeping. Elizabeth of Dreux, the second and much younger wife of Hugh III of Broyes, deposited her dower letter at Clairvaux in order to protect her son's inheritance, as the letter stipulated that her dower lands would pass to him rather than revert to her husband's son by his first wife.[36] In a similar manner Caprarie of Plancy placed with the nuns at the Paraclete her brother Giles's sealed letter promising that she would receive her mother's inheritance.[37] Unfortunately, relatively few strictly lay letters have survived from twelfth-century Champagne. Those deposited in religious archives seldom were copied into the cartularies of those institutions, while the letters exchanged between laymen were discarded after losing their utility or were destroyed by haphazard storage. Letters deposited in the count's chancery archive, on the other hand, were preserved and often copied into the chancery's cartularies, which today contain the richest cache of lay letters.

The earliest aristocratic letters patent appear to have been written by their monastic beneficiaries.[38] Whether the barons also sealed letters drafted by episcopal chanceries or by non-recipient monasteries, as was the case in England, is not yet known.[39] But the chapters of canons established after 1150 do seem to have played a role in the production of private documents in Champagne. Count Henry I created almost two hundred benefices during his thirty-year rule, with major concentrations in Troyes and Provins of secular canons capable of drawing up letters patent.[40] Canons at Saint-Etienne of Troyes, for example, drafted the letters of donation that the count's treasurer,

Artaud, and marshal, Guillaume, sealed and presented to the nuns of the Paraclete before leaving for the Holy Land in 1179.[41] The barons who imitated the count in founding chapters of ten to twelve canons in their castles created virtual mini-chanceries of literate canons capable of preparing their documents. Bartholomew of Vignory's confirmation for Clairvaux was written by his chaplain.[42] Erard I of Chacenay, too, had a local scribe at Chacenay draft his letter confirming the gifts of his ancestors as contained in *their* letters stored in Clairvaux's archive.[43] The ease with which a powerful baron could have his instruments drawn up by his own clerics, by the scribes of his beneficiaries, or by third parties is illustrated by Robert I of Dreux, who used all three.[44] As castle lords acquired personal seals, and as the technology of letter writing moved beyond the monastery and cathedral to the chapter and castle, monastic *scriptoria* and episcopal chanceries lost their monopoly over the production and validation of written instruments. From 1150, letters patent could be produced almost anywhere and validated by anyone with a seal.

Latin remained the preferred language of aristocratic letters patent until circa 1230, when French came into use. More than six hundred original letters in French dated between 1230 and 1270 survive in the regional archives of Champagne, and many more originals and copies are preserved in the Archives Nationales and Bibliothèque Nationale in Paris.[45] The large number of extant instruments, whether in Latin or in French, suggests that the county was awash in self-sealed aristocratic letters in the thirteenth century.[46] As flexible instruments capable of recording a wide range of practices relating to governance, lordship, and familial matters, baronial letters patent remain a major unexplored source for the social history of twelfth- and thirteenth-century France.

THE CHANCERY AND ITS ARCHIVE

A chancery in the formal sense of a stationary writing bureau did not exist in Champagne before Count Henry I the Liberal (1152–81) made Troyes the political and administrative center of his new principality. After building a grand comital residence in the suburb of Saint-Denis just beyond the old city walls, Henry founded the chapter of Saint-Etienne to serve as his chapel, chancery, treasury, and necropolis.[47] The very size of Saint-Etienne (it dwarfed the bishop's cathedral within the old city) and its attachment to the count's residence left no doubt about its role in Henry's new state. Under his chancellor, the physician Guillaume (1149–75), a bureau of scribes drawn from the sixty or so resident canons drafted virtually all of the count's five hundred known acts and the two hundred acts of his regent widow Marie (1181–7, 1190–8) and son

Henry II (1187–90). The comital letters invariably record oral acts – donations, grants, confirmations, quitclaims, and arbitrations – that had transpired at the count's court, either in Troyes or in one of his secondary residences. Thus they also name the witnesses (until 1187), the notary who recorded the event, and the chancellor who presented the sealed document to the beneficiary. No longer did the count's chaplain seal documents written by the beneficiary (in most cases a monastic community).[48]

Like most princely chanceries in the twelfth century, Count Henry's chancery served primarily as a record-producing bureau rather than a record-keeping one.[49] Just what the canons of Saint-Etienne stored in the count's treasury and archive is not clear, because the building was reported to have been seriously damaged by a fire that destroyed much of Troyes on 23 July 1188.[50] Destruction of the comital archive at that time might explain why only eighteen items dated before 1188 can be identified as having been in the archive.[51] On the other hand, the count's feudal rolls (ca 1178), which presumably were stored there, survived the fire, and the treasury-archive was still usable in 1190 when Count Henry II deposited his own feudal rolls there before departing on the Third Crusade.[52] The chapter of Saint-Etienne's collection of its own vital documents, including its foundation charter (1157) and six other items dated before 1188, also survived the fire to be copied into the chapter's cartulary in 1271.[53] It would appear, then, that if fire damaged Saint-Etienne, it did not entirely destroy the comital archive in 1188.

What documents did the archive contain in 1188 beside the rolls of fiefs? There is no evidence that the chancery made copies of the count's outgoing letters, and thus the nine letters of Henry I identified as having been in the archive must have entered it after his death. The oldest item, Henry's 1158 grant to Archambaud of Sully, most likely was returned to the chancery in 1202 after Archambaud's son and grandson quitclaimed their right to redeem the mortgaged fief, as the letter allowed.[54] It is not known under what circumstances the remaining comital letters entered the archive, but it seems highly unlikely that the count's acts or duplicates of them were ordinarily placed in the archive.[55] On the other hand, the five royal letters (four from Louis VII and one from his brother Robert) certainly were on deposit at that time, as was the letter from the chapter of Senlis and the *pariage* agreement from the abbot of Saint-Oyand (see table 2). Those seven, seemingly random items, suggest that the archive may well have held other incoming letters before 1188. Count Henry's active interest in the economic life of his county, his oversight of the expanding trade fairs, and his political engagements with monarchs and regional princes must have generated a large number of directives and missive letters as well, like the ones preserved in the royal chancery at that time, but whether his chancery deliberately preserved them is not known.[56]

Notably absent from the chancery archive, even in the decade after the fire of 1188, are letters from the count's barons. The oldest baronial letter known to have been in the archive is the seneschal Geoffroy V of Joinville's letter of 1199 regarding his tenants living in the count's lands.[57] There is no evidence that the chancery held, either before or after 1188, written declarations of oaths or homages. When Countess Blanche circa 1205 wished to verify that the counts of Blois and Sancerre owed her homage, she was advised by her marshal, Geoffrey of Villehardouin, to consult the rolls of fiefs (*scripta feudorum*) stored at Saint-Etienne; he certainly would have referred to letters of homage in the chancery archive, had they existed.[58] Count Guillaume of Sancerre might well have done homage to Countess Marie when he succeeded in 1191, but he did not seal a letter of attestation at that time.[59] In that respect, he was like the count of Nevers, who said that he had done homage for his castle of Mailly to Countess Marie (ca 1184), then successively to Count Henry II, Thibaut III, and Countess Blanche, but did not seal a letter attesting to his homage until 1207.[60] The lack of letters from the count's barons was not unique to Champagne; the northern French princes collected very few baronial instruments before the 1190s.[61] Even in the royal archive, the earliest letter dealing with royal-baronial relations is the homage of Ida, countess of Boulogne, in 1191.[62] The absence of baronial letters from the royal and princely archives reflects the fact that neither the king nor the northern princes elicited sealed letters from their barons until the very end of the twelfth century, almost a half century after the barons had adopted personal seals to authenticate their private tranactions, and a quarter century after King Henry II of England required his barons (in 1166) to submit letters patent (the *cartae baronum*) attesting to their enfeoffed knights.[63]

King Philip II (1179–1223) began to collect sealed letters from his barons after returning from the Third Crusade in December 1191, and it was clearly at his insistence that he and Count Thibaut III (1198–1201) exchanged sealed instruments testifying to Thibaut's homage in April 1198.[64] The nineteen-year-old count took that example from the king, his uncle, back to Champagne, where he became the first count to collect sealed letters from his own barons. In essence, the king and the count began to exploit for their own purposes the instruments that the barons had been using for their private affairs.[65] The archiving of baronial letters was a natural consequence of that new practice. Within a decade the chancery archive acquired perhaps two hundred letters, and during the next half century it became a vast depository of sealed instruments documenting all facets of governance and feudal tenure.

Table 2
Letters in the Chancery Archive Dated before 1188

Date	Author	Subject	*Layettes*	CR 1	CR 3,4	CR 7
Count Henry I, 1152–81						
1158	Count Henry I	A. of Sully's fief		46		
1160	Robert I of Dreux	Savignies fortress		1	3,4	
1162	chapter of Senlis	notification to count		64	3,4	
1165	Count Henry I	Jouy forest		32	3,4	7.1
1165	Count Henry I	Sourdun forest	1:185	39		7.1
1167	King Louis VII	Savignies	1:208			7.3
1168	King Louis VII	Giles of Seuil's fief	1:215			
1174	Count Henry I	gift by countess Marie				7.1
1176	King Louis VII	merchants of Brienne	1:270			7.1
1176	Count Henry I	gift to Reclus	1:271			7.1
1177	King Louis VII	Traînel's fortification	1:277			7.3
1177	Count Henry I	a mortgaged fief		82	3,4	
1177	Count Henry I	Robert of Mitoy's men				7.1
1179	Count Henry I	Raoul of Combault		45	3,4	7.1
1179	Count Henry I	commune of Meaux	1:299			7.1
Countess Marie, 1181–87						
1186	Countess Marie	La Ferté-Loupière	5:90	37		7.1
Count Henry II, 1187–90						
1187	Count Henry II	dispute over dependents		44		
1187	Abbot of St-Oyand	*pariage* over Sermaize	1:347	74	3	

A bold date indicates an extant letter in the Archives Nationales.
Layettes (volume, edition number): letters existing in the chancery archive when it was transferred to Paris in the fourteenth century.
CR 1 (edition number here): letters copied into the extant folios of the Cartulary of 1211.
CR 3,4: letters copied into cartularies CR 3 and CR 4 (1222).
CR 7: letters copied into cartulary CR 7 (1271).

THE CARTULARY OF 1211

Thibaut III was only twenty-two when he died in May 1201 in the midst of preparations for the Fourth Crusade. His wife of two years, Blanche of Navarre, daughter of Sancho VI the Wise, king of Navarre (1150–94), was in the last weeks of her second pregnancy.[66] Thrust into a role for which she had little preparation and perhaps even less inclination (she had earlier considered a conventual life), the twenty-two-year-old countess quickly rose to the occasion:

she immediately traveled to Sens to do homage to King Philip II, who thus became her protector and *de facto* guardian of the future Thibaut IV, born within days of her return to Troyes. Since the custom in Champagne – and in the realm, as King Philip later declared – was for counts to succeed their deceased fathers at twenty-one, Blanche would be regent for the next twenty-one years (1201–22).[67] The issue was somewhat clouded in Champagne, however, since the posthumous birth of her son potentially activated the inheritance claims of Thibaut III's nieces.[68] But the steadfast support of King Philip, who refused to consider any challenge to Thibaut's succession, made the first decade of Blanche's regency a relatively tranquil one.

In 1210 Blanche may have been jolted when the king insisted that she surrender her nine-year-old son for four years of residence at the royal palace, where Thibaut's cousins Jeanne and Marguerite, heiresses of Flanders, already were in royal custody.[69] Perhaps Blanche's need for a familial presence in Champagne led her to seek out her nephew Remi to fill the office of chancellor, vacant since March 1207.[70] Remi of Navarre, the illegitimate son of her brother Sancho VII the Strong, king of Navarre (1194–1234), appeared as chancellor of Champagne in January 1211.[71] He was the first outsider to hold an office that traditionally had been filled by a canon selected from the ranks of the collegiate chapters in Troyes and Provins.[72] Shortly after October 1211,[73] only nine months after Remi first appeared in Champagne, chancery scribes completed the first-ever comital cartulary (Cartulary-Register 1).[74]

The present fragmentary state of the Cartulary of 1211 makes it difficult to determine its intended purpose. Earlier monastic cartularies for Molesme and Montier-en-Der, and one for the cathedral chapter of Châlons-sur-Marne, bear little ressemblance to the comital cartulary in terms of content and organization.[75] The cartulary of 1211 might have been made as an archival finding-aid for the the convenience of the new chancellor, but it is also possible that Countess Blanche requested the volume as a record of her rule to date, for it was executed with great care: the folios are precisely ruled in a double-column format, the texts are copied accurately and *in toto*, and space has been left for rubrication (see p. viii). Whatever its original purpose, the cartulary in its current state does not reveal whether it was a copy of the entire comital archive or only of items deemed important in 1211.

Organization and Contents

The cartulary initially consisted of five eight-folio quires containing two hundred or more letters.[76] A decade later, when the volume was foliated, it contained only three quires and parts of two others, for a total of thirty-two

Table 3
State of the Cartulary

In 1211 (Quires)	In ca 1222 (Folios)	In 1232 (Quires)	In 15th century (KK 1064: folios)	Edition (numbers)
1	[I–VIII]	(30)		
2	[6 folios–] IX–X[1]	23	254–255	54–62
3	[4 folios–] XI–XIIII[2]	33	256–259	63–89
	[XV–XVI]		259bis[3]	90–91
4	XVII–XXIII [XXIIII]	(34)	260–266	92–122
5	XXV–XXXII	31	238–245	1–53

[missing folio]
(missing quire number)
1 The first six folios of this quire were missing at the time of the original foliation.
2 Folio XIIII is the last folio of a quire.
3 The left half of a single folio.

folios of the original forty folios. Sometime between 1222 and 1232 the entire first quire (folios I–VIII) disappeared, leaving only two intact quires and parts of two others from the original cartulary.[77]

The best preserved quire, the one foliated XXV–XXXII and marked *Littere Baronum* in the 1220s, appears to have been typical of the damaged quires. Four bifolios, each inserted into another, form an eight-folio quire. The folios were lined uniformly in double columns,[78] and fifty-three letters were copied in a steady hand from the beginning to the end, without blank folios and without additions.[79] It is possible that a small volume of forty densely written folios could have contained a complete copy of the chancery archive in 1211.[80]

The surviving folios contain 104 texts copied in 1211 plus seventeen others added between February 1212 and July 1214, for a total of 121 texts.[81] Original letters survive for thirty-eight (31 per cent) of the 121 texts.[82] A comparison of the originals with the cartulary copies confirms both the accuracy and completeness of the copies. The remaining eighty-three texts (69 per cent) are known through copies: twenty-three appear only in the cartulary of 1211,[83] while sixty were copied at least once again directly from the original letters into chancery cartularies in 1222 (Cartulary-Registers 3 and 4) and in 1271 (Cartulary-Registers 7 and 8). In most cases the Cartulary of 1211 gives the best, as well as the earliest, reading.

Fully 84 per cent (102) of the letters are dated between 1198 and 1211, that is, from the three-year rule of Thibaut III and the first decade of Countess Blanche's regency. Within the cartulary the letters are gathered pell-mell in two groups

Figure 2. Quire 31 (*Littere Baronum*)

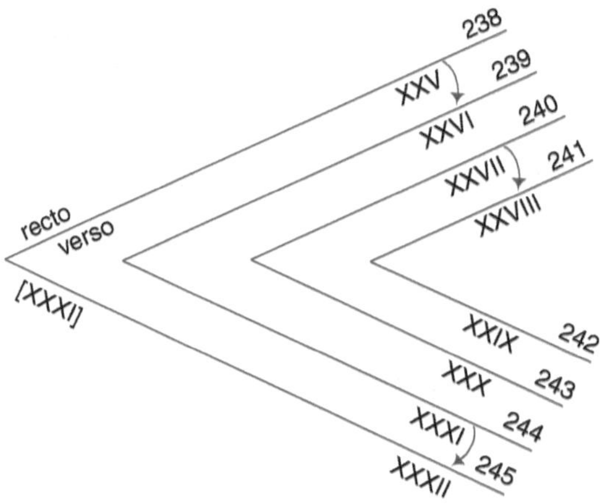

Foliation (15th century) of AN, KK 1064, fols. 238–245
XXV–XXXII: foliation of 1222
[XXXI]: quire number of 1222
↓ text continues from verso to recto

according to whether their authors were lay or religious persons, just as they must have been stored in the archive.[84] Thus the quire marked *littere baronum* consists primarily of letters from laymen: counts, dukes, and castle lords. That lay/religious divide remained the fundamental principle of archival classification through the thirteenth century, even after the chancery introduced subclassifications by subject (as in the cartulary of 1218) and author's title (as in the cartularies of 1222). In 1271 the chancery copied the letters from lay and religious persons into separate cartularies, each arranged hierarchically by author's title and date.[85]

Authors of the Letters

The extant folios of the cartulary contain an approximately equal number of letters from lay (sixty-two) and religious persons (fifty-nine). They are primarily from the barons and prelates of Champagne. Nine are from women.[86] But there are two notable absences among the lay authors. The first is the king: the two royal letters, additional entries of 1213 and 1214,[87] do not reflect the chancery's collection of royal letters at that time, as the later comital cartularies

Table 4
Authors of the Letters

	1158–97	1198–1201	1201–11	1212–14	Total
Lay persons					
King				2	2
Count(ess) of Champagne	7	4	1	2	14
Duke, count	1	3	14		18
Baron, lady		3	22		25
Other			3		3
Subtotal	8	10	40	4	62
Religious persons					
Pope, legate		2	2		4
Archbishop, bishop	1	4	12		17
Abbot, prior	1	4	16	3	24
Dean of chapter	1	1	10	1	13
Military order			1		1
Subtotal	3	11	41	4	59
Total	11	21	81	8	121

contain substantial numbers of letters from Louis VII and Philip II. It is highly likely that the royal letters were in the lost first quire, and that the intact cartulary had a more pronounced lay character than indicated by the surviving folios.[88] The absence of letters from knights, on the other hand, is not unique to this cartulary: very few letters from knights appear in any of the later comital cartularies, even though knights had personal seals by the thirteenth century and presented sealed letters to religious institutions.[89] One of the count's knights, Manasses of Villegruis, took his seal with him on the Third Crusade and sealed his own act at the siege of Acre.[90] But the comital chancery, like the royal chancery, had little direct contact with knights beyond recording their homages and taking their sworn statements during feudal inquests.

Subjects of the Letters

The letters fall into three broad categories of subject matter: castles and fiefs; lordship over rural communities and tenants; and Thibaut IV's succession. The first category, most fully represented by the quire labeled *littere baronum*, deals with castles,[91] homages,[92] and various transactions regarding fiefs.[93] What makes these documents particularly valuable is that they record what, a generation earlier, would have remained entirely oral and thus unrecoverable transactions. The best known of these letters is Count Thibaut III's grant to Jocelin of

Avallon, one of the earliest examples of a letter describing a new fief and probably typical of a class of comital letters dealing with feudal matters that later perished in the hands of their lay recipients. The letter survives because Jocelin's children returned it a decade later when they sold the fief to Countess Blanche.[94] Even more informative are the letters regarding baronial castles. Simon of Châteauvillan described how he initially resisted becoming the count's liegeman, preferring to hold his castle from his older brother (as was his right by custom in Champagne), but how in the end he yielded in return for a fief-rent. Simon's letter exists because the count died before fullfilling their oral agreement and Simon petitioned Countess Blanche for the promised rent.[95] Robert II of Dreux related how the countess licensed him to build a fortification on his allodial property only after he agreed to feudalize the property and surrender the new fortress to her on demand.[96] The details provided by those letters made them far more valuable records than the chancery's own feudal rolls containing brief entries that note only the existence of liegance and feudal service. The county-wide feudal inquest introduced by Henry I (ca 1178) and repeated by Henry II (ca 1190) and Thibaut III (ca 1201) was not employed again for a half-century; in effect, it was displaced by the more informative and probative letters patent.

The case of the count of Sancerre, who resisted doing homage to Countess Blanche, is revealing in this respect. Blanche not only compelled his homage but required him to seal two identical letters, drafted by her scribe, attesting to it. The counts of Brienne and Joigny, who witnessed the homage, jointly sealed another letter prepared by the same scribe. Blanche placed all three letters patent in her chancery archive as proof of the homage, even though the count of Sancerre was listed as her liegeman in an earlier feudal roll.[97] Three years later, in 1212, when Blanche convened her barons to enact a new custom governing the female inheritance of castles, she not only declared their consent, she displayed it in the thirty-three seals of the most prominent barons of Champagne appended to her document.[98] The king made similar demands of her barons, requiring ten named barons to swear oaths accepting his terms for Thibaut's succession *and* to seal letters patent (*litteras patentes*) attesting to their oaths. He stipulated further that when Thibaut eventually succeeded to the county, the same barons or their heirs were to take new oaths and provide new letters patent in attestation.[99] For both the countess and the king, the self-sealed instrument had become an essential tool for controlling the barons. That remarkable shift in practice was captured by the letters copied into the Cartulary of 1211.

The second category of letters in the cartulary encompasses several aspects of nonfeudal lordship, primarily property rights (sales, mortgages, debts, warranties) and the control of dependent men and women (regulations on travel between lordships and exchanges of tenants).[100] The contracts of joint lordship (*pariages*) over villages, both newly founded communities and refounded older ones, suggest a vigorous demographic and economic development of the countryside in the early thirteenth century. In order to attract new settlers to their villages, religious communities associated the count(ess) in lordship over their lands, with half of the revenues and rights. Sermaize, Villiers-en-Argonne, and La Neuville-aux-Larris were entirely new villages sponsored by the count on monastic properties.[101] Chaudefontaine, Esnouveaux, Lavilleneuve-aux-Frênes, and Dierrey-Moirey were refounded older villages.[102] The behind-the-scenes negotiating involved in these joint ventures is illustrated by La Neuville-au-Pont, where Thibaut III had to obtain lands from two monasteries before he could deliver a charter of liberties for a new village near his recently acquired castle of Sainte-Menehould.[103]

The third group of letters, relating to Thibaut IV's succession, would have figured prominently in this edition had the cartulary's first quire with the royal letters survived. Among the notable consequences of Thibaut IV's minority was the king's declaration regarding the age of male majority: in France, said the king in 1209, the custom was that 'no one under twenty-one years of age should be forced to answer about the inheritance that his father held without challenge at his death.'[104] Countess Blanche sent a copy of the letter to Pope Innocent III and to the overlords of the county, requesting their confirmations of that royal declaration.[105] Although the king simply stated the custom, the archbishop of Reims in his confirmation said that the king had approved or confirmed (*approbata*) the custom, and the duke of Burgundy and bishop of Langres claimed that the king had rendered a judgment (*judicium fecit*), that is, he had defined the custom. In effect, he had. The royal pronouncement confirmed what already had become the customary age of male majority within the comital family. But if the king was trying to change the practices of baronial families, he was not successful in Champagne, where the prevailing age of male majority in the absence of a father remained fifteen, as the High Court later affirmed.[106]

Transactions Described in the Letters

The largest number of letters in the cartulary (forty-eight letters or 40 per cent) served as title deeds in grants, sales, mortgages, and exchanges of property.[107] What is most striking, even within the context of the general mobility of property, is the ease with which fiefs circulated among laymen: they were granted, mortgaged, sold, and exchanged, and allodial properties were readily feudalized.[108] A related second category of transactions (thirty-nine letters or 32 per cent) consists of warranties and quittances for debt, letters of non-

Table 5
Subjects of the Letters

Subject	1158–97	1198–1201	1201–11	1212–14	Total
Homage		1	1		2
Castles					
Renderable	1		2		3
Mouvance			5		5
Fiefs					
Grant		2	1		3
Mouvance	1				1
Sale, mortgage, exchange	3	2	10		15
Dowry, dower		1	1	1	3
Subtotal	5	6	20	1	32
Lordship					
Pariage	1	4	6	2	13
Dependents, safeconduct	2	1	13	1	17
Property rights	2	3	18	1	24
Debts		4	10	1	15
Over religious persons	1	2	8		11
Subtotal	6	14	55	5	80
Succession of Thibaut IV			5	2	7
Spiritual matters		1	1		2
Total	11	21	81	8	121

prejudice,[109] recognitions of the count's right to license both the construction of fortresses and the election of an abbess.[110] But the cartulary includes only three feudal recognitions like the ones that became so common in the decades after 1211: Anselm III of Traînel and his mother Hermessend separately attested to their homages for the fortified residence of Villeneuve (1205),[111] and the count of Sancerre declared his liege homage for all his 'major' and 'minor' fiefs.[112] Most notable among the cartulary's confirmations is the *vidimus* of Stephan Langton, archbishop of Canterbury, of Count Henry I's grant to Saint-Martin of Tours and the men of Chablis fifty years earlier.[113]

The third category of transactions consists of agreements and settlements (twenty-four letters or 20 per cent). The process of conflict resolution unfortunately cannot be detected in the agreements that fail to mention any prior *contentio*, *controversia*, or *discordia*,[114] and in the contracts that mention only

Table 6
Transactions Described in the Letters

Type	1158–97	1198–1201	1201–11	1212–14	Total
Grant	1	8	8	1	18
Sale, mortgage, exchange	3	3	23	1	30
Quittance, receipt		3	3		6
Recognition, consent, warranty	3	3	26	1	33
Agreement		2	6	1	9
Dispute resolution	1	1	10	3	15
Notification, directive	3	1	5	1	10
Total	11	21	81	8	121

the peace they established.[115] Some conflicts were resolved directly between the parties themselves.[116] When that proved impossible, the parties resorted to binding arbitration, which often resulted in inquests to determine the facts at issue.[117] We know the outcome of two cases brought before the court of Countess Blanche: the canons of Saint-Quiriace, who claimed a wine tax from the taverners of Provins, were forced to compromise, whereas the monks of Saint-Médard of Soissons were awarded the taxes they sought from the knights of Villegruis.[118] But the disposition of the suit brought by Ade of Avesne, the widowed countess of Grandpré, against her step-son, Henri IV, for her community property and her daughter's dowry, is not known.[119]

Finally, the cartulary includes ten (8 per cent) directives or notifications. They include Count Henry I's orders to his officials to protect his forests,[120] royal and papal directives to the Templars,[121] letters of credence for the collection of debts,[122] and an abbot's request for guidance on how to respond to a royal bailiff's order.[123]

Comparisons with Contemporary Princely Cartularies

The Cartulary of 1211 bears only superficial resemblance to the earlier royal cartularies compiled by Suger of Saint-Denis and Hugh of Champfleury. Abbot Suger collected 164 letters he had received or sent while regent for the absent Louis VII in 1147–9.[124] Hugh, bishop of Soissons, amassed more than 400 letters during his term as royal chancellor from 1152 to 1172.[125] Most of the incoming letters in the two collections are undated reports, requests, and communications from princes and prelates, what we would call 'missive letters' or diplomatic correspondence.[126] Count Thibaut II, for example, complained to Suger about the harrassment of merchants coming to his trade fairs at Provins.[127]

Ida, countess of Nevers, asked Suger's help in recovering a loan in the absence of her husband on crusade.[128] Marie of Champagne, duchess of Burgundy, asked her brother-in-law Louis VII to find a suitable French wife for her son, and inquired about the recently widowed sister of Raoul of Vermandois, the royal seneschal.[129] Those missive letters are quite unlike the constitutive, sealed documents concerning homages, castles, fiefs, and lordship that make up the comital cartulary.[130]

The Cartulary of 1211 is also quite different from the first chancery register of Philip II, Register A of 1205, which consists largely of the chancery's own products, essentially royal acts and administrative lists (inquests, accounts, feudal lists, pledges).[131] Additions made to Register A between 1205 and 1211 are mostly of king's outgoing letters: in fact, 88 per cent of the letters in Register A (255 of 288) are outgoing royal letters, in stark contrast to the comital cartulary, where 88 per cent of the letters are incoming ones.[132] When the royal chancery recopied Register A into a new volume (Register C) in 1212, it reordered the materials into distinct chapters on fiefs, feudal service, revenues, inquests, and royal towns, but the materials it added to that register between 1212 and 1220 continued to be mainly outgoing royal letters.

Much closer in content to the comital cartulary are two princely cartularies from the south, both called *liber instrumentorum* and containing the constitutive acts of castle lords. The cartulary of the Trencavel, viscounts of Béziers and Carcassonne, composed initially in 1186–8, contains 585 texts from the eleventh and twelfth centuries dealing mostly with feudal matters: oaths (55 per cent of all the acts), grants, recognitions, sales, mortgages, and bilateral accords (*convenientiae*).[133] Two decades later the cartulary of the Guilhem of Montpellier copied 570 similar documents.[134] That volume's preface explains that it was compiled in order to preserve two types of written contracts. The first dealt with the lord of Montpellier's possessions in the see of Maguelone (including papal *privilegia* and other *instrumenta*); the second related to his other possessions as described in *placita, pacta, conventiones, constitutiones, donationes vel mutaciones ... et fidelitates factas vel faciendas, cum sacramentis, et cetera.*[135] Those two impressive cartularies stood in the shadow of an even grander collection from Barcelona, the *Liber feodorum maior* of the mid-1190s, containing more than 900 similar instruments spanning the same two centuries.[136] One wonders whether Remi of Navarre knew about the southern cartularies when he had the chancery scribes copy the comital archives shortly after assuming the chancellorship. But if he was inspired by them, he could not have imagined the fate of his own cartulary nor its influence within the comital chancery.

History of the Cartulary

Remi of Navarre's cartulary was completed by October 1211 but received additional entries between February 1212 and July 1214. The latest additions were royal letters affirming support for the countess and her thirteen-year-old son.[137] Inserted haphazardly, in hurried hands, they reflected the recent turn of events in Champagne. A local baron, Erard of Brienne, lord of Ramerupt and scion of one of the most prestigious lineages in the county, had challenged young Thibaut's right to succeed to the county. Erard acted on behalf of his wife Philippa, born to Count Henry II and Queen Isabelle of Jerusalem while Henry II was still count of Champagne. The strong preference in Champagne for succession by descent rather than by collateral transfer (to his brother, Thibaut III) gave Philippa a credible claim to her father's inheritance.[138] Following a series of inconclusive legal maneuverings (1213–16), Erard fomented a revolt by his relatives and fellow barons from south-eastern Champagne that erupted into a full-scale civil war (1216–18). With fierce determination, Blanche overcame the rebel barons, imposed a moderate peace, and assured her son's succession to a county both larger and more tightly controlled than Thibaut III had left it in 1201. Soon after hostilities ended in June 1218, Blanche's chancery – still under Chancellor Remi – created a second cartulary (Cartulary-Register 2) of documents related to the succession conflict and its resolution.[139]

With Thibaut IV's succession in May 1222, the chancery and its archive were thoroughly reorganized under a new chancellor, Guillaume.[140] The archive was closed and hundreds of letters were resorted and copied independently into two new cartularies. The volume known as the 'Cartulary of Countess Blanche' (Cartulary-Register 3) was a selective record of her regency and may well have accompanied her to Argensolles, the Cistercian convent that she founded for her retirement years (1222–9). The second cartulary, with a slightly different selection of letters (Cartulary-Register 4), remained in the chancery as a finding-aid to the closed archive. In those same years, the chancery inaugurated a new system of record-keeping by creating two open-ended registers. One register contained minutes of the count's outgoing letters in chronological order; it was the first attempt in France to keep a systematic register of a ruler's outgoing letters, seventy years before the comparable royal registers under Philip IV.[141] The second register recorded the homages of the count's fiefholders as they were done in Troyes, either directly to him or to a chancery surrogate.[142] By Christmas 1224, when Count Thibaut IV met with his barons in Troyes, his chancery had completed an efficient system for tracking the count's current business with his barons and fiefholders: an open archive of incoming letters received since May 1222, a register of the count's own outgoing letters, and a register of current homages. The closed archive of materials received before Thibaut's accession was accessible through a cartulary finding-aid (Cartulary-Register 4). At that point, the Cartulary of 1211 lost its organic tie to the archive and consequently its utility as a finding-aid; it became instead a commemorative volume, representing the archive (and the county) as it was in 1211. Some of the folios were missing, but a chancery scribe foliated in Roman numerals (I–XXXII) what remained of the cartulary and added the descriptive title *Littere Baronum* to one quire.

In 1232 the chancery recopied all its vital records. That unusual undertaking followed the armed invasion of Champagne by the northern French barons upset by Count Thibaut IV's behavior toward them and the regent queen, Blanche of Castile.[143] As foreign armies overran southern Champagne in 1229–30, there was a distinct possibility that Troyes itself would be torched. The vigorous leadership of the seneschal, Simon of Joinville, averted that fate, but the memory of the great fire of 1188 must have been in the air. The threat to the count's palace and the attached chapter of Saint-Etienne, where the archive and treasury were located, prompted the chancery to make duplicate copies of all its registers. The feudal rolls of Henry I and Henry II, perhaps seventy in all, were copied into a volume later known as the *Feoda Campanie*.[144] Incoming letters received between 1224 and 1231 were copied into a new cartulary (Cartulary-Register 5). Then the four cartularies in the chancery's possession (Cartulary-Registers 1, 2, 4, 5) were disassembled quire by quire and recopied in a composite, duplicate volume (Cartulary-Register 6).[145] The quires of the original cartularies were reassembled and bound together as a single volume that survives as KK 1064 in the Archives Nationales.[146]

That remarkable volume – a veritable compendium of the earliest comital cartularies – remained in the chancery until the fourteenth century, when it was sent with the other registers to the royal Chambre des Comptes in Paris. In the fifteenth century the volume was rebound, foliated, and inventoried with the other administrative registers from Champagne.[147] It was among the few registers from Champagne that later entered the Archives Nationales, where it was placed in the fonds 'Monuments Historiques.' Thereafter the fate of KK 1064 is obscure, and it is the one volume of comital cartularies that Arbois de Jubainville failed to calendar.[148] The existence of the Cartulary of 1211 thus has remained undetected within KK 1064. It is indeed ironic that the duplicate of KK 1064 made in 1232 (Cartulary-Register 6) has become known and cited (as the 'Cartulary of De Thou') because Jacques-Jean de Thou, master of the royal library (1594–1617), made it accessible after appropriating it for his personal library.[149]

NOTES

Numbers in bold type refer to items in the edition.

1 Theodore Evergates, 'The Chancery Archives of the Counts of Champagne: Codicology and History of the Cartulary-Registers,' *Viator* 16 (1985): 159–79.

2 Louis Chantereau-Lefebvre, *Traité des fiefs et de leur origine* (Paris, 1662), and Nicholas Brussel, *Nouvel examen de l'usage général des fiefs en France* (Paris, 1727; 2nd ed., 2 vols., 1750). Chantereau-Lefebvre was the first to understand the significance of the comital cartularies for a study of what he called *l'usage général des fiefs*; Brussel's *nouvel examen* was an even more rigorous examination of those same practices.

3 Henri d'Arbois de Jubainville, *Histoire des ducs et des comtes de Champagne*, 7 vols. (Paris, 1859–69).

4 Auguste Longnon, ed., *Documents relatifs au comté de Champagne et de Brie (1172–1361)*, 3 vols. (Paris, 1901–14).

5 None of the chancery's financial accounts or feudal rolls survive from the twelfth century; the feudal rolls are known through later copies (see Longnon, *Documents*, 1: vi–xix).

6 See below, Comparisons with Contemporary Princely Cartularies.

7 Robert-Henri Bautier, 'Cartulaires de chancellerie et recueils d'actes des autorités laïques et ecclésiastiques,' in *Les Cartulaires*, ed. Olivier Guyotjeannin, Laurent Morelle, and Michel Parisse (Paris, 1993), 369–76. None of the princely cartularies has been published.

8 See p. viii.

9 See the Index Rerum. It is not clear whether scribes in Champagne understood subtle differences in these terms. The royal chancery in England, which began to enroll documents in 1199–1202, did make clear distinctions between the documents that it registered separately as formal royal charters or diplomas (*rotuli chartarum*), as letters close (*rotuli litterarum clausarum*), and as letters patent (*rotuli litterarum patentium*); see Geoffrey W.S. Barrow, 'The English Royal Chancery in the Earlier 13th Century,' *Archiv für Diplomatik* 41 (1995): 243–4. French historians of medieval diplomatic traditionally have preferred charter (*carta*) as a generic term for non-royal letters patent (Arthur Giry, *Manuel de diplomatique* [Paris, 1894], 8–9), but the most recent manual of diplomatic adopts the term 'act' for any constitutive document (Olivier Guyotjeannin, Jacques Pycke, and Benoît-Michel Tock, *Diplomatique médiévale* [Turnhout, 1993], 16, 103–5). See also n. 28 below.

10 **11**, ***62**, **99**, **109** (referring to **77**).

11 Giles Constable, *Letters and Letter Collections* (Turnhout, 1976), p. 12, explains 'missive letter' as conferring no authority or legal right. See n. 56 below.

12 Jean-Luc Chassel, 'L'usage du sceau au XIIe siècle,' in *Le XIIe Siècle: mutations et renouveau en France dans la première moitié du XIIe siècle*, ed. Françoise Gasparri (Paris, 1994), 61–101. The Anglo-Norman barons also began to seal about the same time (T.A. Heslop, 'The Seals of the Twelfth-Century Earls of Chester,' in T.A. Thacker, ed., *The Earldom of Chester and Its Charters* [Chester, 1991], 179–84). The earliest example of an Anglo-Norman baronial letter with an authentic seal is a notification by Nigel d'Aubigny (1109–14) to his brother, in what seems almost a testamentary request to oversee his gifts to several religious houses (D.E. Greenway, ed., *Charters of the Honour of Mowbray, 1107–1191* [Oxford, 1972], 7–10, no. 3).

13 Jean Dufour, ed., *Recueil des actes de Louis IV, roi de France* (*1108–1137*), 4 vols. (Paris, 1992–4), 3: 114–16.

14 Chassel, 'L'usage du sceau,' 66–72.

15 André Duchesne, *Histoire généalogique de la maison royale de Dreux et de quelques autres familles illustres* (Paris, 1631), pt. 5 (Broyes), *preuves*, 20, 1155 (confirmation of a granary to Boulancourt): *Quapropter justis petitionibus vestris, carissimi fratres, libenter acquievi, videns voluntatem vestram esse, ut donum avi mei Hugonis Bardul* [d. ca 1110] *et patris mei Simonis* [d. ca 1132] *ante annos XL factum vestre ecclesie confirmarem impressione sigilli mei. Quia scilicet in tempore illo quo donum factum est, minime consuetudo esset de donationibus cartas sigillare*; *quas malitia dierum istorum non recipit, autoritate evacuans quas non sigillatas conspexit*. In 1131 Simon's father was asked by the abbot and prior of Molesme (perhaps in Troyes on the occasion of Count Thibaut II's confirmation of the foundation of Jully-sur-Sarce) to seal a confirmation of his own father's gifts to Molesme: *eis sigilli mei munimine perpetuo possidenda firmarem* (ibid., *preuves*, 12). That would be the earliest evidence of a baronial seal in Champagne.

16 Charles Lalore, ed., *Cartulaire de l'abbaye de Chapelle-aux-Planches* (Paris, 1878), 19–21, no. 20, 1157: *ego Gaufridus, Jovisville dominus, comitis Henrici senescaldus, notum facio posteris quod dominus Galterus, abbas, fratresque Capelle a me petierunt terras Longueville adjacentes, quas pater meus Rogerus eidem Capelle antiquitus contulerat, sibi collaudari tenoremque suum impressione sigilli mei informari. Quorum petitionibus libenter annuens pacifique et quieti eorum in posterum providens, ego Gaufridus, Felicitate* [of Brienne] *uxore mea, et filio meo Gaufrido, filia quoque Gertrude pariter collaudantibus ... concessi.*

17 Jean Waquet et al., *Receuil des chartes de l'abbaye de Clairvaux*, fascicules 1–2 (Troyes, 1950, 1982), 1: 54–5, no. 30, 1158: *Hanc quidem cartam ego Barthol-*

omeus apud Guanurri in conspectu meo scribere feci, sigillique mei impressione munivi. Bartholomew's chaplain, Matthew, witnessed the confirmation and probably drew up the act. It is the earliest extant baronial letter from Clairvaux's archive.

18 The original document of Bartholomew of Nogent-en-Bassigny (1140–80) is undated (cited in Chassel, 'L'usage du sceau,' 88–9 and n. 127: *amicus meus, dominus abbas de Crista, sigillum hoc de quo presens carta signata est, mihi in domo sua fabricati fecit cum sculptura sua*).

19 Chassel, 'L'usage du sceau,' 67.

20 In 1179 the monks of Clairvaux asked Erard of Chacenay (1179–91) to confirm the letter of his grandfather Anseric II (1107–37), which they presented to him; Erard accepted it as genuine (*cognovi ex authenticis instrumentis antecessorum meorum*) and sealed a letter of confirmation at his castle in Chacenay. At his request, the bishop of Langres later added his seal and noted that fact at the bottom of the letter (Charles Lalore, *Les sires et les barons de Chacenay* [Troyes, 1885], 27–8, no. 55). Twenty-five years later, Erard II of Chacenay (1204–36) sealed a confirmation of his ancestors' letters in Clairvaux's possession (AD Aube, 3 H 10, April 1206 [= Lalore, *Chacenay*, 37–8, no. 78]: *Cartas quas prefata domus Clarevallis habet ab antecessoribus meis et universas donationes eorum ... laudavi et approbavi*).

21 Chassel, 'L'usage du sceau,' 74–5, citing Harry Bresslau, *Handbuch der Urkundenlehre für Deutschland und Italien*, 2 vols., 2nd. ed. (Leipzig, 1912–32), 1: 656–8. The undated decretal (1159–81) reads: *scripta vero authentica, si testes inscripti decesserint, nisi [forte] per manum publicam facta fuerint, ita quod appareant publica, aut authenticum sigillum habuerint per quod possint probari, non videntur nobis alicuius firmitatis robur habere* (Bresslau, *Handbuch*, 1: 657, n. 1).

22 Brigitte Bedos-Rezak, *Form and Order in Medieval France: Studies in Social and Quantitative Sigillography* (Great Yarmouth, 1993), chaps. 9–10.

23 Ade of Meaux jointly sealed two letters with her husband in 1165: Abbé (Alexandre Clement) Boitel, *Histoire du bienheureux Jean, surnommé l'humble, seigneur de Montmirail-en-Brie* (Paris, 1859), 645–6, nos. 10–11. Agathe of Pierrefonds jointly sealed two letters with her husband in 1180: William Mendel Newman, *Les seigneurs de Nesle en Picardie, XIIe–XIIIe siècle*, 2 vols. (Philadelphia, 1971), 2: 171–3, nos. 86–7.

24 Agnes of Brienne: widow of Jacques I of Chacenay (d. 1158) and sister of Gautier III, count of Brienne (Charles Lalore, ed., *Cartulaire de l'abbaye de Basse-Fontaine* [Paris, 1878], 115–16, no. 89, undated [1181–91]). Elizabeth of Pougy, widow of the constable Odo of Pougy (1152–68), gave Montier-en-Der the fief held by Hulduin of Wallecourt and *sigilli mariti mei Odonis, quod meus est,*

impressione corroboravi (AD Haute-Marne, 7 H 13, 1182). Her letter could have been written by either of two witnesses: Bernard, her chaplain, or Guy, a cleric and son of the knight Hugh. Ermengard of Le Plessis, who also lacked a seal in 1188, had her feudal lord Henri, castellan of Vitry, seal her letter of donation to Cheminon (AD Marne, 17 H 135, no. 1); the monks took her letter to Count Henry II for his confirmation (AD Marne, 17 H 135, no. 2, 1188), which mentions her donation but not her letter.

25 Helvide of Dampierre jointly sealed at least five letters with her husband between 1200 and 1208; see **51** and P. Piétresson de Saint-Aubin, 'Notes sur le prieuré de 'Beaumont-lez-Montmirail,' *Nouvelle revue de Champagne et de Brie* 15 (1938), 240–2, nos. 1–2, 1200; and Boitel, *Montmirail*, 654, no. 33, 1207, and 655–6, no. 36, 1208. Isabelle, heiress of Laferté-sur-Amance, and her husband Gautier I of Vignory jointly sealed a letter for Clairvaux in 1202 (AD Aube, 3 H 9, 105, no. 6). Elizabeth of Châteauvillain sealed jointly with her son (**20**, **21**). See also n. 23 above.

26 Charles Lalore, ed. *Cartulaire de l'abbaye du Paraclet* (Paris, 1878), 115–16, no. 91, 1196: *presentem cartam notari feci et sigilli mei munimine roborari*. For Hermesend's life, see *__91__ n. 1.

27 *__91__.

28 Giry, *Manuel de diplomatique*, 815–22 ('Les chartes seigneuriales'), gives a classic description. A more extensive study that bears on practices in Champagne and northern France is R. Weemaes, 'Les actes privées en Belgique depuis le Xe jusqu'au commencement du XIIIe siècle: étude diplomatique,' *Analectes pour servir à l'histoire ecclésiastique de la Belgique*, 3 série, t. 4 [34] (1908): 5–45, 305–40, 416–40. See also the brief remarks in R.-H. Bautier, 'L'authentification des actes privés dans la France médiévale: notariat public et juridiction gracieuse,' in *Notariado público y documento privado: de les orígines al siglo XIV*, 2 vols. (Valencia, 1989), 2: 748–50, and Guyotjeannin, Pycke, and Tock, *Diplomatique médiévale*, 11–12.

29 The comital chancery, too, omitted the names of witnesses after the accession of Count Henry II in 1187.

30 Baronial letters in the Anglo-Norman realm follow the English royal example in remaining undated through the twelfth century; see Michael Gervers, ed., *Dating Undated Medieval Charters* (Woodbridge, 2000).

31 There is only one example in the cartulary of 1211 of autograph crosses appearing in lieu of a seal (**64**).

32 See **44**, **45**, **46**.

33 Waquet, *Receuil des chartes de l'abbaye de Clairvaux*, 2: 145–6, no. 134, 1169.

34 A large number of baronial writs and writ-charters survive in England. The lords of Mowbray, for example, sealed about four hundred letters in the twelfth century,

with seventeen known from Nigel d'Aubigny (1107–29); see Greenway, *Charters of the Honour of Mowbray*, 5–9, nos. 1–17. The earls of Chester produced about two hundred letters, including twenty-six from Ranulf II (1129–53); see John Hudson, 'Diplomatic and Legal Aspects of the Charters,' in Thacker, ed., *The Earldom of Chester*, 153–78.

35 That seems to have been the case with the five dower letters from the Laonnois; see Laurent Morelle, 'Mariage et diplomatique: autour de cinq chartes de douaire dans le laonnois-soissonais, 1163–81,' *Bibliothèque de l'Ecole des Chartes* 146 (1988): 227–8.

36 Duchesne, *Histoire généalogique de la maison royale de Dreux*, pt. 5 (Broyes), *preuves*, 18, 1197 [= Edmund Martène and Ursin Durand, eds., *Thesaurus novus anecdotorum*, 5 vols. (Paris, 1717), 1: 667]. We know about the letter (it was not copied into Clairvaux's cartularies) only because the monks produced a *vidimus* for Countess Blanche in 1201 that was later copied into CR 3, fol. 151r–v.

37 Lalore, *Paraclet*, 94–5, no. 77, 1189. The importance of the act is suggested by the witnesses: Haice of Plancy (her paternal uncle and the count's chancellor), Garnier II of Traînel (her maternal uncle), and two prominent local knights.

38 That was the case for Simon of Broyes and Geoffrey III of Joinville in the 1150s (see nn. 15–16 above).

39 The English barons clearly did rely on local monastic *scriptoria*. For the earls of Chester, see Teresa Webber, 'The Scribes and Handwriting of the Original Charters,' in Thacker, ed., *The Earldom of Chester*, 137–51, and Robert B. Patterson, *The Scriptorium of Margan Abbey and the Scribes of Early Angevin Glamorgan: Secretarial Administration in a Welch March Barony, c.1150–c.1225* (Woodbridge, 2002), an exceptionally detailed study that describes how Margan abbey served as a virtual chancery for the earls of Chester.

40 Patrick Corbet, 'Les collégiales comtales de Champagne (v. 1150–v. 1230),' *Annales de l'Est* 29 (1977): 207–8.

41 Lalore, *Paraclet*, 83–4, no. 64, 1179; 84–5, no. 65, 1179. The two oral acts were witnesssed by the same group of court officials; Artaud's letter contains an additional notation that it was presented to the nuns by the scribe Guillaume at Provins.

42 See n. 17.

43 See n. 20.

44 Andrew W. Lewis, 'Fourteen Charters of Robert I of Dreux (1152–1188),' *Traditio* 41 (1985): 154–5, and 162–3, no. 2, 1155: *Thomas capellanus qui hanc cartam scripsit*. The same Thomas may have written **1** here.

45 The original vernacular documents from Champagne now in the Archives Nationales and Bibliothèque Nationale de France in Paris have yet to be published. Original letters in the regional archives that have been published to date are in: Louis Carolus-Barré, ed., *Les plus anciens chartes en langue française, 1*:

Problèmes généraux et recueil des pièces originales conservées aux Archives de l'Oise, 1241–1286 (Paris, 1964) [202 letters]; Jean-Gabriel Gigot, ed., *Chartes en langue française antérieures à 1271 conservées dans le département de la Haute-Marne* (Paris, 1974) [275 letters, 1232–71]; Dominique Coq, ed., *Chartes en langue française antérieures à 1271 conservées dans les départements de l'Aube, de la Seine-et-Marne et de l'Yonne* (Paris, 1988) [103 letters, 1230–71]; and G. Hérelle and P. Pélicier, 'Chartes en langue vulgaire conservées aux Archives départementales de la Marne (série G), années 1237–1337,' *Bulletin historique et philologique* (1897): 624–717 [30 letters, 1237–70].

46 That phenomenon was not restricted to Champagne. In the cartulary of l'Abbaye-aux-Bois in Picardy, 60 per cent of the 247 letters (1202–79) were sealed by lay persons, primarily as donations and as confirmations of transactions by their fiefholders; see Brigitte Pipon, ed., *Le chartrier de l'Abbaye-aux-Bois (1202–1341)* (Paris, 1996).

47 Corbet, 'Les collegiales,' 198–204.

48 Most of Count Thibaut II's acts after 1129 were sealed by his chaplain, Roaul, without mention of the scribe who wrote the document. In some cases the context of the act suggests that the count directed his chaplain to seal a document drawn up by the beneficiary. The nuns of the Paraclete, for example, appear to have drawn up a document for the count's seal after their donors made an oral presentation before the count and countess at court: *Hec concessio facta est apud Pruvinum in presentia comitis Theobali et Mathildis comitisse, uxoris ejus, et per manum etiam ipsius comitis, qui comes, ut hec stabilis et inconvulsa in perpetuum permaneret, sigilli sui autoritate corroborari precepit. Huic concessioni interfuerunt et testes sunt: Radulphus capellanus comitis Theobaldi qui hanc cartam sigillavit* (Lalore, *Paraclet*, 62–3, no. 45, 1133).

49 The closest analysis of the comital chancery is Hans Eberhard Mayer, *Die Kanzlei des lateinischen Könige von Jerusalem*, 2 vols. (Hannover, 1996), 2: 566–762. The chanceries of the count of Flanders and duke of Burgundy likewise were document-producing bureaus: see Walter Prevenier, 'La chancellerie des comtes de Flandre dans le cadre européen à la fin du XIIe siècle,' *Bibliothèque de l'Ecole des Chartes* 125 (1967): 34–93; Thérèse de Hemptinne, Walter Prevenier, and Maurice Vandermaesen, 'La chancellerie des comtes de Flandre (12e-14e siècle), in *Landesherrliche Kanzleien im Spätmittelalter*, ed. Gabriel Silagi (Munich, 1984), 433–54; and Jean Richard, 'La chancellerie des ducs de Bourgogne de la fin du XIIème au début du XVème siècle,' in *Landesherrliche Kanzleien*, 381–413.

50 Robert of Auxerre, 'Chronicon': *Sancti Stephani basilica, quam comes Henricus fundarat et dotarat reditibus aurique et argenti et ornamentorumque varia supellectile adornarat, ... periit, et cum ea tota illa ornamentorum insignium*

congesta varietas (*Monumenta Germaniae Historica, Scriptores*, 26: 253).

51 See table 2. The archive of Notre-Dame-aux-Nonnains was destroyed by the same fire (only five documents survived); Count Henry II confirmed the convent's lost acts of his father and grandfather (Charles Lalore, 'Documents sur l'abbaye de Notre-Dame-aux-Nonnains de Troyes,' *Mémoires de la Société académique d'agriculture, des sciences, arts et belles-lettres du département de l'Aube* 88 [1874]: 10–12, no. 7, 1188).

52 Milo II Breban of Provins, the treasurer, informed Countess Blanche ca 1205 that he was present (in 1190) when Count Henry II deposited the feudal rolls at Saint-Etienne: *Ad tradendum vero scripta feodorum in ecclesiam Beati Stephani, ego Milo Brebanus interfui, et comes Henricus secum tulit exemplarium ultra mare* (Longnon, *Documents*, 1: xiii, n. 2).

53 A fragment of the original foundation charter survives (AD Aube, G 6); it is edited from the chapter's cartulary copy (BNF, Lat. 17098, Cartulary of Saint-Etienne of Troyes [1271], fols. 31r–32v) in Elizabeth Chapin, *Les villes de foires de Champagne des origines au début du XIVe siècle* (Paris, 1937), 279–82, no. 1.

54 **46**, **86**, **34**. Two other letters dealing with mortgaged fiefs were returned after Henry's death (**45**, **82**).

55 It is not clear why Count Henry I's directives to his forest sergeants (**32**, **39**) were in the archive in 1211.

56 See **64**. The count also received missive letters from his barons and officials, although it is not known where – or whether – they were preserved. In one instance, the count delegated Garnier of Traînel, the younger brother of the butler, Anselm, to settle a dispute between Montiéramy and Larrivour, two important monasteries near Troyes. Garnier's missive letter addressed to the count (*Domino suo natali Henrici, illustri comitis Trecensi, Garnerius de Triangulo, salutem et fidele servicium*) reports what Garnier had 'seen and heard' in the course of reaching a settlement with the aid of several prelates and barons. His letter to the count was sealed but undated (AD Aube, 4 H 1, Cartulary of Larrivour, 31–2, no. 19, ca 1174). Henry's own letter announcing the terms of the settlement borrows directly from Garnier's letter without mentioning it (ibid., 29–30, no. 18, 1174). Apparently Larrivour, as the beneficiary, was presented with both Garnier's report and Henry's formal letter; neither was retained in the chancery archive. See n. 130 for missive letters in the Cartulary of 1211.

57 **14**.

58 See **47** n. 3.

59 See **47**.

60 AN, J 1035, no. 3, 1207 [= Chantereau-Lefebvre, *Traité des fiefs*, 2: 32]. For the context of these homages, see Yves Sassier, *Recherches sur le pouvoir comtal en Auxerrois du Xe au début du XIIIe siècle* (Auxerre, 1980), 197–204.

61 See the *Layettes*, vol. 1, which consists largely of documents stored in princely archives until they were sent to Paris in the late thirteenth and early fourteenth centuries.

62 *Les registres de Philippe Auguste, 1: Texte*, ed. John W. Baldwin in collaboration with Françoise Gasparri, Michel Nortier, and Elisabeth Lalou (Paris, 1992), 1: 472–3, no. 31 (dated from 26 December 1191 to 4 April 1192).

63 King Henry II required his barons and prelates holding in chief to seal letters attesting to the number of knights they had enfeoffed. Each letter (*carta ... de militibus feffatis ex veteri feffamento et novo*) was copied verbatim, under the heading *Certificationes facta de feodis militum*, in a volume later known as 'The Red Book of the Exchequer.' See Hubert Hall, ed., *The Red Book of the Exchequer*, 3 vols. (London, 1896), 1: 186–445. Those returns are analyzed in Thomas K. Keefe, *Feudal Assessments and the Political Community under Henry II and His Sons* (Berkeley, 1983), 6–19.

64 **App. 1**.

65 M.T. Clanchy, *From Memory to Written Record: England, 1066–1307*, 2nd ed. (Oxford, 1993), 19, argues persuasively that in England the demands of royal government accelerated the use of written records and, by extension, practical literacy among lay persons, especially in the thirteenth century. Certainly that was the case in France; yet it is also clear that the barons were sealing letters for their own affairs before being required to do so by the king or the count.

66 Blanche was born in 1179 shortly before the death of her mother, queen Sancha of Navarre (Ann Trindade, *Berengaria: In Search of Richard the Lionheart's Queen* [Dublin, 1999], 47) and thus was about the same age as Thibaut III, who was born 13 May 1179.

67 Blanche's rule is described briefly in Theodore Evergates, 'Aristocratic Women in the County of Champagne,' in *Aristocratic Women in Medieval France*, ed. Theodore Evergates (Philadelphia, 1999), 81–5, and in greater detail in Arbois de Jubainville, *Histoire*, 4: 101–97.

68 In 1190 the unmarried Count Henry II (1187–97) had his barons swear to accept his eleven-year-old brother Thibaut (III) as his successor, should he not return to Champagne after the Third Crusade. But Henry married Isabelle, queen of Jerusalem, and their two daughters would have become his undisputed heirs had he returned to Champagne. After his death in Acre, their claims to Champagne remained problematic as long as Thibaut III was alive. The question of legitimate succession was reopened with Thibaut's death in May 1201, several days before the birth of his son.

69 Blanche had agreed in July 1209 to this surrender (**App. 2**). For Jeanne and Marguerite of Flanders, see Karen Nicholas, 'Countesses as Rulers in Flanders,'

in Evergates, ed., *Aristocratic Women*, 127–33.

70 It is not clear why Blanche kept the chancellorship vacant for more than three years (her letters are marked *vacante cancellaria*). Perhaps she was following the king's example of leaving the royal chancellorship vacant, or she may have been waiting for Remi to reach a suitable age.

71 Remi served as chancellor from January 1211 to February 1220, when he was elected bishop of Pamplona (he assumed that office by May 1220 and died in 1228). See Arbois de Jubainville, *Histoire*, 4: 526–7; and Jose Goñi Gaztambide, *Historia de los obispos de Pamplona, I: siglos IV–XIII* (Pamplona, 1979), 551–66. Nothing is known about Remi in Navarre before 1211. It is possible that he was the Canon Remi to whom Count Henry I granted a life income of 2.5 *modii* of grain in 1178 (AD Aube, G 2857 [copy of 1527]: to a *domino Remigio sacerdoti*). In 1196 Henry II promised that on Remi's death that revenue would pass to two priests in the cathedral chapter of Saint-Pierre of Troyes; the count identified Remi as *dominus Remigius, succentor ecclesie sancti Stephani, capelle mee* (Mayer, *Die Kanzlei*, 2: 920, no. 18, 1 October 1196, done at Acre). This Remi entered Saint-Pierre of Troyes in 1178, became sub-chanter in the comital chapter of Saint-Etienne, and then accompanied Henry II on the Third Crusade.

72 If the Remi mentioned in n. 71 was in fact Remi of Navarre, he would fit the requirement of being previously associated with a local chapter. The twelfth-century chancellors are listed in Arbois de Jubainville, *Histoire*, 3: 132–5, and 4: 525–6. For the role of collegiate chapters in the comital administration, see Corbet, 'Les collégiales comtales de Champagne,' 225–8.

73 The latest text in the cartulary's original folios is dated October 1211 (**75**).

74 I have used 'cartulary-register' (CR) to decribe the comital cartularies in order to distinguish these volumes concerned with governance from the ecclesiastical cartularies devoted primarily to possessions and rights (Evergates, 'The Chancery Archives,' 160 n. 7). Stein classified as cartularies all codex copies of archived records, including the royal cartularies of Philip II and Louis IX (Stein, *Bibliographie générale des cartulaires français*, 196–8). But the practice of recent historians, following Léopold Delisle, is to call the royal cartularies 'registers' to underscore the fact that the early ones (Registers A,C,E) are primarily copies of internally generated records rather than of archived incoming letters.

75 Warin, canon of the cathedral chapter of Châlons-sur-Marne, compiled a small cartulary in the early twelfth century (L.P. Pélicier, ed., *Cartulaire du chapitre de l'église cathédrale de Châlons-sur-Marne, par le chantre Warin* [Paris, 1897]). Montier-en-Der's first cartulary dates to circa 1127; see Laurent Morelle, 'The Metamorphosis of Three Monastic Charter Collections in the Eleventh Century (Saint-Amand, Saint-Riquier, Montier-en-Der),' in *Charters and the Use of the*

Written Word in Medieval Society, ed. Karl Heidecker (Turnhout, 2000), 190–4. Molesme's first cartulary was drawn up circa 1142 (Jacques Laurent, ed., *Cartulaires de l'abbaye de Molesme, 916–1250*, 2 vols. [Paris, 1907, 1911], 1: 20–2).

76 The best preserved quire (KK 1064, fols. 238–54) contains 53 letters (**1–53**); five completed quires would have contained at least 200 texts.

77 The first quire (folios I–VIII) probably included letters from Louis VII and Philip II.

78 The folios measure 19.5 by 27.5 cm, with a text area of 15.5 by 19.5 cm (each column is 7 to 7.3 cm wide).

79 The same hand copied the fourth and fifth quires (fols. XVII–XXIII, XXV–XXXII).

80 The fifty-three letters of quire 31 represent 6.6 letters per folio.

81 One late addition (***90**, a duplicate of **15**) is not counted here.

82 See the Chronological Table of the Letters.

83 Three items are unique to this cartulary and otherwise unknown (***88**, **105**, ***117**); twenty items were recopied into CR 6 (**24**, **34**, **36**, **44**, **46**, **49**, **50**, **51**, **52**, **59**, **60**, **72**, **81**, **83**, ***89**, **108**, ***114**, ***116**, ***121**, ***122**).

84 The Cartulary of 1211 displays little evidence of any subclassification of letters within those two broad headings, but the additional texts inserted after the completion of the volume in October 1211 suggest that the chancery had begun to group letters by subject matter, as with the king's treaty with Countess Blanche and Pope Innocent's confirmation of it (***61**, ***62**), the letters from the abbot of Saint-Denis (***112**, ***113**), Count Thibaut III's foundation of La Neuville-au-Pont (***114**, ***115**), and the finances of powerful widows (***116**, ***117**).

85 Cartulary-Registers 7 and 8.

86 They are from: Countess Marie (**37**), Countess Blanche (**36**, ***116**, ***121**), the abbess of Fontevraud (**103**), Hermesend of Traînel (***91**), Isabelle of Château-villain (**20**, **21**), and Helvide of Montmirail (**51**).

87 ***62**, ***88**.

88 See n. 77.

89 The cartulary contains only one letter from a knight (**70**).

90 Manasses of Villegruis sealed an instrument by which he augmented the fief held from him by Milo II Breban of Provins, the count's treasurer (Mayer, *Die Kanzlei*, 2: 914–16, no. 15, 1191: *litteris meis annotatum sigillo mea communivi*). Manasses was listed in the feudal roll for Provins (Longnon, *Documents*, 1: 56, no. 1523, ca 1178).

91 **1**, **4**, **13**, **15**, **25**, ***91**, **102**.

92 **6**, **47**, ***62**, **102**. See also **App. 1**, **App. 2–3**

93 **10, 29, 34, 45, 81, 86, 96.**

94 **12**. The count's letter granting a fief to Raoul *Plunquet* may have been returned for a similar reason (see ***122**).

95 **5**. The High Court reaffirmed (ca 1270) the right of younger sons to hold their inheritances from their oldest brothers: *il est encor coustume que se I vauvesourz muert qui ait enfanz, li ainnez des enfanz doit repanre dou signour et li autre enfant on chois de repanre de l'ainné frere ou dou signour de cui li herritaiges muet*; Paulette Portejoie, ed., *L'ancien coutumier de Champagne* (*XIIIe siècle*), (Poitiers, 1956), 159, art. 12.

96 **4**. See also **15**.

97 **47**. Robert II of Dreux also sealed a letter drawn up by countess Blanche's scribes in the same year (**25**).

98 AN, J 198, no. 20 [= *Layettes*, 1: 385–6, no. 1031].

99 ***62**. Fifteen years earlier, when he received Thibaut III's homage, the king demanded only the confirming oaths of eleven Champenois barons, not their letters patent (**App. 1**).

100 For property transactions, see n. 107 below. Regulation of travel and settlement: **17, 28, 30** (see also **5**). Exchanges of men with lay lords: **2, 3, 14, 20, 44**. Exchanges of men with religious lords: **40, 58, 75, 97, 111**, ***112**.

101 **74, 94, 98**.

102 **54, 84, 101, 105**, ***119**.

103 **43, 100**, ***114**, ***115**. See also Blanche's rewriting of the contract of association over Chaudefontaine (**54, 105**).

104 **App. 2**.

105 **61, 48, 65, 38**.

106 Portejoie, *L'ancien coutumier de Champagne*, 148–50, art. 5 (decision of the High Court, 1178): *hons est hors d'avoerie an quinzainme an* (and must do homage for his fiefs).

107 Sales: **9, 41, 66, 67, 70, 87**. Mortgages: **53, 82**. Debts: **7, 8, 27, 42, 49, 50, 72, 103**, ***117** (see also n. 109 below). Warranties: **26, 52**. Property disputes: **33, 35, 55, 60, 76**.

108 Fiefs were granted (**12**, ***122**), mortgaged (**46, 82**), sold (**31, 45**), exchanged (**18**), and allods feudalized (**4**).

109 Warranties for debt: **24, 51**, ***121**. Quittances for debt: **73, 78, 80**. Letters of non-prejudice: **69, 79, 95, 107**. Other warranties: **26, 52**.

110 License to construct a fortress: **4, 25.** License to elect an abbess: **108**.

111 **15**, ***91**.

112 **47**.

113 **104**. See also **109**.

114 **4, 10, 14, 110**.

115 **64, 109, *118.**
116 **1, 5, 13, 30, 96, 102, *118.**
117 **28, 33, 35, 92, 109, *113.** Inquests: **30, 33.**
118 **76, 99.**
119 ***116.**
120 **32, 39.**
121 ***88, 89.**
122 **8, 49.**
123 **60.**
124 André Duchesne, *Historiae Francorum Scriptores*, 5 vols. (Paris, 1636–49), 4: 491–546, published it from a now-lost manuscript under the title 'Epistolae Sugerii abbatis S. Dionysii.' M.J.J. Brial republished Duchesne's text in the *RHF* 15 (1808): 483–532, but rearranged the undated letters into chronological order and added related letters not in the collection. Michel Nortier has suggested that Suger's collection constitutes the earliest royal cartulary (comment in *Les cartulaires*, 377).
125 The original manuscript survives as Vatican Reg. Lat. 179. Duchesne, *Historiae Francorum Scriptores*, 4: 557–762, published it in its original order (hierarchically by title, beginning with the letters of Alexander III). M.J.J. Brial republished Duchesne's edition in the *RHF*, 16 (1814): 2–170, but rearranged the letters into chronological order. An analysis is in Françoise Gasparri, 'Manuscrit monastique ou registre de chancellerie?: à propos d'un recueil épistolaire de l'abbaye de Saint-Victor,' *Journal des Savants* (1976): 131–40.
126 For the definition of missive letter, see n. 11.
127 *RHF*, 15: 503, no. 56, 1148; 511, no. 73, 1149.
128 *RHF*, 15: 491, no. 21, 1147–48.
129 *RHF*, 16: 67, no. 213, ca 1163.
130 The Cartulary of 1211 contains four undated letters lacking mention of seals (**57, 59, 60, 71**). See nn. 11, 56.
131 John W. Baldwin, *The Government of Philip Augustus* (Berkeley, 1986), 412–18. None of the royal registers has been edited *in toto*, but the first three (Registers A, C, E) – exclusive of the royal letters and feudal lists published elsewhere – are edited in a composite volume, *Les registres de Philippe Auguste, 1: Texte.* Register A is best seen in the photographic reproduction by Léopold Delisle, *Le premier registre de Philippe-Auguste: reproduction héliotypique du manuscrit du Vatican* (Paris, 1883).

The present state of Register A eludes any reliable reconstuction of its quires: Michel Nortier, 'Les actes de Philippe Auguste: notes critiques sur les sources diplomatiques du règne,' in *La France de Philippe Auguste: le temps des mutations*, ed. Robert-Henri Bautier (Paris, 1982), 435–42, has resuscitated the opinion that it was preceded by an earlier cartulary (consisting of the urban charters that make up the most stable folios of the present Register A). The chaotic state of the register, with incomplete and careless copies of many texts, has led Jean Dufour to question whether that royal chancery at that time can even be called an organized bureau ('Peut-on parler d'une organisation de la chancellerie de Philippe Auguste?,' *Archiv für Diplomatik* 41 [1995]: 249–68).

132 Register A contains only thirty-three *carte diverse* dated before 1212 (*Les Registres de Philippe Auguste*, 1: 441–512). Nortier, 'Les actes de Philippe Auguste,' 436, counts 255 royal letters in Register A (they are edited in the *Recueil des actes de Philippe Auguste*). In the extant folios of the Cartulary of 1211, only fourteen of the 121 letters (11.5 per cent) are comital acts (see table 4).

133 Hélène Débax, 'Le cartulaire des Trencavel (*Liber instrumentorum vicecomitalium*),' in *Les cartulaires*, 291–9; and Joseph Dovetto, *Cartulaire des Trencavel: analyse détaillée des 617 actes, 957–1214* (Carcassonne, 1977). See also Fredric Cheyette, 'The Castles of the Trencavels: A Preliminary Aerial Survey,' in *Order and Innovation in the Middle Ages: Essays in Honor of Joseph R. Strayer*, ed. William C. Jordan, Bruce McNab, and Teofilo F. Ruiz (Princeton, 1976), 255–72, and Elisabeth Magnou-Nortier, 'Fidélité et féodalité méridionales d'après les serments de fidélité,' in *Les structures sociales de l'Aquitaine, du Languedoc et de l'Espagne au premier âge féodale* (Paris, 1969), 119–28.

134 *Liber instrumentorum memorialium, cartulaire des Guilhems de Montpellier*, ed. Alexandre C. Germain, 2 vols. (Montpellier, 1884, 1886). See also Jean Baumel, *Histoire d'une seigneurie du Midi de la France: naissance de Montpellier (985–1213)*, 3 vols. (Paris, 1969), esp. vol. 1, and Hideyuki Katsura, 'Serments, hommages et fiefs dans la seigneurie des Guilhem de Montpellier (fin XIe–début XIIIe siècle),' *Annales du Midi* 104 (1992): 141–61.

135 *Liber instrumentorum memorialium*, 1–2.

136 *Liber feudorum maior*, ed. Francisco Miguel Rosell, 2 vols. (Barcelona, 1945, 1947). See Adam J. Kosto, 'The *Liber feudorum maior* of the Counts of Barcelona: The Cartulary as an Expression of Power,' *Journal of Medieval History* 27 (2001): 1–22.

137 ***62**, ***88**.

138 See n. 68.

139 Evergates, 'The Chancery Archives,' 165–6.

140 Guillaume was chancellor from April 1222 to December 1232 (Arbois de Jubainville, *Histoire*, 4: 528).

141 Evergates, 'The Chancery Archives,' 168–9. It is not clear whether the draft copies of the count's acts were made directly from dictation or copied from notes recorded on wax tablets.

142 The Book of Homages (1222–9) was edited by Longnon as the sixth register of the *Feoda Campanie* (Longnon, *Documents*, 1: 133–80).

143 Arbois de Jubainville, *Histoire*, 4: 198–254.

144 The 127-folio volume entitled *Feoda Campanie* was inventoried in the fifteenth century as volume 'J' in the Chambre des Comptes (Longnon, *Documents*, 2: 573). It disappeared in the fire of 1737, but Longnon reconstructed the volume from copies made in the fourteenth and sixteenth centuries (Longnon, *Documents*, 1).

145 The 'Cartulary of Countess Blanche' (1222) seems to have remained at Argensolles after Blanche's death (1229).

146 Evergates, 'The Chancery Archives,' 163.

147 In 1489 it was inventoried as volume 'B' (Longnon, *Documents*, 2: 572).

148 He intended to study to volume, but the Archives Nationales in Paris would not send it to Troyes, where he was archivist of the Archives Départementales de l'Aube (see Arbois de Jubainville, *Histoire*, 5: 8).

149 Evergates, 'The Chancery Archives,' 174–5.

EDITORIAL PRINCIPLES

The order of the edition, with one exception, follows the sequence of quires established by the scribes who foliated them in the 1220s and largely preserved in the fifteenth-century rebinding and foliation of KK 1064 (see table 3). In the absence of the cartulary's first quire (folios I–VIII), the edition begins with the second quire, the one labeled *littere baronum* and the most complete of the surviving quires.[1]

An asterisk identifies a text added after 1211 to the completed folios of the cartulary. Added texts are evident by their placement (at the end of folios), script (usually hurried), and date (after October 1211).

The edited texts are based on the cartulary of 1211 except when an original letter survives; in that case, the original is edited here, with variant (and usually incidental) cartulary readings noted. The cartulary scribes in fact made exceptionally accurate copies. In the absence of original letters, significant variants to the cartulary readings are noted only from later chancery copies made directly from the originals, specifically Cartulary-Registers 3 and 4 (1222) and Cartulary-Registers 7 and 8 (1271). Variants in later copies and editions based on those same chancery cartularies (as in Chantereau-Lefebvre and Brussel) are ignored here.[2]

Abbreviations have been expanded according to current conventions. In a few questionable cases, and in the absence of the original documents, the readings of Cartulary-Register 3 (1222) have been adopted as the nearest contemporary reading of the originals. It should be noted that chancery scribes did not retain the orthography of the original letters but employed their own, characteristic set of abbreviations. The cartulary scripts are unremarkable, with the exception of *i*/*j*: an initial or final *i* often was lengthened into *j* (for example, *huj* abbreviated for *hujus*).[3] In this edition, and in accordance with modern editorial practices in France, an *i* before a vowel is rendered *j*. In like manner, a *u* before a vowel is rendered *v*. Punctuation is inserted to aid the modern reader, and vernacular terms are printed in italics.

The comital chancery and most of the smaller writing bureaus in Champagne and in adjacent lands began the year with Easter, and so the dates of twenty letters have been converted to new style (n.s.), that is, with the year commencing 1 January.[4]

Placenames are given their modern French forms. Personal names, however, are more problematic. They are rendered in French except for persons already well-known in their English forms, for example, the counts of Champagne (Henry for Henri) and kings of France (Philip for Philippe). Biographical citations are furnished with a person's first appearance in the edition.

NOTES

1 The recopyists in 1232 numbered it quire 31; the lost first quire would have been quire 30 of KK 1064 (see table 3).

2 Chantereau-Lefebvre and Brussel both consulted the original *Liber Principum* (CR 7) and CR 6. Chantereau-Lefebvre generally distinguishes the 'Cartulaire de Champagne' (CR 7), which he saw in the Chambre des Comptes, from the 'Cartulaire de le Bibliothèque de M. de Thou (CR 6). Brussel, *Nouvel examen*, xxxii–xlii, identifies the four cartularies he consulted: CR 3 and CR 6 (in Colbert's library), CR 7 (in the Chambre des Comptes), and CR 8 (in the royal library).

3 This practice is characteristic of the scribe of quires 31 and 34 (fols. 238–45, 260–6).

4 In a few cases, the context of the letter requires such a conversion; for example, **65** (dated January 1209) must be dated January 1210 because it follows **App. 2** (dated July 1209).

ABBREVIATIONS

*	Text added to a completed quire of CR 1 after 1211
>	Text of CR 1 recopied into CR 6
n.s.	Date converted from Easter style (year begins on Easter) to new style (year begins on 1 January)
AD	Archives Départementales
AJ	Catalogue in Arbois de Jubainville, *Histoire*, vols. 3–4
AN	Archives Nationales (Paris)
BNF	Bibliothèque Nationale de France (Paris)
CR	Cartulary-Register of the counts:
	CR 1 (1211) = AN, KK 1064, fols. 238–45, 254–66 (*Littere Baronum*)
	CR 2 (1218) = AN, KK 1064, fols. 208–37, 246–53, 372–9
	CR 3 (1222) = BNF, Lat. 5993 ('Cartulary of Countess Blanche')
	CR 4 (1222) = AN, KK 1064, fols. 1–207
	CR 5 (1231) = AN, KK 1064, fols. 267–371
	CR 6 (1232) = BNF, Lat. 5992 ('Cartulary of De Thou'); copy of KK 1064
	CR 7 (1271) = *Liber Principum* (destroyed in 1737). A seventeenth-century copy is BNF, Cinq Cents de Colbert, vols. 56 (7.1), 57 (7.2), 58 (7.3). A slightly later copy is BNF, nouv. acq. Lat 2454.
	CR 8 (1271) = BNF, Lat. 5993A (*Liber Pontificum*)
Layettes	*Layettes du Trésor des Chartes*
PL	*Patrologia Latina*
RHF	*Recueil des historiens des Gaules et de la France*

LITTERE BARONUM

THE CARTULARY

[quire 31: fols. 238r–245v]

1

1160, Orléans

Robert I, count of Dreux,[1] *announces the resolution of his dispute with Count Henry I of Champagne over his residence at Savignies,*[2] *where he has constructed a fortification with a moat. Henry allows it to remain but prohibits the building of a palisade. In the event of war between them, Robert will render the structure immediately to Henry, who will return it at the end of hostilities in the same condition he received it. Robert sealed this letter in the presence of several of Henry's officials, and Robert's chaplain presented it to Henry at Orléans.*[3]

COPIES: CR 1, fol. 238r (>CR 6, fol. 140v). CR 3, fol. 142v–143v. CR 4, fol. 21v. CR 7.1, fols. 269r–270r.

EDITIONS: Duchesne, *Histoire généalogique de la maison royale de Dreux*, pt. 1 (Dreux), *preuves*, 236. Brussel, *Nouvel examen*, 1: 382 note b (from CR 7, fol. 180).

CALENDARED: AJ, no. 77.

1 Robert I, count of Dreux and lord of Braine (1152–88), was the younger brother of King Louis VII; a brief biography is in Lewis, 'Fourteen Charters of Robert I, count of Dreux.'

2 Arbois de Jubainville and Guyotjeannin (*Episcopus et comes*, 25, 159) identify Savignies (dép. Oise, ar. Beauvais); Bur (*Le château*, 90) prefers Savigny-sur-Ardres (dép. Marne, ar. Reims).

3 In 1167 Count Henry transferred Savignies to Bartholomew, bishop of Beauvais, who had one of his knights promise to render service for it (*Layettes*, 1: 94, no. 208: letter of Louis VII). Henry's roll of fiefs for Meaux (ca 1178) lists the bishop: *Episcopus Belvaci, de feodo de Savignies* (Longnon, *Documents*, 1: 40, no. 1042).

Ego Robertus comes, frater regis Francie, notum fieri volo tam presentibus quam futuris quod quadam controversia erat inter comitem Henricum et me de domo quadam que nominatur Savignicum, partem cujus jam firmaveram cum fossato duorum jactuum. Hujus vero rei compositio tali pacto terminata est, ita videlicet quatenus illud quod jam firmatum fuerat cum fossato duorum jactuum remaneret; reliquum vero cum uno jactu fossati tantum et sepe sine britheschia firmetur.

Si vero guerram erga eum vel erga quemlibet alium haberem, domum jam predictam statim ei redderem. Hoc fide et per obsides ei firmavi. Ipse vero michi concessit quod domum sepedictam et stagna et molendinos bona fide et absque malo ingenio michi servaret, et ita munita ut ei ea committerem, finita guerra, statim michi redderet.

Et ut hoc firmius et memoriter teneatur, sigilli mei impressione confirmari precepi. Hujus autem rei testes interfuerunt: Odo comitis Henrici constabularius, Hugo de Planceio, Matheus Lothoringus, Petrus Britaudus, Petrus Bursaudus, Goffridus Brulardus, Girardus Eventatus, Hugo Stunulus, Milo Balena, Reinerus de Brena, Ado de Curia Landonis, Ohelardus de Brena. Actum est hoc anno ab incarnatione Domini M C LX, Lodovico rege Francorum regnante, Sansone Remensium archiepiscopo existente. Tradita fuit carta apud Aurelianum per manum Thome capellani.

2

1206 April

Thibaut I, count of Bar-le-Duc and Luxemburg,[1] *announces that he and Countess Blanche of Champagne have exchanged jurisdiction over their women who married men of the other lord. Thibaut agreed that the children from future intermarriages will belong to Blanche, but he retains jurisdiction over the children of his men and women who live in Champagne and marry among themselves.*

COPIES: CR 1, fol. 238r (>CR 6, fols. 140v–141r). CR 3, fol. 107r–v. CR 4, fol. 49r. CR 7.2, 97–8.

EDITIONS: Chantereau-Lefebvre, *Traité des fiefs*, 2: 30 (from CR 7). Laplace, *Actes des comtes de Bar*, no. 50.

1 Thibaut I, count of Bar-le-Duc (1191–1214) and Luxemburg (1197–1214); see Poull, *La maison souveraine et ducale de Bar*, 129–57, and Parisse, 'Thiébaut, comte de Bar et de Luxembourg.'

CALENDARED: AJ, no. 650. *Layettes*, 5: 57, no. 160 (reference to AN, J 911, no. 1, a notarized copy made from CR 7 on 7 March 1561). Grosdidier de Matons, *Catalogue*, no. 186.

Ego Theobaldus, comes Barri et Luceburgensis, omnibus ad quos presentes littere pervenerint, notum facio quod ego dedi Blanche, comitisse Campanie, et heredibus Campanie duas filias Girardi la Pore, unam videlicet quam Grancherus habet in uxorem et aliam quam Guillelmus Monachus habet in uxorem, cum heredibus earum. Et comitissa concessit et dedit mihi et heredibus meis in excambium filiam Garneri prepositi, quam Adam la Pore habet in uxorem, et filiam Petri Lorni quam Tierricus *la Pore* habet in uxorem, cum heredibus earum.

Fuit autem excambium istud factum inter me et comitissam tali modo, quod si homo meus vel femina mea se maritaverint in homines vel feminas comitisse, liberi inde nati erunt comitisse sine parte mea. Et si ego adduxero homines meos vel feminas meas de castro meo de Bormont apud Trecas, vel de alio loco qui sit de feodo domini Campanie, et ego maritavero eos in homines meos vel in feminas meas, liberi inde nati erunt mei et heredum meorum sine parte comitisse. Et hoc factum fuit salva libertate maritagiorum predictorum comitisse et salvo jure vicecomitatus. Hoc autem actum est sub testimonio sigilli mei, anno ab incarnatione Domini M CC VI, mense aprili.

3

1205 November

Guy II of Dampierre[1] *quit to Countess Blanche the jurisdiction over certain named men and women at Wassy and Flornoy; in exchange she gave him her feudal and domanial rights at Troisfontaines.*

COPIES: CR 1, 238r–v (>CR 6, fols. 141r–v). CR 3, fol. 71r–v. CR 4, fol. 104r–v. CR 7.2, 248–9.
CALENDARED: AJ, no. 635.

1 Guy II, lord of Dampierre (1179–1216), was son of the constable Guillaume and ranked among the most prominent barons of Champagne. He accompanied Count Henry II on the Third Crusade (1190–2), was pledge for Thibaut III's homage to the king in 1198, and appeared in that same capacity for Blanche in 1201 and 1213 (*__62__). Guy also moved within the royal orbit; he is listed circa 1203–6 among the *barones* of King Philip II (*Les registres de Philippe Auguste*, 1: 328). In 1197 Guy married Mathilda, heiress of Bourbon, after her divorce from Gaucher of Vienne. Savetiez, 'Maison de Dampierre-Saint-Dizier,' 116–25, provides a brief biography.

Ego Guido de Donpetra notum facio presentibus et futuris quod ego quitavi karissime domine mee Blanche, illustre comitisse Campanie, quicquid juris clamabam in hominibus de Waisseio et de Florneio qui sunt isti: Fraillez, Hatez, Hugo et soror eorum, Girardus filius Huelin, Lorencez filius Lorei, Henricus de Hubertcort, Vaslinus filius suus, Johannes filius Renardi de Sancta Leneria, Galterus Vaslierus, Robertus furnerius, Adam serviens et soror sua, Johannes de Florneio, Girardus frater ejus, Symonez Liedevid et familia ejus, Helena filia ejus. Ipsa vero comitissa in excambium hujus quitationis donavit mihi quicquid juris habebat apud Tres Fontes modis omnibus et commodis in banno et justitia, in feodo et custodia et dominio, ita quod nec ipsa aliquem de hominibus meis nec ego aliquid de suis, nisi fuerit homo Petri Dervensis, a nuper preterito festo Omnium Sanctorum in posterum poterit retinere, preter illos homines qui sunt in hoc excambio, quorum nomina sunt hec: Gyonez de Vilers, Emelina, Johannes Beleveue, Liedevid, Hugo li Mannaius, Maria soror presbiteri, filia Liethondi, Perrinus filius Liebaldi et mater sua, filius Thiebaldi, Girardez, Johannes filius Ficenne, gener Alardi, Huguet Foliers, Genez, Gauterius frater Viviani, Dominicus Potarius, Garinus major, Ingerus Ernolez, Hodiardis filia Reimbaldi, Androcta uxor Maserii. Quod ut ratum permaneat in futurum, presentes litteras fieri volui et sigilli mei munimine roborari. Actum anno Domini M CC quinto, mense novembri.

4

1206 April, Provins

Robert II of Dreux and Braine[1] *announces the agreement he made with Countess Blanche at Provins regarding his fortified residence at Torcy. He promised not to enlarge Torcy before Thibaut IV attains his majority; in return, Blanche allowed him to construct a fortification on his allodial property at Fère-en-Tardenois, which he converted into a liege fief. Robert will render that fortification to the countess at her need, and she will return it in the same condition forty days after finishing with it. Robert promised further not to construct any other fortification between Fère and Champagne without her license. One of Blanche's knights swore an oath on her behalf that she will observe this agreement.*

COPIES: CR 1, fol. 238v (>CR 6, fols. 141v–142v). CR 3, fols. 146v–147v. CR 4, fols. 21v–22v. CR 7.1, fols. 277r–278r.

1 For Robert II (1188–1218), see Duchesne, *Histoire généalogique de la maison royale de Dreux*, pt. 1 (Dreux): 43–5.

EDITIONS: Duchesne, *Histoire généalogique de la maison royale de Dreux*, pt. 1 (Dreux), *preuves*, 252–3 (from CR 7). Brussel, *Nouvel examen*, 386–7, note a (from CR 7, fol. 186).
TRANSLATION: Evergates, *Documents*, 5–7, no. 5.
CALENDARED: AJ, no. 647

Ego Robertus comes, dominus Drocarum et Brane, notum facio presentibus et futuris [quod] inter me et karissimam dominam meam Blancham, comitissam Campanie, tales conventiones esse super domo mea de Torciaco. Conventiones enim tales sunt: quod domus mea de Torciaco remansit in illo puncto in quo erat die qua conventiones apud Pruvinum facte fuerunt. In conventionibus est, et ego id cognosco, quod domus mea de Torciaco non poterit altius levari et quod in illa vel circa illam nichil aliud fieri poterit donec Theobaldus, filius comitisse, sit ad etatem tenendi terram. Et si, quod absit, Theobaldus interim decederet, ita remaneret donec heres Campanie esset ad etatem terram tenendi.

Comitissa vero michi concessit per istas conventiones quod ego possim facere unam fortericiam in allodio meo de Fara, videlicet vel in parco meo de Fara vel in loco ita propinquiori domui Fare sicut parcus est qui est de allodio. Ego vero parcum de Fara et vivarium meum et forestam meam de Daula, cum alio feodo meo de Brana, posui in feodo ligio comitisse et filii sui Theobaldi vel si, quod absit, decederet, in feodo domini Campanie. Et similiter posui in eorum feodo ligio totum allodium meum quod est in dominio Brane et Fere, quod videlicet allodium a domino non tenebam. Et sciendum quod de hoc allodio quod posui in feodo ligio comitisse et filii sui Theobaldi et dominorum Campanie, totus ligius sum comitisse et filii sui et dominorum Campanie, et exinde totus eorum ligius erit unus heredum meorum qui erit dominus Brane et Ferre.

In hiis enim que posui in feodo comitisse et filii sui Theobaldi et dominorum Campanie, sicut dictum est, faciam unam fortericiam, et ipsa forastericia erit jurabilis et reddibilis ad magnam vim et ad parvam tam ipsi comitisse quam filio suo Theobaldo vel domino Campanie; ita quod quotienscumque voluerint et petierint pro negocio suo fortericiam illam, ego tradam eam eis sine aresto vel senescallo suo vel constabulario vel buticulario vel marescallo suo, tali modo quod quadraginta diebus postquam essent de suo negotio liberati, fortericiam meam michi reddent in eodem puncto et integritate in qua eam eis tradidissem.

Sciendum est preterea et ita est in conventionibus nostris quod inter Branam et Faram et terram domini Campanie ego vel heres meus non possum facere nisi per comitissam Campanie et filium suum Theobaldum vel dominum Campanie aliam fortericiam quam illam que per supradictas conventiones concessa est michi ad faciendam in supradicto allodio meo quod, sicut dictum est, posui in feodo ligio comitisse et filii sui Theobaldi et dominorum Campanie.

Omnes autem conventiones que sunt in presenti carta juravi ego me bona fide et sine malo ingenio perpetuo servaturum tam ipsi comitisse quam filio suo Theobaldo et dominis Campanie. Ipsa autem comitissa, de observandis conventionibus istis, michi et heredibus meis fecit sacramentum suum jurari per unum militum suorum. Quod ut ratum permaneat et firmum, presentem cartam fieri volui et sigilli mei testimonio roborari. Actum Pruvinum, anno incarnati Verbi M CC sexto, mense aprili.

5

1208 May

Simon of Châteauvillain[1] *makes known that he had a dispute with Count Thibaut III over his castle at Châteauvillain, which he preferred to hold from his older (half-)brother Simon (II of Broyes), lord of Commercy.*[2] *However, Simon relented and became liegeman to the count in return for a 30* l. *rent. But the count died before assigning the rent, and what Countess Blanche later assigned Simon as rent infringed on the rights of the priory of Silvarouvres. So the countess and Simon agreed that, in lieu of the rent, she will not allow any of Simon's men at Châteauvillain who owe him service to settle in her lands.*

ORIGINAL: AN, J 193, no. 3 (missing pendant seal).
COPIES: CR 1, fols. 238v–239r (>CR 6, fols 142v–143r). CR 3, fols. 61r–62r. CR 4, fol. 107r–v. CR 7.3, fols. 93v–94v.
EDITION: *Layettes*, 1: 320, no. 848.
TRANSLATION: Evergates, *Documents*, 4–5, no. 4.
CALENDARED: AJ, no. 683.

1 Simon was the only son of Hugh III of Broyes (d. 1199) and his second wife Elizabeth/Isabelle of Dreux; Duchesne, *Histoire généalogique de la maison royale de Dreux*, pt. 5 (Broyes), 31–3. Elizabeth's dower included Châteauvillain, for which Simon did homage circa 1201 (Longnon, *Documents*, 1: 91, no. 2439: *Dominus de Castro Villani est homo ligius comitis Campanie et tenet castrum Villanum cum omnibus feodis appendentibus a comite Campanie*). Elizabeth/Isabelle of Dreux died in 1239 (see **20**, n. 1). Simon was still lord of Châteauvillain in 1258 (Gigot, *Chartes en langue française*, 92–4, no. 85).

2 Simon II of Broyes and Commercy (1166–1202) was the oldest son of Hugh III of Broyes by his first marriage; see Duchesne, *Histoire généalogique de la maison royale de Dreux*, pt. 5 (Broyes), 25–6.

Ego Symon, dominus Castrivillani, notum facio presentibus et futuris quod discordia quedam fuit[a] inter me et comitem Theobaldum super eo quod dictus comes volebat quod Castrumvillanum, quod de feodo domini Campanie cognoscebam, caperem de ipso ligie et tenerem. Ego autem castrum illud de Symone, domino Commarceii, fratre meo primogenito, volebam capere et tenere. Tandem castrum illud cepi ligie de predicto comite Theobaldo. In cujus rei compensationem jam dictus comes mihi triginta libratas terre annuatim debuit assignare. Sed cum morte preventus illud quod promiserat adimplere non posset, dedit in mandatis karissime domine mee Blanche, comitisse Campanie, uxori sue, et voluit quod illam terram[b] mihi assignaret. Illa vero mandatum viri sui comitis Theobaldi exequi cupiens et tenere, mihi, pro illis triginta libratis terre, assignavit quicquid dominus Campanie habebat apud Silvam Rouram, Sanctum Leodegarium et Dintevillam. Sed cum prior Silve Roure cartam comitis Campanie haberet quod custodia hominum et rerum prioris Silve Roure a manu domini comiti Campanie non posset alienari,[3] ego et dicta comitissa Campanie composuimus in hunc modum: quod ego ei et domino Campanie quitavi in perpetuum custodiam illam et quicquid ad prioratum Silve Roure pertinebat, et ita habebo, sicut dictum est, quicquid dominus Campanie habebat apud Santum Leodegarium et Dintevillam et Silvam Rouram excepta predicta custodia et exceptis rebus ad prioratum Silve Roure pertinentibus, que remanent in manu domini Campanie. Ipsa vero propter hoc mihi concessit quod in tota terra sua nullum hominum manencium apud Castrumvillanum vel in castellaria, de quo servicium habuerim, poterit retinere. Et si quis hominum illorum in terram suam veniret, si probare possem per legitimos testes, sine vadio duelli, quod servicium habuissem de illo, sine contradictione aliqua illum hominem rehaberem. Hec autem omnia concessa sunt et statuta inter me et predictam comitissam Campanie, salva carta comitis Campanie quam habet prior Silve Roure. Et ut hoc ratum permaneret et firmum, presentem cartam fieri volui sigilli mei appensione munitam. Actum anno Domini M CC octavo, mense maio.

[a] fuit quedam *in CR 1.* [b] terram terram *in CR 1.*

3 Perhaps a reference to Count Henry I's act of 1149 (in Blampignon, *Bar-sur-Aube*, 399–402, no. 21).

6

1200

Odo III, duke of Burgundy,[1] *announces that he has received the homage of Thibaut III, count of Troyes, just as his father, Hugh III, received the homage of Thibaut's father, Henry I.*[2]

ORIGINAL: AN, J 198, no. 7 (missing pendant seal).
COPIES: CR 1, fols. 239r (>CR 6, fol. 143v). CR 3, fol. 31r. CR 4, fol. 53r. CR 7.1, fol. 171v.
EDITIONS: Chantereau-Lefebvre, *Traité des fiefs*, 2: 14 (from CR 7). Longnon, *Documents*, 1: 468, no. 4. *Layettes*, 1: 224, no. 605.
CALENDARED: AJ, no. 539. Petit, *Histoire*, 3: 376, no. 1019.

Ego Odo, dux Burgundie, notum facimus universis tam presentibus quam futuris quod nos, de tota terra quam comes Henricus, pater, tenuit de patre nostro Ugone, duce Burgundie, karissimum[a] consanguineum et fidelem nostrum Theobaldum, comitem Trecensem, dicti comitis filium, in hominem nostrum recepimus, sicut pater ejus, comes Henricus, homo fuit patris nostri. Concessimus etiam eidem Theobaldo quod tam nos quam heredes nostri in perpetuum ipsi et heredibus suis garantiemus terram illam contra omnem

1 Odo III, duke of Burgundy (1192–1218), was the grandson of Odo II (1143–62) and Marie of Champagne (sister of Count Henry I). See Petit, *Histoire des ducs de Bourgogne*, 3: 87–251 (for Odo III), and 2: 252–305, 3: 1–86 (for his father Hugh III, 1165–92).

2 Count Thibaut II (1125–52) did homage (*fecit homagium*) to his son-in-law, Odo II, duke of Burgundy, in 1143 (Longnon, *Documents*, 1: 466, no. 1). Odo II's wife, Marie of Champagne, was Count Henry I's sister and thus Odo III's grandmother and Count Thibaut III's paternal aunt. Henry I must have done homage to Hugh between 1165 and 1179.

Count Thibaut III may have sought assurances before leaving on the Fourth Crusade that the duke would recognize his heirs rather than Henry II's daughters. Duke Odo III sealed another letter in Provins in 1200, perhaps on the same occasion:

Ego Odo, dux Burgundie, notum facio tam presentibus quam futuris quod, cum karissimus consanguineus et fidelis meus Theobaldus, comes Trecensis, Dominice crucis vexillum assumpsisset et vellet Jherosolimam proficisci, ad precum ejus instantiam, ipsi et heredibus ejus in perpetuum concessi quod nec ego nec heredes mei de feodo quod dictus comes de me tenet, de quo eum in hominem meum recepi et de quo comites Campanie homines fuerunt ducum Burgundie, permittemus ipsum vel heredes suos in nostra vel in alicujus alterius curia in causam trahi aut modis aliquibus fatigari. Set contra omnem hominem vel feminam de feodo illo, ego et heredes mei prefato comiti et heredibus suis in perpetuum portabimus garantiam. Quod ut notum permaneat et ratum habeatur, litteris annotatum sigilli mei munimine roboravi. Actum apud Pruvinum, anno incarnati Verbi M ducentesimo (AN J 198, no. 6 [=*Layettes*, 1: 224, no. 606]).

creaturam que possit vivere et mori, eosque ad terram illam pacifice ac quiete tenendam, toto posse nostro, juvabimus bona fide. Quod ut notum permaneat et ratum teneatur, presentem cartam fieri voluimus in testimonium et sigilli nostri munimine roborari. Actum anno incarnati Verbi, millesimo[b] ducentesimo.

[a] carissimum *in CR 1.* [b] M. *in CR 1.*

7

1210 June, Troyes

Guy II of Dampierre[1] makes known the agreement by which the Jew Bandin will pay his father Valin's debts to Countess Blanche.[2] Guy's own Jews, who are named, heard the terms for repayment and stood surety for Bandin and his wife, who will be imprisoned again by the countess if the debts are not repaid.

COPIES: CR 1, fol. 239r–v (>CR 6, fols. 234v–235r). CR 3, fols. 71v–72r. CR 4, fols 104v–105r. CR 7.2, 250–1.

EDITIONS: Monicat and Fournoux, *Chartes du Bourbonnais*, 56–7, no. 34 (from CR 3). Grayzel, *The Church and the Jews*, 351–2, no. 3 (from CR 7.2).

CALENDARED: AJ, no. 743.

Ego Guido de Dampetra notum facio universis presentes litteras inspecturis quod, cum Bandinus, judeus, cum karissima domina mea Blancha, comitissa Trecensi, finem fecisset hoc modo, quod de omnibus debitis Vaalini, patris sui – exceptis illis que domina comitissa jam finaverat – medietatem redderet domine comitisse terminis subscriptis, sicut compotus afferret, videlicet tertiam partem ad proximum festum Omnium Sanctorum, aliam[a] tertiam partem ad Pascha subsequens, ultimam tertiam partem ad aliud festum Omnium Sanctorum.[a] Alteram vero medietatem quam ei commodabat domina comitissa, eidem redderet ad submonitionem suam. Audivi judeos meos subscriptos, videlicet Sampsonem Rufum de Dampetra, Helium de Sancto Justo, Sachinum de Dampetra, Soninum et Samuelem fratres, Cochinum de Sancto Desiderio, et Salaminum, fratrem Samsonis Rufi, in presentia domine comitisse et mea, recognoscentes se esse debitores et redditores de fine illo, tali videlicet modo, quod si Bandinus in aliqua dictarum solutionum deficeret, ipsi solutionem illam facerent vel corpus Bandini vel corpus Belle, uxoris sue, ponerent in

1 See **3** n. 1.
2 Valin made several large loans to monasteries between 1196 and 1210 (Arbois de Jubainville, *Histoire*, 4: 829–30). See also **27**, **42**, **72**.

captione domine comitisse, sicut erant antequam finis iste factus fuisset; ita quod Bandinus et uxor ejus recognoscerent se esse judeos domine comitisse et quod aliam medietatem quam domina comitissa commodavit Bandino, si Bandinus illam non redderet ad submonitionem domine comitisse, tenerentur predicti judei mei reddere similiter domine comitisse, vel corpus Bandini et corpus Belle, uxoris sue, ponere in captione ejusdem domine mee ita quod ipsi recognoscerent se esse judeos domine comitisse, sicut predictum est. Sed sciendum quod eo die quo littere iste facte fuerunt, erant omnia debita judeorum meorum in manu mea pro redemptione sua. Ut autem hec omnia nota permaneant, ego, ad preces et requisitionem predictorum judeorum meorum, presentes litteras feci sigillare sigillo meo. Actum Trecas, anno gratie M CC X, mense junio.

[a] aliam *through* Sanctorum *omitted in Monicat and Fournoux.*

8

1201 August, Sézanne

Geoffroy V of Joinville, seneschal of Champagne,[1] *makes known that at his request Countess Blanche ordered the Templars to pay his kinsman Guy of Le Plessis the 500* l. *that Count Thibaut III had bequeathed to Guy's brother, Eustace of Conflans.*[2] *Both Guy and Eustace's widow Marie affirmed that the money was legitimately due.*

COPIES: CR 1, fol 239v (>CR 6, fol. 235r). CR 7.2, 459–60.
EDITIONS: Chantereau-Lefebvre, *Traité des fiefs*, 2: 20 (from CR 7). Delisle, *Mémoire sur les opérations financières des Templiers*, 95, no. 1 (from CR 6).
CALENDARED: AJ, no. 553. Delaborde, *Jean de Joinville*, no. 116.

Ego Gaufridus de Jonivilla, Campanie senescallus, notum facio presentibus et futuris quod quingentas libras pruviniensis monete, quas pie recordationis Theobaldus, quondam comes Campanie, legaverat karissimo consanguineo meo Eustachio de Cofflans, domina Blancha, illustris comitissa Campanie, ad

1 The most recent summary of the life of Geoffroy V (1190–1203) is Lusse, 'D'Etienne à Jean de Joinville: l'ascension d'une famille seigneuriale champenoise,' 16–18.

2 Guy of Le Plessis and Eustace of Conflans appear to have been distantly related to the Brienne and thus also to the Joinville. The brothers shared a fief in the late 1170s (Longnon, *Documents*, 1: 48, no. 1215) and were among the knights who planned to join Thibaut III on the Fourth Crusade. Eustace left Champagne in the company of Gautier III of Brienne by April 1201 and must have died before August 1201 (Longnon, *Les compagnons de Villehardouin*, 21).

requisitionem meam, reddi fecit Guidoni de Plaisseto, fratri ejusdem Eustachii, per manus Templariorum qui eas servabant. Ego autem eidem domine comitisse creantavi et concessi quod, si idem Eustachius vel alius dicte domine vel Templariis aliquid interrogaret, domina comitissa ad totum feodum meum quod de ea teneo, se sine fide mentita vertere poterit donec de predicta pecunia et de dampnis, si aliqua proinde incurrerit,[a] creantum suum habuerit.

Similiter etiam Maria, uxor prefati Eustachii, et Guido frater ejus, me presente, domine comitisse creantaverunt quod, si per memoratum Eustachium vel per alium super predicta pecunia dampnum incurrerit, ad feoda sua que de ea tenent, sine fide mentita, se vertat donec ei super hoc fuerit satisfactum.[b] In cujus rei testimonium et confirmationem, presentes litteras feci sigilli[c] mei munimine roborari. Actum anno incarnati Verbi, M CC primo, mense augusto, apud Sezanniam.

[a] incurrerit *in CR 1 and CR 7.2*, occurrerint *in Delisle.* [b] satisfactum *in CR 1 and CR 7.2*, emendatum *in Delisle.* [c] feci sigilli *in CR 1 and CR 7.2*, feci fierri [et] sigilli *in Delisle.*

9

1208 November

Anselm III of Traînel[1] *announces that, with the consent of his mother Hermesend,*[2] *his wife Ida,*[3] *and his sister Marie, lady of Charmoy,*[4] *he has sold all his possessions at Pont-sur-Seine to Countess Blanche and has compensated his mother and sister for their shares of this property.*[5]

COPIES: CR 1, fol. 239v (>CR 6, fol. 235r–v). CR 7.2, 515–16.
CALENDARED: AJ, no. 697. Lalore, 'Documents pour servir à la généalogie des anciens seigneurs de Traînel,' no. 176.

Ego Ansellus, dominus Trianguli, notum facio omnibus presentibus et futuris quod, laude et assensu karissime matris mee Hermesendis, domine Trianguli, et

1 Anselm III, lord of Traînel (1185–1210), predeceased his mother by one year; see Lalore, 'Documents pour servir à la généalogie des anciens seigneurs de Traînel,' 187–8, 230–4, and Roserot, *Dictionnaire historique*, 3: 1491.
2 See **91** n. 1.
3 See **62** n. 9.
4 For Marie, lady of Charmoy (1198–1231), see Roserot, *Dictionnaire historique*, 1: 344.
5 The castellany of Pont-sur-Seine was among Countess Blanche's dower lands assigned at her marriage in 1199 (*Layettes*, 1: 204, no. 49; tr. in Evergates, *Documents*, 58–9, no. 40). See also **19**.

Yde, uxoris mee, et Marie, domine Charmei, sororis mee, vendidi karissime domine mee Blanche, illustri comitisse Trecensi palatine, quicquid habebam apud Pontes super Sequanam in pedagio, in hominibus, in aquis, in nemoribus, in plano et in omnibus modis et commodis, et quicquid predicte mater et soror mee ibidem habebant in omnibus modis et commodis, pro quo competens excambium eis dedi. Ita tamen quod soror mea in manu sua retinuit XX libras in pedagio Pontium quas Domui Dei de Triangulo dederat antequam venditionem supradicta. Quod ut ratum permaneat et firmum, presentem cartam fieri volui sigilli mei appensione munitam. Actum anno Domini M CC VIII, mense novembri.

10

1205 December

Renier II of Nogent-en-Bassigny[1] *announces a marriage contract whereby his daughter's husband, Renier, the son of Josbert of Chaumont,*[2] *will be Countess Blanche's liegeman for Ageville and will owe one month's castle-guard annually at Chaumont. Countess Blanche gave that property to Josbert and his heirs in exchange for their quitclaim to Chaumont and to the inheritance of Lady Chaumonde.*[3] *If either spouse dies without heir, that property will revert to Josbert and his heirs.*[4]

ORIGINAL: AN, J 193, no. 14 (missing pendant seal).
COPIES: CR 1, fol. 239v (>CR 6, fol. 235v). CR 3, fol 59r–v. CR 4, fol. 119v. CR 7.3, fols. 87v–88r.
EDITION: *Layettes*, 1: 298, no. 789.
TRANSLATION: Evergates, *Documents*, 39–40, no. 26.
CALENDARED: AJ, no. 637.

Ego Renerus de Nogento notum facio[a] omnibus, tam presentibus quam futuris, quod cum filius domini Joiberti de Calvomonte ceperit[b] filiam meam in uxorem, ipse erit ligius homo domine comitisse et dominorum Campanie, et debebit unum mensem custodie apud Calvummontem in anno de terra Agiville

1 For the life of Renier II (1183–1237), see Faget de Casteljau, 'A la recherche des anciens seigneurs de Nogent-en-Bassigny,' 62–7.
2 For Josbert of Chaumont (ca 1140–1203) and his son Renier (ca 1170/80–1218), see Dessargues, 'Notes d'histoire généalogique,' 10, 13 (genealogical table).
3 See **96** n. 2.
4 See **55**, **96**.

et de furno et molendino Albe Petre, et ex hoc quod habet apud Albam Petram, que domina mea comitissa Campanie dedit eidem Joiberto et heredibus suis pro quittatione caduci domine Chaumonde et Calvimontis. Sed sciendum quod si filius domini Joiberti moriatur sine herede de filia mea, terra illa veniet ad dominum Joibertum et ad suos heredes; et similiter, si filia mea sine herede de filio domini Joiberti moriatur, terra illa veniet ad dominum Joibertum vel[c] ad suos heredes. Quod ut ratum permaneat in futurum, presentem cartam sigillo meo roboravi. Actum anno Domini M CC V, mense decembri.[d]

[a] facio *in the original and in CR 1*, fiero volo *in Layettes.* [b] ceperit *in the original and in CR 1*, recipiet *restored by Layettes.* [c] et *in CR 1.* [d] decembri *in the original and CR 1*, decembris *in Layettes.*

11

1200 May

Jean I of Montmirail[1] makes known that he has assigned his wife Helvide[2] a new dower to replace the one they alienated. He warrants that dower against the fief he holds from Count Thibaut III, and he promises to obtain sealed letters from the prelates of Reims and Soissons confirming the new dower. He describes the dower lands and identifies the dower house as being at Condé-en-Brie.

COPIES: CR 1, fol. 240r (>CR 6, fol. 236r). CR 3, fol. 96r. CR 4, fol. 89r. CR 7.2, 491–2.

EDITIONS: Chantereau-Lefebvre, *Traité des fiefs*, 2: 16 (from CR 6). Martène and Durand, *Thesaurus novus anecdotorum*, 1: 765.

CALENDARED: AJ, no. 515.

1 Jean was the sole heir of André of Montmirail and Hiliard of Oisy. Born circa 1165, Jean lost his mother circa 1177 and his father circa 1179; his step-mother, Alix of Courtenay, used her familial ties to send him to the royal court, where he became close to Prince Philip, who was about the same age. Jean accompanied King Philip II on the Third Crusade, fought with him in Normandy against Richard Lionheart, and became a habitué of tournaments. Jean married Helvide, the sister of Guy II of Dampierre (after 1185), and thereafter Jean and Helvide appeared together in jointly sealed acts (see **51**). In 1210 Jean left his wife and four children to take the Cistercian habit at Longpont, where he died in 1217 after an exemplary monastic life. His tomb was the site of miracles, and in 1236 the monks wrote his *vita* in an attempt to have him canonized. See Mathieu, *Montmirail en Brie*, 60–100.

2 Helvide was third daughter of Guillaume I of Dampierre (constable, 1133–72). After Jean of Montmirail left her to take the habit at Longpont (1210), Helvide assumed the lordship of Montmirail for eight years in custody for her eldest son, then retired to her dower lands; she died in 1225. See Boitel, *Histoire du bienheureux Jean*, 650–6.

In nomine sancte et individue Trinitatis. Ego Johannes, Montis Mirabilis dominus, notum facio tam presentibus quam futuris quod ego pono comitem Campanie et ejus successores obsides super feodum quod ab eo teneo de dote quam reddo Helvidi, uxori mee, pro excambio de Sonsois, quam ego et ipsa quitamus. Hujus rei pono omnes homines meos legios plegios, ita quod si ego vel filii mei super hoc vellemus ei nocere, ad eam absque fidei lesione liceret reverti. Indeque debet fieri secura per litteras pendentes Remensis archiepiscopi et Suessionensis episcopi. Divisio autem ista extenditur a Mollenum usque ad crucem super Sparni et inde ad crucem de Chamcharuum. Idem ad Vardum. Item extenditur a Mollenum ad vivarium. Inde ad Corboin. Inde ad Antrenne. Inde ad Cressanti. Inde ad Molins. Inde ad Barrum. Inde ad Capellam. Inde ad Euri. Quicquid infra predictas metas habeo in omnibus proficuis et etiam predicte mete continentur infra dotem quitto et laudo. Domusque de Conde continetur in dote. Quod ut ratum remaneat, sigilli mei testimonio feci confirmari. Actum istud anno ab incarnatione Domini, M CC, mense maio.

12

1201 (n.s.) January, Chaudun

Count Thibaut III gives the village of Gillancourt in fief to Jocelin of Avallon.[1] *For that, Jocelin becomes the count's liegeman after a prior liegeance to Gérard of Arcy,*[2] *the duke (Odo III) of Burgundy,*[3] *and Pierre (II of Courtenay), count of Auxerre.*[4]

1 Jocelin was a Burgundian knight with lands on the border between Champagne and Burgundy. The count's chancery extracted the basic facts from this letter in the roll of fiefs for the castellany of Laferté-sur-Aube (Longnon, *Documents*, 1: 76, no. 2129: *Jocelinus de Avalone, ligius de Gillencort, salvo ligeitate Girardi de Arseio et ducis Burgundie et comitis Autissiodorensis* [added:] *Jocelinus filius ejus fecit homagium*). Thibaut's letter of 1201 must have been returned to Countess Blanche after she repurchased the fief in 1210 (**16**, **31**).

2 Gérard, lord of Arcy, descended from a castle knight of Mailly (Sassier, *Recherches sur le pouvoir comtal en Auxerrois*, 118–22).

3 See **6** n. 1.

4 Pierre II of Courtenay, grandson of King Louis VI, married Agnes, heiress of Nevers, Auxerre, and Tonnerre in 1184. He ruled her lands in her name until her death (1188), then as guardian for their only daughter Mathilda/Mahaut until her marriage to Hervé IV of Donzy (1198). Hervé became count of Nevers in Mathilda's name, while Pierre retained control of Auxerre and Tonnerre from 1192 (when Agnes's mother gave up her dower lands to enter a convent) until his death in Constantinople in 1218. See Fromageot, *Tonnerre et son comté*, 67–77, and Lespinasse, *Le Nivernais et les comtes de Nevers*, 1: 398ff.

COPIES: CR 1, fol. 240r (>CR 6, fol. 236r–v). CR 3, fol. 65r. CR 4, fol. 9v.
EDITIONS: Chantereau-Lefebvre, *Traité des fiefs*, 2: 14 (from CR 6). Quantin, *Recueil*, 1–2, no. 2 (from Chantereau-Lefebvre).
TRANSLATION: Evergates, *Documents*, 4, no. 3.
CALENDARED: AJ, no. 530.

Ego Theobaldus, comes Trecensis palatinus, notum facio tam presentibus quam futuris quod Jocelino de Avalone et heredibus suis in feodo dedi villam que dicitur Gilleincort, que est de castellaria Firmitatis super Albam; et quicquid idem Jocelinus adquirere poterit in eadem villa, ipsi et heredibus suis concessi in augmento feodi illius. Concessi etiam ei quod in nulla villa mea libera retinebo homines qui sint de hoc dono. Idem autem Jocelinus propter hoc devenit homo meus ligius, salva tamen ligietate Girardi de Arseio et domini ducis Burgundie et Petri comitis de Autissiodoro. Actum apud Choaudon. Teste me ipso. Anno dominice Incarnationis M CC, mense januario. Datum per manum Galteri, cancellarii mei. Nota Milonis.

13

1203 September, Sézanne

Henri III, count of Grandpré,[1] *makes known the resolution of his dispute with Countess Blanche over the castle of Saint-Jean-sur-Tourbe.*[2] *Giles of Saint-Jean-sur-Tourbe will hold the fortress there as a liege fief directly from the countess, but he will hold the town from Henri, who in turn will hold it from the countess.*[3]

ORIGINAL: AN, J 202, no. 1 (missing pendant seal).
COPIES: CR 1, fol 240r (>CR 6, fol. 236v). CR 3, fol. 145r–v. CR 4, fol. 23r–v. CR 7.2, 136–7.

1 For the rule of Henri III (1190–1211), see Barthélemy, 'Notice historique sur la maison de Grandpré,' 101–2.
2 For the castle, see Bur, *Vestiges d'habitat seigneurial fortifié du Bas-Pays Argonnais*, 90–2.
3 Countess Blanche insisted on direct control of this fortress because it lay on the road to Sainte-Menehould, the new castle acquired by Thibaut III in 1200 where he had sponsored new villages (see **100**). Soon after this agreement, the count's chancery noted that Giles held his fortress as a *domus jurabilis* (Longnon, *Documents*, 1: 80, no. 2227). In 1218 Blanche confiscated Saint-Jean-sur-Tourbe because of Giles's disloyalty during the war over Thibaut IV's succession; she regranted it to Gaucher II of Nanteuil-la-Fosse (Chantereau-Lefebvre, *Traité des fiefs*, 2: 101–2, December 1218 [= Bur, *Vestiges d'habitat seigneurial fortifié du Bas-Pays Argonnais*, 91])

EDITIONS: Martène and Durand, *Thesaurus novus anecdotorum*, 1: 784. Bur, *Vestiges d'habitat seigneurial fortifié du Bas-Pays Argonnais*, 91.
CALENDARED: AJ, no. 593. *Layettes*, 1: 245, no. 694

Ego Henricus, comes Grandis Prati, notum facio et testificor omnibus presentibus et futuris quod cum inter me et karissimam dominam meam Blancham, comitissam Trecensem palatinam, discordia esset de castro Sancti Johannis, tandem pacificata et declarata est in hunc modum: quod fortericia primi fossati quod est circa motam, et preterea homines Sancti Remigii Remensis et Sancti Petri de Advenaio et Sancti Martini de Spernaco, sunt et remanent in feodo ligio domine mee comitisse, et hec omnia tenet[a] de ea Gilo de Sancto Johanne. Preterea Gilo de Sancto Johanne tenet de me burgum in quo ecclesia sedet una cum justitia et banno, tam intus quam extra, et ego teneo de domina mea comitissa. Quod ut permaneat firmum, presentem paginam fieri volui et sigilli mei testimonio roborari. Actum apud Sezannam, anno Domini M CC tercio, mense septembri.

[a] tenent *in CR 1.*

14

1199 July, Provins

Geoffroy V of Joinville, seneschal of Champagne,[1] *makes an agreement with Count Thibaut III by which Geoffroy's men are prohibited from buying and mortgaging land in the count's custody, except by the count's license.*

ORIGINAL: AN, J 1032, no. 2 (damaged; missing pendant seal).[2]
COPIES: CR 1, fol. 240r–v (>CR 6, fols. 236v–237r). CR 3, fol. 59v. CR 4, fols. 112v–113r. CR 7.2, 458–9.
EDITION: *Layettes*, 5: 44, no. 127 (based on the original and copies).
CALENDARED: AJ, no. 486. Delaborde, *Jean de Joinville*, no. 111.

Ego Galfridus de Junivilla,[a] Campanie senescallus, notum facio presentibus et futuris quod cum domino meo Theobaldo, comite Trecensium, hanc habeo pactionem quod de terris hominum in custodia et advocatia sua existentium, homines mei nichil emere vel in vadium sumere de cetero poterunt, nisi prius ab

1 See **8** n. 1.
2 This is the oldest baronial letter that has survived from the comital archive (see also ***91**). The oldest original comital letter is **39**. See also **46** n. 1.

ipso comite licentia fuerit impetrata. Et si absque ipsius licentia de predictis terris emerent amodo vel in vadium ceperint,[b] emptionem suam et gageriam amittent juxta ejusdem domini voluntatem. De terris autem illis quas homines mei a prefatis hominibus jam emerunt vel in vadium ceperunt, idem homines mei, secundum quantitatem et valorem emptionis vel gagerie sue, eidem domino reddent consuetudinem que proinde antea solvebatur. Quod ut notum permaneat et ratum teneatur, litteris annotatum sigilli mei munimine roboravi. Actum Pruvini, anno incarnati Verbi M C nonagesimo nono, mense julio.[c]

[a] Joinvilla *in Layettes.* [b] sumerent *in Layettes.* [c] julii *in Layettes.*

15

1205 July

Anselm III of Traînel[1] *recognizes that he holds the fortified residence at Villeneuve-aux-Riches-Hommes*[2] *as a liege fief from Countess Blanche. He promises that if he ever is unable to warrant it, he will dismantle it at her will.*[3]

ORIGINAL: AN, J 196, no. 1 (missing pendant seal).
COPIES: CR 1, fol. 240v[4] (>CR 6, fol. 237r–v). CR 3, fol. 101v. CR 4, fols. 93v–94r. CR 7.2, 516–17.
EDITIONS: Chantereau-Lefebvre, *Traité des fiefs*, 2: 27 (from CR 7). *Layettes*, 1: 566, no. 777bis.
CALENDARED: AJ, no. 625.

Ego Ansellus de Triangulo notum esse volo[a] presentibus et futuris, et animo bono cognosco, domum nostram[b] de Villa Nova Parva Divitum Hominum esse de feodo ligio karissime domine mee ligie Blanche, illustris Campanie comitisse, et heredum suorum tali modo, quod de quacumque hora verbum inde veniret per quod domus illa esse posset de alterius feodo quam de feodo domine comitisse, et ego domum hanc, quam recognosco esse de feodo ligio comitisse

1 See **9** n. 1.
2 The Traînel possessed Villeneuve since the early twelfth century, when Milo (of Traînel), bishop of Troyes, confirmed the church there to the monks of Molesme. Little else is known about the place before this letter, which reveals the existence of a fortified residence, perhaps of a recent date. For the subsequent history of Villeneuve, see Roserot, *Dictionnaire historique*, 3: 1818–21. See also Higounet, *Défrichements et villeneuves*, 108.
3 Anselm and his mother, Hermesend, appear to have done homage to Countess Blanche at Troyes, as noted in Hermesend's almost identical letter (***91**).
4 Same as ***90**.

et heredum suorum, non possem garantire, creanto ei tamquam domine mee et promitto, supra omne quod de illa teneo, quod domum ipsam ex tunc diruam ad voluntatem ejus vel illius quem ad id faciendum mitteret. Quod si non facerem, ex tunc volo quod domina comitissa licenter se capiat ad me et ad feodum meum, salva fide sua erga me, usquedum hoc, sicut dictum est, fiat. Actum anno gratie M CC V[c], mense julio.

[a] facio *in lieu of* esse volo *in* ***90**. [b] meam *in CR 1 and in* ***90** *and* ***91**.
[c] quinto *in CR 1.*

16

1211 (n.s.) January

Odo III, duke of Burgundy,[1] *warrants that the brother and sister of Jocelin II of Avallon, on reaching the age of consent,*[2] *will consent to Jocelin's sale of the fief that Count Thibaut III had given to his father.*[3]

ORIGINAL: AN, J 205, no 1 (missing pendant seal).
COPIES: CR 1, fol. 240v (>CR 6, fol. 237v). CR 3, fol. 33r. CR 4, fols. 54v–55r. CR 7.1, fol. 175r.
CALENDARED: AJ, no. 760. *Layettes*, 1: 362–3, no. 957. Petit, *Histoire*, 3: 437, no. 1251.

Ego Odo, dux Burgundie, notum facio presentibus et futuris quod cum dilectus et fidelis meus Jocelinus, miles de Avalone, vendidisset Blanche, comitisse palatine Trecensis, feodum quod Theobaldus, maritus ejusdem comitisse, dederat patri dicti Jocelini apud Gilencort, quia frater et soror ejusdem Jocelini ad annos laudandi et etatem nondum pervenerant, sepedictus Jocelinus predicte comitisse et ejus heredibus me constituit responsorem quod quando dicti frater et soror ejus ad etatem laudandi pervenirent, ab eisdem predictam venditionem laudari faceret et concedi. Et post laudationem per annum et diem, secundum jus, garantiam dicte comitisse et heredibus ipsius portaret. Quod ut ratum habeatur, presens scriptum sigillo meo confirmavi. Actum anno gratie M CC decimo, in januario.

1 See **6** n. 1.
2 They had already given their consent as minors (**31**).
3 See **12**.

17

1210 October

Odo III, duke of Burgundy,[1] *makes known his agreement with Countess Blanche: he will not allow her Jews to reside in his lands, and she in turn will not allow his Jews to reside in her lands.*

COPIES: CR 1, fol. 240v (>CR 6, fol. 238r). CR 3, fol. 32v. CR 4, fol. 54v. CR 7.1, fols. 174v–175r.

EDITIONS: Brussel, *Nouvel examen*, 580 note a (from CR 6). Grayzel, *The Church and the Jews*, 352, no. 4 (from CR 3, CR 7.1).

CALENDARED: AJ, no. 750. Petit, *Histoire*, 3: 432, no. 1233.

Ego Odo, dux Burgundie, notum facio presentibus et futuris quod inter me et dominam Blancham, comitissam palatinam Trecensem, talis facta est de judeis nostris conventio: quod nec ego judeos ipsius sub me mansuros retinere possum, nec ipsa meos sub se mansuros retinere potest. Quod ut ratum habeatur, presens scriptum sigillo meo confirmavi. Actum est hoc anno incarnati Verbi M ducentessimo decimo, in octobris.

18

1200 (n.s.) February

Gautier III, count of Brienne,[1] *makes known that he has acquired the* mouvance *of four villages (Trannes, Jessains, Onjon, and Pel-et-Der) from Count Thibaut III, who gave in exchange the village of Villeloup with permission to sell it.*[2]

COPIES: CR 1, fol. 240v (>CR 6, fol. 238r). CR 3, fol. 121v. CR 4, fol. 16r. CR 7.2, 68.

CALENDARED: AJ, no. 498. Arbois de Jubainville, 'Catalogue d'actes des comtes de Brienne,' no. 111.

---

1 See **6** n. 1.

1 For Gautier III (1192–1205), see Roserot, *Dictionnaire historique*, 1: 244; Longnon, *Les compagnons de Villehardouin*, 15–18; and Arbois de Jubainville, 'Catalogue d'actes des comtes de Brienne,' 162–8.

2 This letter represents only part of a complex exchange. According to Thibaut III, Abbot Nevel of Molesme (1163–6) had mortgaged Villeloup to count Henry I for 1000 *l.* and Abbot Gaucher redeemed the property in 1199 (Socard, 'Chartes inédites extraits des cartulaires de Molesme,' 291). Subsequently the monks must have sold the village to Thibaut, who here transfers it to the count of Brienne.

Ego Galterus, comes Brene, notum facio presentibus et futuris quod karissimo domino meo Theobaldo, comiti Campanie, concessi per excambio Ville Lupi, quam mihi vendere concessit, ut Traine et Gesseing et Onjons et Peix et Derf, quo de feodo meo erant, sint in perpetuum de feodo dicti comitis Campanie. In cujus rei testimonium, presentem cartam sigilli mei robore confirmavi. Actum anno incarnationi Verbi M C nonagesimo nono, mense februario.

19

1209

Garnier III of Traînel, lord of Marigny,[1] *announces that, with his wife's consent, he has sold to Countess Blanche all that he had in the tolls of Pont-sur-Seine.*[2]

COPIES: CR 1, fols. 240v–241r (>CR 6, fol. 238r–v). CR 7.2, 514–15.
CALENDARED: AJ, no. 732. Lalore, 'Documents pour servir à la généalogie des anciens seigneurs de Traînel,' no. 177.

Ego Garnerus de Triangulo notum facio tam presentibus quam futuris quod, laude et assensu Agnetis, uxoris mee, vendidi karissime domine mee Blanche, illustri comitisse Trecensi, quicquid habebam in pedagio Pontium super Sequanam, et tam ipsi comitisse quam heredibus suis perpetuo habendum concessi. Quod ut notum permaneat et ratum teneatur,[a] litteris annotatum sigilli mei munimine roborari. Actum anno incarnati Verbi, ducentessimo nono.

[a] habeatur *in CR 7.2.*

1 Garnier III (1195–1218) was the first cousin of Anselm III of Traînel. Although Garnier carried the Traînel name, his properties were located primarily around the castle of Marigny; see Lalore, 'Documents pour servir à la généalogie des anciens seigneurs de Traînel,' 221–37.

2 Garnier and his cousin Anselm III of Traînel inherited property and revenues at Pont-sur-Seine through their fathers, the brothers Anselm II (butler of Champagne) and Garnier II of Traînel (see also **9**).

20

1209 April

Isabelle (Elizabeth) of Châteauvillain[1] *and her son Simon*[2] *jointly seal a letter by which they exchange several men and women with Countess Blanche.*

COPIES: CR 1, fol. 241r (>CR 6, fol. 238v). CR 7.3, fol. 95r–v.
CALENDARED: AJ, no. 737.

Ego Isabellis, domina Castrivillani, et Symon, filius meus, notum facimus tam presentibus quam futuris quod nos karissime domine nostre Blanche, comitisse Trecensi, pro Christiano de Longo Campo, uxoris ejus, liberis eorum et Rolandino, fratre dicti Christiani, hominibus suis, dedimus in excambium custodiam uxoris Galteri de Esternay et liberorum suorum et Milonis de Trefos et Foberti, fratris sui, et uxoris sue et liberorum suorum. De hac autem custodia tenemur dicte comitisse rectam garantiam portare. Et ut hoc ratum permaneat et firmum, presentem cartam fieri voluimus sigillorum nostrorum munimine roboratam. Actum anno incarnati Verbi, M CC X, mense aprili.

21

1211 (n.s.) February

Elizabeth (Isabelle) of Châteauvillain[1] *and her son Simon*[2] *make known that they have given to Countess Blanche their castle of Baudement and all that they possess in its castellany, including its fiefs and adjacent villages.*[3]

1 Elizabeth was one of four daughters of Robert I of Dreux (see **1** n. 1) and Agnes of Baudement. In 1178 she became the second wife of Hugh III of Broyes (d. 1199), and in 1197 she received Châteauvillain in dower (Martène and Durand, *Thesaurus novus anecdotorum*, 1: 667), with the provision that it be her son Simon's inheritance (see **5**). She died in 1239 (Aubri of Trois-Fontaines, 'Chronicon,' 945).

2 See **5** n. 1.

1 See **20** n. 1.

2 See **5** n. 1.

3 Baudement was Elizabeth's maternal inheritance. It is not clear whether the castellany of Baudement in fact contained all the items listed in this letter of sale, for Elizabeth's grandfather, the seneschal André of Baudement, had given all his possessions there – except the fortress and fiefs – to the Templars in 1133 before joining the Cistercians (Carrière, *Histoire et cartulaire des Templiers de Provins*, 101, no. 81). For the castle, see Bur, *Vestiges d'habitat seigneurial fortifié en Champagne central*, 22–5. See also **36**.

ORIGINAL: AN, J 195, no. 59 (two missing pendant seals).
COPIES: CR 1, fol. 241r (>CR 6, fols. 238v–239r). CR 3, fol. 62r. CR 4, fol. 107v. CR 7.3, fols. 94v–95r.
EDITION: Chantereau-Lefebvre, *Traité des fiefs*, 2: 42 (from CR 7).
CALENDARED: AJ, no. 764. *Layettes*, 1: 365, no. 962.

Ego Elyzabeth, domina Castrovillani, et ego Symon de Castrovillani, filius ejus, notum facimus universis tam presentibus quam futuris quod nos motam et forteriçiam Baudemanti et quicquid in tota castellaria habebamus in hominibus, in terris, in aquis, in consuetudinibus, in justicia, in feodis, et in omnibus modis et commodis et quicquid habebamus in villis adjacentibus, videlicet Corbeson, Soisi, Thommes, Estrechi, et Waisiam, similiter in omnibus modis et commodis proprio motu et spontanea voluntate dedimus et concessimus karissime domine nostre Blanche, illustri comitisse Trecensi, et Theobaldo, filio suo, et eorum heredibus quiete ac pacifice perpetuo possidendum. Quod ut notum permaneat et ratum teneatur, litteris annotatum sigillorum nostrorum fecimus munimine roborari. Actum anno Verbi incarnati millesimo ducentessimo decimo, mense februario.

22

1205 April, Provins

Jean of Brienne[1] *makes known that he has sold the village of Fontaine-Mâcon to Countess Blanche for 800* l. *Jean notes that Count Thibaut III had given the village to Blanche in dower but then gave it to Jean without Blanche's consent.*[2] *Jean warrants good title to the village and promises to place 400* l. *worth of property in fief within Blanche's dower lands. Eight barons pledge 100* l. *each that if Jean reneges on this agreement, they will place themselves in captivity in Sézanne and remain there until each pays the countess 100* l.

1 Jean (b. 1148) was the third son of Erard II, count of Brienne (1143–91). He spent his early years at Clairvaux but in 1162 abandoned monastic life to follow the tournament circuit, and he later held several small lordships. At the death of his brother Gautier III (count of Brienne, 1191–1205), Jean became guardian (1205–21) for his nephew, Gautier IV, but spent most of the time in the Holy Land. He married Marie, daughter of the queen Isabelle of Jerusalem and Conrad of Montferrat (1210), and became regent of Jerusalem (1212–25), then co-emperor of Constantinople (1231–7). See ***88** and Arbois de Jubainville, *Recherches sur les premières années de Jean de Brienne*.

2 See **29**.

COPIES: CR 1, fol. 241r–v (>CR 6, fol. 239r–v). CR 7.2, 75.

EDITIONS: Chantereau-Lefebvre, *Traité des fiefs*, 2: 28 (from CR 7). Brussel, *Nouvel examen*, 833 (incomplete copy from CR 7, fol. 202). Martène and Durand, *Thesaurus novus anecdotorum*, 1: 801–2.

CALENDARED: AJ, no. 614.

Ego Johannes de Brena notum facio omnibus presentibus quam futuris quod ego villam que dicitur Fontaine Macon, que est de dotalicio reverende domine mee Blanche, illustris comitisse Trecensis – quam villam dominus meus, vir ejus, inclite recordationis comes Theobaldus, postquam eam duxit in uxorem et ei dotalicium fecit, mihi sine assensu ipsius dederat in feodum et casamentum – eidem comitisse vendidi octingentis libris; et quicquid habebam in villa illa in omnibus commodis, ipse comitisse quittavi et perpetuo habendum concessi. Pro hoc autem contractu inter me et dominam comitissam sic facto, ponam quadringentas libras in feodo ipsius comitisse in loco qui sit de dotalitio suo, quando ab ipsa fuero requisitus, et ipsa me videbit super hoc ahisatum, competenter et habere opportunitatem id faciendi. Fiduciavi etiam manu mea propria quod si aliquis vel aliqua super eadem villa voluerit aliquid reclamare, aut dictam comitissam super hoc modis aliquibus fatigare, ego inde ipsi rectam garantiam portabo. Statuo etiam et concedo quod heredes mei, si forte decessero, vel quicumque terram meam tenebunt, hec omnia que predixi dicte comitisse tenere et facere teneantur sicut ego nunc teneor. Et si forte in illis tenendis in aliquo deficerent, domine comitisse liceat inde se capere, sine fidem mentiri, ad ea omnia que ipsi de terra mea tenerent. De predictis autem, sicut dictum est, a me tenendis fidejussores dedi domine comitisse de octingentis libris, scilicet Garnerum de Triangulo de C libris, Galcherum de Joigniaco de C libris, Simonum de Jonvilla de C libris, Robertum de Milliaco de C libris, Ogerum de Sancto Karauno de C libris, Odardum marescallum Campanie de C libris, Hugonem de Sancto Mauricio de C libris, Odonem de Barris de C libris. Isti autem prenominati fidejussores, si ego in predictis tenendis aliquo modo deficerem, infra quindenam postquam a domina comitissa fuerint requisiti, tenebunt captionem apud Sezannam, de villa non exituri donec domine comitisse reddiderint octingentas libras, scilicet singuli C libris vel vadia valencia C libris. Ut autem hec omnia nota permaneant et rata teneantur, litteris annotatum sigilli mei munimine roboravi. Actum Pruvinum, anno Domini M CC quinto, mense aprili.

23

1209

Odo III, duke of Burgundy,[1] *states that when Countess Blanche disppossesed Milo of Montréal*[2] *of the oaths owed by the men of Chablis,*[3] *Milo objected, claiming that he had been in possession of that right since the time of Count Thibaut III.*[4] *At Odo's request, Blanche restored Milo's right, at the same time preserving the privileges granted by Count Henry I to Saint-Martin of Tours, as described in a document that the monks retain.*[5]

ORIGINAL: AN, J 195, no. 57 (missing pendant seal).
COPIES: CR 1, fol. 241v (>CR 6, fols. 239v–240r). CR 3, fol. 31r–v. CR 4, fol. 53r–v. CR 7.1, fol. 174r–v.
EDITION: *Layettes*, 1: 344, no. 908.
CALENDARED: AJ, no. 731. Petit, *Histoire*, 3: 421–2, no. 1195.

Ego Odo, dux Burgundie, omnibus presentibus et futuris notum fieri volumus quod, cum dilecta et fidelis nostra Blancha, illustris comitissa Trecensis palatina, Milonem de Monteregali dissaisivisset de sacramento hominum Chableiarum, Milo vero super hoc injuriam sibi fieri quereretur, asserens se sacramentum illud habuisse tempore karissimi consanguinei nostri comitis Theobaldi, ejusdem comitisse mariti. Tandem dicta comitissa, ad instantiam precum nostrarum, dictum Milonem de sacramento illo resasivit, salva tamen dicte comitisse et heredibus suis custodia dicte ville, et salvo gistio, et salvo omni jure quod ipsis in eadem villa competit vel competere poterit in futurum, salvis etiam cartis et privilegiis que ecclesia Beati Martini Turonensis habet de comite Henrico, et salvo similiter jure predicti Milonis. In hujus autem rei testimonium, presentem cartam fieri volumus sigilli nostri munimine roboratam. Actum anno gratie M CC nono.

1 See **6** n. 1.
2 Milo, the third son of Anseric II of Montréal (d. 1190), was also known as Milo 'of Chablis' (Bouchard, *Sword*, 338–40).
3 An undated twelfth-century notice states: *Omnes homines, quotquot sunt, apud Chableias, sive milites sive filii militum qui habent etatem, cujuscunque sint conditionis, debent esse jurati comiti sub hac forma*: '*Ego juro quod ego ero fidelis comiti, de cetero, et quod ego servabo membro ejus et honorem ejus pro posse meo, sic me Deus adjuvet, et hac sancta salva fidelitate Beati Martini*' (CR 6, fols 166v–167r [= Chantereau-Lefebvre, *Traité des fiefs*, 2: 13–14 = Brussel, *Nouvel examen*, 775–6, note a = Quantin, *Cartulaire général de l'Yonne*, 2: 437–8, no. 183]).
4 Apparently Count Thibaut III had renewed Henry I's original grant of 1152 to Milo's father (Anseric II) or grandfather (Anseric I).
5 Henry I promised never to alienate his right to the fidelity of the residents of Chablis (see **104**). See also **71**.

24

1205 September, Pont-sur-Seine

Hugh IV of Broyes[1] *acknowledges that his mother*[2] *owes 1440* l., *payable in four annual payments of 360* l., *to Countess Blanche's Jew, Manasses the Black. If his mother's income is inadequate to meet the payments, her provost, Robert of Sézanne,*[3] *and Nathan of Broyes will collect a* taille *from her dower lands in the castellany of Broyes that Manasses holds as security. Hugh promises to repay his mother's debt if she dies before repaying it.*

COPIES: CR 1, fol. 241v (>CR 6, fol. 240r).
CALENDARED: AJ, no. 631.

Ego Hugo, dominus Brecarum, notum esse volo omnibus presentibus et futuris quod karissima domina et mater mea debet Manasserio Nigro, judeo illustris domine mee Blanche, Campanie comitisse, mille quadringentas et quadraginta libras pagandas eidem judeo ad quatuor annos. Quarum prima paga incipiet ab octabis proximi festi Sancti Remigii in unum annum, ita quod ex tunc annuatim inde recipiet trecentas et sextaginta libras ad predictum terminum, ita quod si domina mea mater de terra sua plenus recipiat quas trecente libras sint illud reddet pro paga Menassero si voluerit. Si vero minus ipsa perficiet, sciendum etiam quod per manum Nathons de Brecis et Roberti, prepositi de Sezannia, fiet tallia in illa terra domine mee matris quam tenet pro dotarium in castellaria Brecarum, que est in manu Manasseri pro debito memorato. Sed si mater mea infra illos quatuor annos possit totum debitum pagare super Manasserum, cadet summa usure, que erit ad rationonem et mensuram termini qui remaneret. Si vero mater mea infra illos quatuor annos morietur, ego creantavi domine mee Blanche, Campanie comitisse, et adhuc creanto quod conventiones istas erga Manaserum tenebo. Actum apud Pontes, anno gratie M CC V, mense septembri.

25

1209 March, Lagny

Robert II, count and lord of Dreux and Braine,[1] *makes known that when he acquired Lizy-sur-Ourcq with the intention of building a residence there,*

1 For Hugh IV (1205–27), see Duchesne, *Histoire généalogique de la maison royale de Dreux*, pt. 5 (Broyes), 28–30 and *preuves*, 24–7.
2 Her identity is not certain; see Parisse, *Noblesse et chevalerie*, 372.
3 See also **36**.
1 See **4** n. 1.

Countess Blanche was warned that he intended to construct a fortress. Therefore Robert appeared at her court at Lagny and promised never, ever to fortify that place without her license, and that if he or his heirs ever should do so, she may dismantle it without reprisal.[2]

COPIES: CR 1, fol. 241v (>CR 6, fol. 240v). CR 3, fol. 146v–147r. CR 4, fols. 22v–23r. CR 7.1, fols. 278v–279r.
EDITION: Duchesne, *Histoire généalogique de la maison royale de Dreux*, pt. 1 (Dreux), *preuves*, 253 (from CR 7).
CALENDARED: AJ, no. 730.

Ego Robertus comes, dominus Drocarum et Brane, notum facio tam presentibus quam futuris quod cum ego plateam quandam acquisivissem prope Lisiacum super aquam et in ea domum edificarem, insinuatum fuit karissime domine mee Blanche, comitisse Trecensis, quod ibidem forteritiam faciebam. Propter quod apud Latiniacum comparvi coram ipsa, et ipsi bona et firmiter creantavi quod nec ego nec heredes mei ullo unquam tempore ibidem fortericiam faciemus nisi de assensu et voluntate dicte comitisse et successorum ejus dominorum Campanie, quod si ego vel heredes mei ibidem forteritiam faceremus sine assensu et voluntate dicte comitisse vel dominorum Campanie, ipsi possent eam diruere sine interpresura. Quod ut notum permaneat et ratum teneatur, litteris annotatum sigilli mei munimine roborari. Actum Latiniaci, anno incarnationi Verbi M ducentesimo nono, mense martio.

26

1208 August

Pierre of Joigny[1] *states that at his request Countess Blanche warranted the 300* l. *rent that his father Guillaume I, count of Joigny, had given him, as described in her letter and in the king's letter.*[2]

---

2 This letter appears to have been written by a chancery scribe, perhaps at the direction of the countess. The text states only that Robert sealed the letter, not that he requested it, suggesting that it was presented to him for sealing and then deposited in the comital archive. See also **47** n. 3.

1 Pierre was the son of Guillaume I, count of Joigny (1177–1221), and Adele of Courtenay, countess of Joigny (1179–86) until her divorce. Pierre must have attained his majority of twenty-one by 1208 and would have been in his mid-thirties when he succeeded his father in December 1221; he died four months later in April 1222 (Newman, *Les seigneurs de Nesle*, 2: 333–6).

2 King Philip II confirmed Blanche's pledge (*Receuil des actes de Philippe Auguste*, 3: 107, no. 1040).

COPIES: CR 1, fol. 242r (>CR 6, fols. 240v–241r). CR 3, fol. 172v. CR 4, fol. 143v. CR 7.3, fols. 198v–199r.

EDITIONS: Chantereau-Lefebvre, *Traité des fiefs*, 2: 34 (from CR 7), 2: 35 (from CR 6). Quantin, *Recueil*, 33, no. 72 (from Chantereau-Lefebvre).

CALENDARED: AJ, no. 689.

Ego Petrus de Jovigniaco notum facio, tam presentibus quam futuris, quod cum domina mea karissima Blancha, comitissa Trecensis illustris, se ad preces meas plegiam constituisset pro me erga dominum et patrem meum Willelmum, comitem Jovigniaci, quod ratas tenerem et firmas conventiones illas quas habeo erga dictum patrem meum de trecentis libratis terre quas mihi assignavit, sicut in litteris domini regis et in litteris ipsius comitisse plenius continentur. Ego dicte comitisse concessi quod, si pro plegeria ista dampnum aliquod incurrerit, inde se capiat ad feodum quod de ipsa teneo et ad aliam terram meam sine fidem suam mentiri. In hujus autem rei testimonium, presentes litteras fieri volui sigilli mei[3] appensione munitas. Actum anno gratie M CC VIII, mense augusto.

27

1204 November

Odo III, duke of Burgundy,[1] reports that Countess Blanche seized the revenues that Guillaume of Champlitte and his brother Odo[2] collected from the fairs of Champagne after Guillaume borrowed 300 l. *from Pierre Capitulus. When the duke paid off Guillaume's debt, the countess allowed Odo to collect up to 300* l. *from those revenues; but Odo then assigned that revenue to Valin, a Jew of Troyes,[3] in order to pay off his own debt.*

3 This appears to have been his personal seal, not the comital seal (Newman, *Les seigneurs de Nesle*, 2: 336, f: *quando vero primum sigillum comitis Jovigniaci habuero, presentes letteras faciam sigillo roborari*).

1 See **6** n. 1.

2 The brothers Guillaume and Odo II of Champlitte (viscount of Dijon) were the sons of Odo I 'the Champenois' of Champlitte who in 1125 was dispossessed of the county of Champagne by his father, Count Hugh. The two brothers participated prominently on the Fourth Crusade. Odo II died in May 1202, while Guillaume was seriously wounded the next year but recovered sufficiently to lead the conquest of the Peleponnese, where he became the first prince of the crusader principality of the Morea (Longnon, *Les compagnons de Villehardouin*, 209–12).

3 See **7** n. 2.

COPIES: CR 1, fol. 242r (>CR 6, fol. 241r). CR 3, fols. 33v–34r. CR 4, fol. 55v. CR 7.1, fol. 173r.

CALENDARED: AJ, no. 610. Petit, *Histoire*, 3: 397–8, no. 1097.

Ego Odo, dux Burgundie, omnibus ad quos littere iste pervenerint. Notum facio quod cum dilecta et fidelis nostra Blancha, comitissa Campania, pro trecentis libris quas Guillermus de Chanllita abstulerat Petro Capituli, saisiisset redditus quos Odo, frater Guillermi, et Guillermus habebant in nundinis. Nos easdem trecentas libras pro honore dicte comitisse fecimus Petro Capituli reddi, et ipsa comitissa ad predictos redditus quos saisierat, nos assignavit pro illis trecentis libris quas voluit nos rehabere. Nos autem ad eosdem redditus assignavimus pro debito nostro Vallinum, judeum Trecensem, usque dum habuerit totas illas trecentas libras. Et comitissa hanc assignationem debet Vallino garantire pro nobis. Actum anno Domini M CC IIII, mense novembri.

28

1204 (n.s.) March

Pierre II of Courtenay, count of Auxerre and Tonnerre,[1] *accepts the mediation of King Philip II in reaching a compromise with Clarembaud IV of Chappes*[2] *over the travel of his men to Ervy (in Champagne).*[3]

COPIES: CR 1, fol. 242r (<CR 6, fol. 241r). CR 3, fol. 3v. CR 4, fol. 137r.

EDITIONS: Chantereau-Lefebvre, *Traité des fiefs*, 2: 24 (from CR 7). Brussel, *Nouvel examen*, 1010.

CALENDARED: AJ, no. 598.

Ego Petrus, comes Altissiodorensis et Tornodorensis, notum facio presentibus et futuris quod per manum domini mei Philippi, regis Francie, compromisi in Clarembaudum de Capis super percursu Herviaci et captione Hugonis Salvagii. Quicquid super hiis per sacramentum suum dixerit ratum habiturus. Actum anno gratie M ducentesimo tercio, mense martio.

1 See **12** n. 4.

2 Clarembaud IV of Chappes, viscount of Troyes (ca 1170–1204), participated on the Third Crusade and died on pilgrimage to Saint Jacques of Compostella (Roserot, *Dictionnaire historique*, 1: 330).

3 See **30**.

29

1201 (n.s.) March, Troyes

Jean of Brienne,[1] *guardian of the county of Brienne for his brother Gautier III,*[2] *announces his exchange with Count Thibaut III. In return for Herbisse, Thibaut gave Jean property at Fontaine-Mâcon, Onjon, Luyères, Avant-lés-Marcilly, and Longsols, as well as two men and 780* l. *in cash. Because of an existing debt, Jean places that cash in his brother's domain land, but after redeeming the debt, he must use the money to purchase land that will be a comital fief.*[3] *Jean also guarantees good title to Herbisse against claims by the heirs of his deceased brother Guillaume.*

COPIES: CR 1, fol. 242r (>CR 6, fol. 241v). CR 7.2, 72–3.
EDITION: Chantereau-Lefebvre, *Traité des fiefs*, 2: 16 (from CR 7).
CALENDARED: AJ, no. 536. Arbois de Jubainville, 'Catalogue d'actes des comtes de Brienne,' no. 119.

Ego Johannes de Brena notum facio omnibus presentibus et futuris quod karissimus dominus meus Theobaudus, illustris comes Campanie, pro excambio Herbitie, mihi assedit et assignavit quicquid ipse habebat apud Fontem Maconis et apud Onjon et Luerias et Avanz et Lonsost, et unum hominem apud Pex et alterum apud Ruilliacum, et octingentas libras, viginti libras minus, quas posui in gageria quam a fratre meo Galtero, comite Brene, accepi, videlicet quicquid ipse in proprio dominio habebat inter Sequanam et Albam. Ita quidem quod gageria illa sit de feodo domini comitis Campanie. Et cum redempta fuerit, pecunia predicta ponetur in terram que similiter erit de feodo comitis Campanie. Ego autem eidem domino comiti creantavi quod heres defuncti Willermi de Brena aut quicumque pro eo juste poterit reclamare adversum me de omnibus predictis, in tali jure et querela erit in quali esset de Herbicia. In cujus rei testimonium presentem cartam volui fieri et sigilli mei munimine roborari. Actum Trecis anno Domini M CC, mense martio.

1 See **22** n. 1.
2 Jean's oldest brother, Gautier III, count of Brienne (1192–1205), had left Champagne to claim his wife's inheritance in Sicily, where he died in April 1205 (Longnon, *Les compagnons de Villehardouin*, 15–18).
3 See also **22**.

30

1205

Pierre II of Courtenay, count of Auxerre and Tonnerre,[1] declares that an inquest among local residents has verified the right of his men and of Countess Blanche's men to travel between his town of Tonnerre and her towns of Ervy and Saint-Florentin.[2]

COPIES: CR 1, fol. 242r–v (>CR 6, fol. 194r). CR 3, fol. 2r. CR 4, fol. 136v. CR 7.2, 10–11.

EDITIONS: Chantereau-Lefebvre, *Traité des fiefs*, 2: 27 (from CR 7). Brussel, *Nouvel examen*, 1009 (from CR 7, fol. 202).

CALENDARED: AJ, no. 643.

Ego Petrus, comes Autissiodorensis et Tornodorensis, notum facio tam presentibus quam futuris quod cum discordia esset inter me et dominam meam Blancham, illustram comitissam Trecensem, super percursu inter Tornodorum, ex parte mea, et Herviacum et Sanctum Florentinum, ex parte ipsius comitisse; tandem rei veritate, de assensu et voluntate dicte comitisse et mea, diligenter ab indigenis super hoc inquisita, didicimus percursum esse inter dictas villas et ita percursus ille fuit cognitus et probatus.

Preterea quittavi contentiones et querelas quas adversus Hernulphum Grossum super dei judicio quod mihi arramiaverat et adversus Columbum Bornum super caduco matris sue habebam. Actum anno gratie M ducentesimo quinto.

31

1210

Guillaume of Nanteuil-la-Fosse[1] states that he has received the consent of Jocelin II of Avallon and his wife, brother, and unmarried sister to the sale of Gillancourt to Countess Blanche.[2]

1 See **12** n. 4.

2 See **28**.

1 Guillaume of Nanteuil-la-Fosse (d. ca 1214), lord of Autrèches, was the brother of Gaucher II, lord of Nanteuil, and Milo of Nanteuil, provost of Reims and later bishop of Beauvais (see **81** n. 1).

2 Jocelin II's brother and sister were still minors at this time (see **16**). See also **12**.

COPIES: CR 1, fol. 242v (>CR 6, fol. 194r). CR 3, fol. 57r. CR 4, fol. 47r. CR 7.2, 433.
CALENDARED: AJ, no. 761.

Ego Willelmus de Nantholio notum facio presentibus et futuris quod accepi laudationem et concessum a domino Jocelino de Avalone et uxore ejus et fratre ejus et sorore ejus nondum maritata super hiis que vendidit domine comitisse Campanie apud Gillencort. Actum anno incarnationi Verbi M CC decimas.

32

1165, Provins

Count Henry I notifies his sergeants and all who see this letter that no one may touch the trees in his forest of Jouy, except those who live there, on pain of fine and loss of limb.[1]

COPIES: CR 1, fol. 242v (>CR 6, fol. 194v). CR 3, fol. 168v. CR 4, fol. 9r. CR 7.1, fol. 119r–v.
EDITION: Arbois de Jubainville, *Histoire* 3: 453, no. 129 (from CR 3).
CALENDARED: AJ, no. 132.

Ego Henricus, Trecensium palatinus comes, omnibus servientibus meis et universis qui presens scriptum viderint, notum facio quod in foresta mea de Joyaco quercum, fagum, pomum, pirum, esculum, alierium, et corberium proprie defensionis mee et proprii juris mei ita habeo, quod nemo nisi illi soli quorum nemora fuerint ad predictas arbores manum apponat. Illi vero ad solum herbergagium suum eas poterunt accipere. Si quis vero alius eas attentare presumpserit, non solum pecunie sed et membrorum reus erit. Quod ut notum permaneat et illibatum, litteris annotari et sigilli mei impressione firmari precepi. Datum Pruvini, anno incarnati Verbi M C LX quinto, per manum Guillelmi, cancellarii.

1 See the identical restrictions for the forest of Sourdan (**39**).

33

1208 August

Renaud of Dammartin, count of Boulogne,[1] *announces that Gaucher III of Châtillon-sur-Marne, count of Saint-Pol,*[2] *and Guillaume III des Barres*[3] *will conduct an inquest in order to resolve his dispute with Countess Blanche over the residence and village of Brégy. The village has been held by Count Henry I, Countess Marie, Count Henry II, and Renaud's father, Alberic. The inquest will also determine who may collect the head tax at Brégy.*

COPIES: CR 1, fol. 242v (>CR 6, fols. 194v–195r). CR 3, fol. 120v. CR 7.1, fols. 265v–266r.

EDITIONS: Chantereau-Lefebvre, *Traité des fiefs*, 2: 34 (from CR 6). Brussel, *Nouvel examen*, 100 (from CR 7, fol. 176 and CR 3, fol. 120v).

CALENDARED: AJ, no. 690.

Ego Reginaldus, comes Bolonie, omnibus presentes litteras inspecturis, notum facio quod super discordia que erat inter me et dominam meam Blancham, comitissam Trecensam palatinam, de domo et villa Brigiaci et appendiciis, in Galcherum, comitem Sancti Pauli, et Guillermum de Barris compromisimus in hunc modum: quod ipsi bona fide inquirent jus meum et jus predicte comitisse super predictis, sicut comes Henricus pater and comitissa Maria, uxor ejus, et Henricus comes, filius eorum, et Albericus, comes Donni Martini, pater meus,

1 See Malo, *Un grand feudataire*: *Renaud de Dammartin*.

2 Gaucher III (b. ca 1164/5) was the second son of Guy II of Châtillon and Adele of Dreux. In 1191 Gaucher succeeded to Châtillon after the death of his older brother Guy on the Third Crusade, and in 1196 he married the heiress of Saint-Pol. Thereafter he appeared prominently in Champagne and in royal circles until his death in 1219. See Duchesne, *Histoire de la maison de Chastillon sur Marne*, 47–69; *preuves*, 31–8; and Mathieu, 'Châtillon-sur-Marne.'

3 Guillaume III des Barres was in the military service of King Philip II from 1186 until his death in 1233. The 'des Barres' family had property in Paris since the early twelfth century, and a younger son, Ebrard, became grand master of the Templars, 1149–52 (Lombard-Jourdan, *Paris*, 107, 226 n. 489, and Bulst-Thiele, *Sacrae Domus Militiae Templi Hierosolymitani Magistri*, 41–52). Guillaume was celebrated for his charitable deeds as much as his military ones; his generosity to the nuns of Fontaines-les-Nonnes in Meaux was commemorated in an obituary notice (*Obituaires*, 4: 190, of 24 March: *karissimus atque dulcissimus amicus et benefactor noster, dominus Willelmus de Barris, venerabilis miles*). The nuns also drew up a mortuary roll in his name that circulated among one hundred twenty-seven religious communities: at the beginning of the seventeen-membrane roll, Guillaume is depicted on his deathbed, covered by a simple draped cloth and attended by the bishop of Meaux, two priests, and standing nuns of Fontaines (Grésy, *Etude historique et paléographique*).

tenuerunt, et quid inde jus meus michi dabunt et comitissa suum. Similiter de capitalibus que apud Brigiacum dicebam comitissam levasse, et que ipsa inde me levasse dicebat, de quibus inter nos erat discordia. Inquirent duo predicti veritatem et illi jus meum michi dabunt et comitissa suum. Si autem ipsi duo non potuerint concordare, dominus rex Francorum erit desuper et quod inde nobis dederit tam[a] ego quam comitissa[a] ratum habebimus et inconcussum. Actum anno Domini M CC VIII, mense augusto.

[a] tam *through* comitissa *omitted in CR 1.*

34

1202

Archambaud II, lord of Sully,[1] *quitclaims the rent that his grandfather, Archambaud I, had received from Count Thibaut II, then mortaged to Count Henry I.*[2]

COPIES: CR 1, fol. 242v (>CR 6, fol. 195r).
CALENDARED: AJ, no. 580.

Ego Erchembaudus, dominus Soliaci, notum facio omnibus ad quos littere iste pervenerint quod ego quitavi in perpetuum dominam Blancham, comitissam Campanie, ab omne querela seu jure quod requirere poteram super redditas quas bone memorie Theobaldus, quondam comes Blesensis, dedit domino Erchembaldum de Soliaco, avo meo, quod etiam idem Erchembaudus postmodum comiti Henrico, filio supradicti Theobaldi, consanguineo suo, pignori obligavit. Ita quod ipsa domina comitissa me sine omni contradictione omne beneplacitum suum faciat et statuat. In hujus itaque quitationis testimonium quam dicte comitisse feci et heredibus suis, presentem cartam sigilli mei feci impressione signari. Actum anno incarnati Verbi M CC secundo.

1 Archambaud II was the son of Giles II, lord of Sully, and nephew of Odo (of Sully), bishop of Paris (see **46** n. 2).
2 The dispute resolved by this quitclaim arose because Count Henry I's letter (**46**) allowed Archambaud's heirs to redeem the loan whenever they wished (see also **86**).

35

1204, Troyes

The dean Jean and chapter of Saint-Pierre of Troyes announce the resolution of their dispute with Henri of Chennegy.[1] *Henri claimed that he long had collected a grain rent from the villages of Orvilliers, Vallant, and Saint-Georges as a commutation of his right to justice and other taxes from the men of those villages. Under the auspices of Countess Blanche, three arbitors – the abbot of Pontigny, the archdeacon of Troyes, and the chancellor of Champagne – decided that Henry had to quitclaim all his rights over the three villages and half of the revenue he used to collect there, for which he received 450* l. *He will continue to receive the other half of the rent but will collect it from the chapter's agents rather than directly from the villagers.*[2]

ORIGINAL: AN, J 195, no. 3 (missing pendant seal).
COPIES: CR 1, fol. 243r (>CR 6, fols. 195r–196r). CR 8, fols. 420v–421r.
CALENDARED: AJ, no. 611. *Layettes*, 1: 272, no. 740.

Ego Johannes decanus totumque capitulum Beati Petri Trecensis. Notum facimus tam presentibus quam futuris quod cum inter nos et Henricum de Chinigiaco discordia verteretur super justicia, vieria et quibusdam consuetudinibus quas idem Henricus clamabat in tribus villis dicte ecclesie nostre, scilicet Orvilers, Valanz, et Sancto Georgio, in potestate etiam et hominibus earumdem villarum, asserens nos memoratas justiciam, vieriam et alia predicta a suis predecessoribus et ab ipso sub admodiatione duodecim modiorum avene diutius possedisse. Que omnia nos ei negabamus. Tandem, post multas rationes hinc inde propositas per dominam nostram Blancham, illustrem Campanie comitissam, et per venerabiles viros ..[a] abbatem Pontigniaci, Galterum cancellarium Campanie, et Milonem Trecensem archidiaconum, in quos tam a nobis quam ab ipso Henrico fuerat compromissum.

De predicta discordia inter nos et ipsum compositum est in hunc modum: Henricus de Chinigniaco predictam justiciam, vieriam et consuetudines predictas ecclesie nostre et nobis dimisit in perpetuum et quittavit. De duodecim autem modiis avene quos prefatus Henricus et predecessores sui in tribus villis prefatis ab antiquo precipere solebant, ecclesie nostre et nobis dimisit sex

1 Henri of Chennegy, lord of Saint-Mesmin (1196–1230) succeeded to his father Dudo's fief circa 1190 (Longnon, *Documents*, 1: 72, no. 1998); see also Roserot, *Dictionnaire historique*, 1: 374–5.

2 Countess Blanche sealed an almost identical letter for the canons (Lalore, *Cartulaire de Saint-Pierre de Troyes*, 109–11, no. 107, 1204).

modios in perpetuum et quittavit. Et quicquid juris in tribus prenominatis villis in potestate etiam et hominibus earumdem villarum habebat vel habere poterat, similter ecclesie nostre et nobis dimisit in perpetuum et quittavit, excepto feodo quod Guido Gasteble[3] tenet de ipso, quod feodum remanet in justicia nostra, et exceptis hominibus quibusdam quos ipse Henricus in memoratis villis habet, qui homines similter remanent in justicia nostra et salvamento nostro.

Pro predictis autem quittationibus dedimus sepedicto Henrico quadringentas et quinquaginta libras Pruvinensis monete. Alios vero sex modios reddent ei vel ejus mandato majores vel servientes nostri singulis annis in perpetuum infra octavas Sancti Remigii, et adducent ei apud Sanctum Memorium in domum suum ad rectum bichetum Trecense, recte et legitime mensurandos. Sed occasione hujus bladi non poterit ipse Henricus vel ejus heredes aliquid aliud in memoratis villis in potestate vel hominibus earum in posterum reclamare. Si vero isti sex modii avene soluti non fuerint in integrum termino constituto, Henricus de rebus hominum dictarum villarum, sine injuria aliqua ecclesie vel nobis aut etiam ipsis hominibus propter hoc inferenda, capere poterit usque ad valentiam defectus vel usque ad valentiam sex modiorum integrorum si nichil adhuc receperit, donec de sex modiis avene creatum ejus fiat. Hanc itaque compositionem et quittationes predictas voluit et laudavit Verderia, uxor Henrici. Ut autem hec omnia nota permaneant et rata teneantur, litteris annotata sigilli nostri fecimus munimine roborari. Actum Trecis, anno gratie millesimo ducentesimo quarto.

[a] *The scribe made two dots to indicate the absence of a name for the abbot of Pontigny.*

36

1203 June

Countess Blanche grants the causeway of Baudement and the right to collect the toll there for the next seven years to Robert, provost of Sézanne,[1] *Froger of Méry-sur-Seine, Isembard of Barbonne-Fayel, and Pierre of Baudement. They*

3 Guy Gasteblé (of Traînel) also held a comital fief in the castellany of Bray-sur-Seine: he appears in the feudal rolls of 1178 and 1201 (Longnon, *Documents*, 1: 51, no. 1326; 1: 100, no. 1226: two fiefs, each owing six weeks castle-guard). He later retired to the Cistercian monastery of Pontigny, where at an advanced age in 1217 he testified about the siege of Saint-Aignan castle in 1153 (see Sassier, *Recherches*, 88–90, and Evergates, *Documents*, 38–9, no. 25).

1 See **24**.

must repair one-seventh of the causeway each year,[2] *and the countess will furnish the necessary timber for repairing the two large bridges there.*[3]

COPIES: CR 1, fol. 243r–v (>CR 6, fol. 196r).

EDITIONS: Mortet and Deschamps, *Recueil de textes*, 196–7, no. 94 (from CR 6). Mesqui, *Les routes*, 149, fig. 17 (photograph of CR 6, fol. 196r).

TRANSLATION: Mesqui, *Les routes*, 185. Brunel and Lalou, *Sources d'histoire médiévale*, 511.

CALENDARED: AJ, no. 588.

Ego Blancha, comitissa Trecensis palatina, notum facio omnibus ad quos littere presentes pervenerint quod ego Roberto preposito Sezannie et Frogero de Meriaco et Isembardo de Barbona et Petro de Baudement concessi quod a festo proximo Pentecostes quod fuit anno Domini M CC III usque ad septem annos habeant in manu sua calceiam de Baudement, ita quod omne pedagium et cathenam recipiant exceptis decem libras quas ecclesia Beati Stephani Trecensis habet ibidem. Et est conventio quod singulis annis debent facere septinam parcem calceie, et ego debeo mittere magnum marremum sine planchis ad opus duorum magnorum pontium. Ipsi autem in fine septimi anni debent reddere caliceam totam pavimentatam. In cujus rei testimonium, presentes litteras fieri volui et sigilli mei testimonio roboravi. Actum anno Domini M ducentesimo tercio, mense junio.

37

1186

Countess Marie and her son Henry II make known that Pierre II of Courtenay, count of Nevers,[1] *allowed Guillaume I, count of Joigny,*[2] *to hold the fief of La Ferté-Loupière directly from Marie, but that four of her officials advised her that the fief should be held directly from the count of Nevers. Therefore she agreed that the count of Joigny will hold that fief directly from the count of Nevers, who in turn will hold it from the countess.*[3]

2 See **71** for a seven-year lease of the provost's revenues at Chablis.

3 At the expiration of this contract, the countess purchased the castle of Baudement from its heiress (**21**), thus bringing that castle town on the Aube River completely under comital control.

1 See **12** n. 4.

2 For Guillaume I, count of Joigny (1177–1221), see **26** n. 1 and Newman, *Nesle*, 2: 335.

3 By circa 1201, however, the count of Joigny held La Ferté-Loupière directly from Countess Blanche, as reported in a roll of fiefs: *comes de Jovigniaco est homo ligius domini Campanie et tenet Jovigniacum ... et Feritatem Luperie* (Longnon, *Documents*, 1: 91, no. 2432).

ORIGINAL: AN, J 1035, no. 1 (missing pendant seal).
COPIES: CR 1, fol. 243v (>CR 6, fol. 196v). CR 7.1, fols. 151v–152r.
EDITIONS: Chantereau-Lefebvre, *Traité des fiefs*, 2: 9 (from CR 7, printed twice). Quantin, *Cartulaire général de l'Yonne*, 2: 378 (from Chantereau-Lefebvre).
CALENDARED: AJ, no. 350. *Layettes*, 5: 31, no. 90.

Ego Maria, Trecensis comitissa, et Henricus, filius meus, notum facimus presentibus et futuris quod Petrus, comes Nivernensis, nobis concessit ut Guillermus, comes Jovigniaci, feodum de Firmitate de Luparia de nobis teneat in capite, quousque Drogo de Merloto, Petrus de Tusquino, Gilo de Torneello, et Milo de Pruvino nobis dicant quod feodum illud reddamus ipsi comiti Nivernensi. Et quando ipsi hoc nobis dixerint, nos illud ei reddemus et tunc comes Jovigniaci illud tenebit de comite Nivernensi, et comes Nivernensis de nobis illud tenebit. Quod ut ratum teneatur, litteris annotatum sigillo nostro firmavimus. Testibus: predictis Drogone, Petro, Gilone et Milone. Actum anno incarnatione Domini M C LXXX sexto. Data per manum Haicii, cancellarii. Nota Willermi.

38

1210 April

Alberic, archbishop of Reims,[1] *approves of the treaty between King Philip II and Countess Blanche, a copy of which he has received from the king.*[2] *The archbishop restates the main provision of that treaty: Philip will not hear any challenge to Thibaut's inheritance before Thibaut attains twenty-one, at which time he will receive Thibaut's homage. But the king will hear any charge brought by an ecclesiastical person.*

ORIGINAL: AN, J 198, no. 18 (missing pendant seal).
COPIES: CR 1, fol. 243v (>CR 6, fols. 196v–197r). CR 3, fol. 4v. CR 4, fol. 139v. CR 8, fol. 111r.
EDITIONS: Chantereau-Lefebvre, *Traité des fiefs*, 2: 40 (from CR 6). *Layettes*, 1: 349, no. 918.
CALENDARED: AJ, no. 735.

1 For Archbishop Alberic of Humbert (1207–18), see Desportes, *Reims et les Rémois*, 151, and *Fasti Ecclesiae Gallicanae*, 156–7.

2 See Philip's letter (**App. 2**). The pope (***61**) and the bishop of Langres (***120**) also alluded to the king's letter. See also **48**, **65**.

Albericus, Dei gratia Remensis archiepiscopus, omnibus ad quos littere iste pervenerint, in Domino salutem. Noverint universi quod nos laudamus et approbamus consuetudinem a domino Philippo, rege Francorum, per suas litteras approbatam, sicut eam vidimus in suo auctentico contineri, secundum quam Theobaldus, filius dilecte et fidelis nostre Blanche, illustris comitisse Campanie, et eadem Blancha, mater ipsius, non possunt trahi in causam de aliquo quod pater ejusdem Theobaldi sine placito tenebat quando decessit, donec idem Theobaldus vicesimum primum compleverit annum. Si tamen aliqua ecclesia vel ecclesiastica persona conquereretur de eis, non obstante hac consuetudine, plenam eis justiciam faceremus. Postquam autem idem Theobaldus vicesimum primum annum compleverit, ipsum in hominem recipiemus de omnibus que predecessores sui a nostris predecessoribus tenuerunt, sub ea forma qua solent homagia recipi. Actum anno gratie M CC decimo[a], mense aprili.

[a] X *in CR 1.*

39

1165, Provins

Count Henry I notifies his sergeants and all who see this letter that no one may touch the trees in his forest of Sourdun, except those who live there, on pain of fine and loss of limb.[1]

ORIGINAL: AN, J 203, no. 1 (missing pendant seal).[2]
COPIES: CR 1, fol. 243v (>CR 6, fol. 197r). CR 7.1, fols. 118v–119r.
EDITION: *Layettes*, 1: 89–90, no. 185.
CALENDARED: AJ, no. 133.

Ego Henricus, Trecensium palatinus comes, omnibus servientibus meis et universis qui presens scriptum viderint, notum facio quod in foresta de Surdulio querqum,[a] fagum, pomum, pirum, esculum, alierium, et corberium proprie[b] defensionis et proprii juris mei ita habeo quod nemo, nisi illi soli quorum nemora fuerint, ad predictas arbores manum apponat. Illi autem ad solum herbergagium suum eas poterunt accipere. Si quis vero alius eas attentare[c] presumpserit, non solum pecunie[b] sed et membrorum reus erit. Quod ut notum

1 See the identical restrictions for his forest at Jouy (**32**).

2 This is the oldest original document to survive from the comital archive (see table 2). The oldest baronial letter is **14**.

permaneat et illibatum, litteris annotari et sigilli mei impressione firmari precepi. Datum Pruvini, anno incarnati Verbi M C LX V,[d] per manum Guillelmi, cancellarii.

[a] quercum *in CR 1.* [b] *The original document indicates a final e with cedilla, which is ignored by CR 1 and CR 8.* [c] attemptare *in CR 1.* [d] quinto *in CR 1.*

40

1202 December, Epernay

Abbot Hugh and the community of Saint-Martin of Epernay make known that they have exchanged a woman with her children and future progeny in return for a 20 s. *rent from Countess Blanche's toll at Epernay. The rent will be paid on the anniversary of Count Thibaut III.*[1]

ORIGINAL: AN, J 197, no. 3 (missing pendant seal).
COPIES: CR 1, fol. 244r (>CR 6, fol. 197r–v). CR 3, fol. 54v. CR 4, fol. 162r–v. CR 8, fol. 276v.
CALENDARED: AJ, no. 570. *Layettes*, 1: 238, no. 654.

Noverint tam presentes quam futuri quod ego Hugo, Sparnacensis ecclesie dictus abbas, totusque ecclesie nostre conventus commutavimus domine nostre Blanche, nobili Trecensis comitisse palatine, Helvidem, uxorem Hugonis Coranth, et filios et filias ejus omnemque generationem que ex ipsius in posterno egredietur, tam predicte comitisse quam successoribus ejus, perpetuo possidendam pro viginti solidos in theloneo Sparnacensis. Et in parte ejus nobis assignatis singulis annis in die anniversarii comitis Theobaldi, viri et domini sui, ecclesie Sparnacensis persolvendis. Quod ut ratum esset et notum, presentem cartam inde fieri voluimus et sigilii nostri testimonio roboravimus. Actum apud Sparnacum, annum Domini M CC secundo, mense decembri.

1 The monks retained Countess Blanche's reciprocal letter:
Ego Blancha, comitissa Trecensis palatina, notum facio presentibus et futuris quod dilecti mihi abbas et conventus ecclesie Sparnacensis concesserunt mihi habendam Helvidem, uxorem quondam Hugonis Coranth, et filios et filias ejus omnemque eorum generationem que ab ipsis post modum egredietor, tam mihi quam successoribus meis perpetuo possidendam pro viginti solidis in thelonio meo Sparnacensi et in parte mea assignatis singulis annis die anniversario karissimi domni et viri mei, illustris quondam comitis Theobaldi, Sparnacensi ecclesie persolvendis. Actum apud Sparnacum, anno M CC II, mense decembri. Datum per manum cancellarii Galteri (Nicaise, *Epernay et l'abbaye Saint-Martin*, 2: 147, no. 20).

41

1205

Abbot Simon and the chapter of Saint-Paul of Cormery approve the sale of woods at Courtioux[1] *by the prior of Notre-Dame of Pont-sur-Seine*[2] *to Countess Blanche for 300* l.

COPIES: CR 1, fol. 244r (>CR 6, fol. 197v). CR 3, fol. 116v. CR 4, fol. 158r. CR 8, fol. 261r.
CALENDARED: AJ, no. 646.

Ego Symon abbas et universum capitulum Beati Pauli Cormeracensis notum facimus presentibus et futuris quod frater Renaudus, prior Beati Marie de Pontibus, karissime nostre Blanche, illustri comitisse Trecensium palatina, per III C libris vendidit centum arpentum nemoris de Cortol juxta nemus Templariorum. Nos autem venditionem volentes et laudantes, presentem cartam in hujus rei testimonium sigillorum nostrorum appensionibus roboravimus. Actum anno Domini millesimo ducentesimo quinto.

42

1208 (n.s.) February, Dijon

Robert, bishop of Langres,[1] *and Arnaud, abbot of Cîteaux, grant papal authorization for Saint-Bénigne of Dijon to sell the residence of Morains to Countess Blanche for 1700* l.[2] *The monks owe that amount to the Jew Valin*[3] *and are unable to repay either the debt or the interest.*

COPIES: CR 1, fol. 244r (>CR 6, fols. 197v–198r). CR 3, fol. 161r. CR 4, fol. 124v. AD Aube, 3 H 10, Cartulary of Clairvaux, 281, no. 2.[4]
CALENDARED: AJ, no. 677.

Ego Robertus, Dei gratia episcopus Lingonensis, et ego frater Arnaudus, abbas Cystercii, notum facimus universis presentibus et futuris quod abbas Adam et

1 Identification by Roserot, *Dictionnaire historique*, 1: 448–9.
2 The priory of Notre-Dame, dependent on the monastery of Cormery, had existed at Pont-sur-Seine for several centuries (Roserot, *Dictionnaire historique*, 2: 1170).
1 Bishop Robert (1204–9) was the brother of Gaucher III of Châtillon-sur-Marne.
2 Countess Blanche then gave the house to Clairvaux (AD Aube, 3 H 10, Cartulary of Clairvaux, 281, no. 1, February 1208, n.s.).
3 See **7** n. 2.
4 Clairvaux's own copy no doubt derived from an identical letter in its archive.

totus conventus ecclesie Sancti Benigni Divionensis dederunt et concesserunt, de assensu nostro qui plenam habebamus auctoritata apostolica patrem tam in capite quam in membris ecclesie Sancti Benigni, super venditionem possessionum suorum ad solutionem debitorum ejusdem ecclesie faciendam nobili domine Blanche, illustri comitisse Trecensium palatine: domum de Morans cum omnibus tenementis et appenditiis suis per mille et septingentis libris pruvinensium, et usuris earum que cucurrerant per XI annos et unaquaque libra tres denarios per ebdomadam lucrabatur in manu Vaallini judei. Nos autem attendentes tantam esse paupertatem ecclesie quod alio competentiori modo nunc minus dampnoso non posset memoratum debitum vel lucrum solvi. Hanc donationem ratam habemus et auctoritate apostolica quam fungimus confirmamus. Actum mense februario apud Divionem, anno an incarnatione Domini, M CC VII.

43

1200 October

Abbot Milo and the chapter of Châtrices make known that they have given in perpetuity to Count Thibaut III the land and forest whose perimeter is described here for the establishment of a village (La Neuville-au-Pont).[1] *The monks reserve certain rights there, as well as the tithes.*

COPIES: CR 1, fol. 244r–v (>CR 6, fol. 198 r–v). CR 3, fols. 133v–134r. CR 4, fol. 188r. CR 8, fol. 341r.
CALENDARED: AJ, no. 525.

Ego Milo dictus abbas totumque capitulum de Castriciis notum facimus presentibus et futuris quod domino Theobaldo, illustri comiti Campanie, communi assensu dedimus et habenda perpetuo concessimus totam terram et nemus nostrum a loco qui dicitur *la Concye Clarel* usque ad rivum de Noyer, et usque ad costam de *Myroaut* per chalediam Galteri, ultra usque ad *marcheyz* de Antre juxta rivum de deserte *meys* sursum directe ad lineam usque ad caput terre Sancti Dyonisii, et usque ad *la Concye Clarel*, et quicquid infra terminos illos habebamus in omnibus modis et commodis, preter grossam decimam et minutam que nobis retinuimus et preter presbiterium si forte illic villa fuerit constituta. Dominus autem comes nobis concessit usuarium nostram ad usus perpetuos in omnibus predictis et ad edificandum et ad comburendum. Si autem in predictis dampnum faceremus, dampnum sine forisfacto aut emenda restitueremus.

1 See **100**, ***114**, ***115**.

Concessit etiam nobis quod predicta nullo modo alienari poterunt de manu heredis sui qui Vitriacum tenebit et quod res nostre per Sanctam Meneheldym sine consuetudine que ad ipsum pertineat libere transient et quiete. In cujus rei testimonium et confirmationem, presentem cartam sigilli nostri munimine duximus roborare. Actum anno domini M CC, mense Octobri.

44

1187, Sézanne

Count Henry II announces that he has resolved a dispute his father had with Haice of Plancy[1] *by exchanging rights over five men.*

COPIES: CR 1, fol. 244v (>CR 6, fol. 198v).
CALENDARED: AJ, no. 356.

Ego Henricus, Trecensis comes palatinus, notum facio presentibus et futuris quod cum pie memorie pater meus, comes Henricus, domino Haicio de Planciaco quosdam homines de quibus inter ipsos querela vertebatur, Thadeum scilicet, Johannem de Rumilli, Fovion, Becelinum et Girardum fratrem ejus, dedisset in augmento casamenti sui, et quicquid juris in eis habebat sive de albanagio sive de jure alio ei quietum clamasset, ita etiam quod ipsi Haicio, si vellet, liceret eos alii dare qui ipsos de ipso comite teneret in feodo. Postea idem Haicus prefatos Johannem, Fovion, Becelinum, et Girardum michi dimisit et quietos clamavit. Ego vero predictum Thadeum ei demisi in feodo predicto modo quo de patre meo illum tenebat, ita scilicet quod liceat ei dare eundem Thadeum alii qui ipsum de me teneat in feodo. Quod ut ratum teneatur, litteris annotatum sigillo meo confirmavi. Actum anno ab incarnatione Domini M C LXXX septimo. Data Sezannie per manum Guidonis, cancellarii. Nota Guillermi.

---

1 Haice, the brother of Hugh II, lord of Plancy (1138–89), entered the newly founded chapter of Saint-Etienne of Troyes in 1160 and rose to become its dean. At the same time he was a canon in the cathedral chapter of Saint-Pierre of Troyes, where he also became dean. In 1181 Countess Marie appointed him chancellor; in 1191 he was elected bishop of Troyes (1191–3). See Arbois de Jubainville, *Histoire*, 3: 134–5; Roserot, *Dictionnaire historique*, 3: 1577–8; and Mayer, *Die Kanzlei*, 2: 589–93.

45

1179, Provins

Count Henry I announces that since Raoul of Combault[1] *sold a fief, with the count's consent, to Robert of Cuiry-Housse*[2] *for 50* l., *Raoul must replace that fief with 50* l. *worth of property. Raoul's brother Gaucher likewise must invest 50* l. *in property to be held as a comital fief, that is, the 25* l. *he already has received from the count and the 25* l. *he will receive from the count's butler, Anselm II of Traînel.*[3]

COPIES: CR 1, fols. 244v–245r (>CR 6, fol. 199r). CR 3, fol. 13r–14r. CR 4, fols. 11v–12r. CR 7.1, fols. 121r–122v (dated 1178).
CALENDARED: AJ, nos. 286 (dated 1178), 298.[4]

Ego Henricus, Trecensi comes palatinus, notum facio presentibus et futuris quod cum Radulphus de Combellis Robertum de Curia, hominem suum, de me teneret in feodo, ipse illum, me assentiente, vendidit precio L librarum tali conditione, quod ipse Radulpus has L libras ponet in feodo meo que quidem L libre jam posite sunt in commendatione in ecclesia beate Marie de Chagia. Cum etiam idem Radulfus de eodem Roberto prius habuisset XXX libras, ipse illas positurus est in feodo meo, et exinde fidejussorem habeo Galcherum de Combellis, ita etiam quod licet michi redditus suos quos habet apud Latiniacum capere et detinere quousque hee XXX libre in feodo meo posite sint.

Preterea notum facio quod Galcherus de Combellis L libras positurus est in feodo meo, quarum XXV libras jam a me recepit; alias autem XXV libras traditurus est ei ex precepto meo dominus Ansellus de Triangulo, si prius illas XXV libras quas jam recepit in feodo meo posuerit. Prefatum itaque pecuniam dicti Radulphus et Galcherus ponent in feodo meo, sive in vadio sive in emptione, ad laudamentum vel testimonium et dispositionem Odonis de Poenci et Johannes, prepositi Meldensis, Hugonis de Montguillon, Johannis de Pommura, et Bartholomei de Porta Sancti Meloti. Illud autem sciri volo, quoniam si

1 Raoul of Combault is listed in the feudal roll for Coulommiers (Longnon, *Documents*, 1: 47, no. 1190, ca 1178).

2 Robert of Cuiry-Housse purchased at least one other comital fief in the 1180s (Longnon, *Documents*, 1: 33, no. 888; 35, no. 918; 123, no. 3324).

3 Anselm II, lord of Traînel and butler of Champagne (1152–85), was perhaps Count Henry I's closest companion and the one who witnessed most of the count's acts; see Lalore, 'Documents pour servir à la généalogie des anciens seigneurs de Traînel,' 185–7, 208–25; and Roserot, *Dictionnaire historique*, 3: 1490–1. See also his widow, Hermesend of Bar-sur-Seine (***91**).

4 Arbois de Jubainville catalogued the same document twice: as no. 286 (from the copy in CR 7.1 that is dated – erroneously – 1178) and as no. 298 (from the copy in CR 3 dated 1179).

vel ipse Radulfus vel Galcherus istam pecuniam in vadio ponerent, cum vadium redimerent, ponerent pecuniam in custodia in ecclesie de Chagia, nec ad ipsam pecuniam manum apponerent quousque illam in vadio vel emptione possuissent in feodo meo. Quod ut notum permaneat et ratum teneatur, litteris annotatum sigilli mei impressione firmavi, testibus domino Ansello de Triangulo, Garnero fratre ejus, Willermo marescallo, Deimberto de Ternantis, Girardo Eventato, Willermo de Gloisa, Artaudo camerario, et Milone de Pruvino. Actum Pruvini, anno incarnati Verbi, M C LXX nono.[a] Data per manum Stephani, cancellarii. Nota Guillermi.

[a] *CR 1, CR 3, and CR 4 give 1179; CR 7.1 gives 1178 by error; see n. 4.*

46[1]

1158, Château-Thierry

Count Henry I makes known that he regranted to Archambaud I of Sully[2] *the fief of 120* l. *rent that Count Henry's father, Thibaut II, had given him.*[3] *But then Archambaud mortgaged that revenue to Henry for 550* l., *on the understanding that his heirs could redeem it whenever they wished.*[4]

COPIES: CR 1, fol. 245r (>CR 6, fol. 199v).
EDITION: Chantereau-Lefebvre, *Traité des fiefs*, 2: 4 (from CR 6).
CALENDARED: AJ, no. 53.

Ego Henricus, Trecensis comes palatinus, presentibus et futuris notum fieri volo quod Theobaldus, comes Blesensis, pater meus bone memorie, Archambaudo de Solliaco, nepoti suo, VI^{xx} libras pruvinensis monete singulis annis in feodum dedit, quas ego ipse post decessum patris mei sibi reddidi, et ipse Archambaudus propter V^{c} et L libras pruvinensis et meldensis et trecensis monete michi invadiavit, tali siquidem conditione, quod ipse vel heres suus

1 This is the oldest document known to have been in the chancery archive in 1211 (see table 2 and **14** n. 2, **39** n. 2). It seems to have entered the chancery in 1202, after Archambaud's son and grandson quitclaimed their right to redeem the mortgaged fief (see **34**, **86**), but was discarded after being copied into the Cartulary of 1211, as it does not appear in any later cartulary.

2 Archambaud I of Sully was the eldest son of Guillaume of Blois-Chartres and grandson of Count Etienne-Henri of Blois-Chartres-Meaux (1089–1102), and Countess Adele of Blois (1089–1120, d. 1137). Countess Adele arranged Guillaume's marriage to Agnes, heiress of Sully, in effect displacing him as heir of Blois-Chartres-Meaux in favor of his younger brother, Thibaut IV (II of Champagne, 1125–52). See Devailly, *Le Berry*, 363–5, 486 (genealogical table), and LoPrete, 'Adela of Blois,' 31–2.

3 Count Henry renewed the grant shortly after becoming count in January 1152, angering the monks of Saint-Martin of Tours (**104**).

4 See **34**, **86**.

quocumque termino voluerint, redimere poterunt. Hujus rei testes sunt ex parte Archambaudi: Gilo Meschinus de Sancero, idem Archambaudus, Guillermus de Castro. Ex parte vero mea testes sunt hii: Ansellus de Triangulo, Hugo de Planceio, Odo constabularius, Petrus Bursaudus, Matheus Lotharingus, Gauterus marescallus. Anno incarnati Verbi M C L VIII. Tradita est apud Castrum Theoderici per manum Guillermi, cancellarii.

47

1209, Nogent-sur-Seine

Guillaume, count of Sancerre,[1] *declares that he is a liegeman of Countess Blanche for Sancerre and the fiefs that move from Sancerre, namely four 'great fiefs' (held by the lords of Montfauçon, Sully, La Tour de Vèvre, and Léré) and certain unnamed 'small fiefs,' as well as Saint-Brisson and Châtillon-sur-Loing.*[2]

ORIGINALS: AN, J 198, nos. 15, 17 (two identical acts by the same scribe; missing pendant seals).[3]

---

1 Guillaume, count of Sancerre (1191–1219), eldest son of Count Etienne I of Sancerre (1152–90), had been under the guardianship first of his aunt, Queen Adele, then of Count Thibaut III (see **68**).

2 The fiefs listed here appear in the feudal roll of 'great fiefs' of circa 1201 (Longnon, *Documents*, 1: 90, no. 2427).

3 The fact that Countess Blanche demanded two sealed letters underscores the importance of this recognition, which Guillaume apparently had denied or tried to obscure. In circa 1205 Geoffroy of Villehardouin, marshal of Champagne who at the time was in Constantinople, advised Countess Blanche that 'count Thibaut (V) of Blois and count Etienne of Sancerre are your liege men (*homines ligii*)' (Longnon, *Documents*, 1: xiii, n. 2). Jean, count of Brienne, and Guillaume I, count of Joigny, jointly sealed a letter (written by the same scribe who wrote Guillaume's two letters) attesting to having witnessed Guillaume's recognition:

Ego Johannes comes Brene et ego Willermus comes Jovigniaci notum facimus tam presentibus quam futuris quod dilectus et fidelis noster Willelmus comes Sacrii Cesaris in presentia karissime nostre Blanche, illustris comitisse Campanie, nobis presentibus, recognovit se tenere Sacrum Cesaris de dicta comitissa cum omnibus pertinentiis suis, tam in feodo quam in dominio. Hec autem sunt magna feoda que movent de Sacro Cesaris, videlicet feodum domini Montis Falconis, feodum domini Soilliaci, feodum domini de Woevre, Lereium cum omnibus pertinentiis suis tam in feodo quam in dominio. Hec predicta cum aliis minutis feodis que inde movent de Sacro Cesaris, tenet dictus comes de predicta comitissa. Similiter tenet de ipsa Sanctum Britium cum omnibus pertinentiis suis tam in feodo quam in dominio, Castellione super Loain cum omnibus pertinentiis suis tam in feodis quam in dominio. De hiis omnibus fuit pater ejus, inclite recordationis, comes Stephanus, homo ligius comitis Campanie. Et ipse similiter de omnibus predictis homo ligius est prefate comitisse ante omnes homines. Ut autem hec nota permaneant et rata teneantur, litteris annotata sigilli nostrorum munimine fecimus roborari. Actum anno gratie M CC nono (AN, J 198, no. 16, 1209; missing pendant seal [= Martène and Durand, *Thesaurus novus anecdotorum*, 1: 814]).

COPIES: of AN, J 198, no. 15: CR 1, fol. 245r (>CR 6, fols. 199v–200r). CR 3, fol. 2v–3r. CR 4, fol. 138v. CR 7.2, 33–4.
COPY: of AN J 198, no. 17: CR 7.2, 34–5 ('Alia littera de eodem').
EDITIONS: Chantereau-Lefebvre, *Traité des fiefs*, 2: 35 (from CR 7). *Layettes*, 1: 343, no. 904.
CALENDARED: AJ, no. 733.

Ego Willelmus, comes Sacri Cesaris, notum facio tam presentibus quam futuris quod, in presentia karissime domine mee Blanche, illustris comitisse Trecensis, recognovi et adhuc bene recognosco me tenere de ipsa Sacrum Cesaris cum omnibus pertinentiis suis tam in feodo quam in dominio. Hec autem sunt magna feoda que movent de Sacro Cesaris, videlicet: feodum domini Montis Falconis, feodum domino Soilliaci,[a] feodum domini de Woevre,[b] Lereium cum omnibus pertinentiis suis tam in feodo quam in dominio. Hec predicta, cum aliis minutis feodis que inde movent et de Sacro Cesaris, teneo de predicta comitissa. Similiter teneo de ipsa Sanctum Britium cum omnibus pertinentiis suis tam in feodo quam in dominio, Castellionem super Loain cum omnibus pertinentiis suis tam in feodo quam in dominio. De hiis omnibus fuit pater meus, inclite recordationis, comes Stephanus, homo ligius comitis Campanie. Et ego similiter de hiis omnibus predictis homo ligius sum prefate comitisse ante omnes homines. Ut autem hec nota permaneant et rata teneantur, litteris annotata sigilli mei munimine roboravi. Actum Nogenti, anno gratie millesimo ducentesimo nono.

[a] Seilliaci *in AN, J 198, no. 15 and in CR 1.* [b] Waevre *in AN, J 198, no 15 and in CR 1.*

48

1209 September

Odo III, duke of Burgundy,[1] *approves of the treaty between King Philip II and Countess Blanche according to which the king will not hear any challenge to Thibaut's inheritance until he reaches twenty-one.*[2]

1 See **6** n. 1.

2 The duke refers to the king's legal judgment (*judicium*), the same term used by the bishop of Langres in a similar letter (**65**). The duke and the bishop sealed longer letters on the same subject in January 1210 (see ***120**). The documents sealed by Philip and Blanche (**App. 2**) refer to an accord or agreement (*conventiones*). See also **38**, ***61**.

ORIGINAL: AN, J 198, no 14 (missing pendant seal).
COPIES: CR 1, fol. 245r (>CR 6, fol. 200r). CR 7.1, fol. 199r.
CALENDARED: AJ, no. 712. *Layettes*, 1: 333, no. 880. Petit, *Histoire*, 3: 428, no. 1218.

Ego Odo, dux Burgundie, notum facio omnibus presentibus et futuris quod ego laudo, approbo et concedo judicium illud quod karissimus dominus meus Philippus, illustris Francorum rex, fecit de Theobaldo, filio karissimi et consanguinei et fidelis mei comitis Theobaldi et de Blanche, matre ejus, que comitatum Campanie tenebat per advocatiam, videlicet quod nec ipse Theobaldus nec Blanche, mater ejus, respondere debent de terra de qua dictus consanguineus meus Theobaldus tenens erat cum decederet, antequam dictus Theobaldus, filius ejus, haberit viginti et unum annum. In cujus rei testimonium, presentem cartam fieri volui sigilli mei munimine roboratam. Actum anno Domini M ducentesimo nono, mense septembri.

49

[1199–1201][1]

Guillaume V, count of Vienne and Mâcon,[2] *notifies his brother-in-law, Count Thibaut III, that by his letter he has authorized R. of Beaune to collect the 150* l. *that he is owed annually at the fairs of Bar-sur-Aube and Troyes. He requests that Thibaut pay that sum in cash as 3000* solidi.

COPIES: CR 1, fol. 245r (>CR 6, fol. 200v).
CALENDARED: AJ, no. 1517 (dated 'probably 1222').

Dilectissimo domino et karissimo fratri suo Theobaldo, Campanie comiti, Willelmus, comes Viennensis et Masticensis comes suus, in omnibus salutem fraternamque dilectionem fraternitati vestre. Notum sit quod ego assignavi R. de Biaune, littere presentium, ad nundinas Barri VI^{xx} et V libras et ad primas nundinas de *Troies* post nundinas Barri XXV libras. Unde vobis mando et precor quod predicto R. predictam pecuniam in pace ex parte mea permittatis recipere et sic habebit MMM solidos.

1 This letter must be dated between Guillaume V's accession in 1199 and Thibaut's death in May 1201.

2 Guillaume V, count of Vienne and Mâcon (1199–1234), married Count Thibaut III's sister Scholastique; see Bouchard, *Sword*, 278–9.

50

1204 (n.s.) January

Hugh, castellan of Vitry,[1] *makes known the arrangement he has made for repaying his 400* l. *debt to the Jews of Guy II of Dampierre.*[2] *Count Hugh II of Rethel (his uncle) has lent him the money without interest for that redemption, on condition that he is repaid in two installments.*[3] *Hugh authorizes Countess Blanche to seize the fiefs he holds from her if he does not redeem that debt before 2 February.*

COPIES: CR 1, fol. 245v (>CR 6, fols. 200v–201r).
EDITION: Chantereau-Lefebvre, *Traité de fiefs*, 2: 24 (from CR 6).
CALENDARED: AJ, no. 597.

Ego Hugo, castellanus Vitriaci, notum facio omnibus presentibus et futuris quod ego in plegiam misi dominam meam ligiam Blancham, illustrem Campanie comitissam, erga comitem Registestis de quatuor centum libris pruvinensis monete, de quibus si usque ad Purificationem Beate Marie fecero quod judei Guidonis de Donnipetro quitent comitem. Conventio est inter me et ipsum quod comes faciet mihi dari respectum sine usura de medietate usque ad Pascha proximo venturum, et de alia usque ad festum Sancti Remigii. Si vero usque ad Purificationem Beate Marie non fecero quitationem fieri a judeis, sicut dictum est, ego creanto et concedo domine comitisse quod ex tunc infra quindenam qua comes eum submoneret, possit se capere ad omne feodum quod teneo de ea, tam pro predictis quam pro catallis, salva erga me fide sua, et quod propter hoc non sint quiti illi plegii quos propter hoc comiti dedi. Actum anno domini M CC III, mense januario.

1 Hugh was the son of Helvide and Henri of Rethel, castellan of Vitry (d. ca 1190). Helvide remarried by circa 1191 to Renard II of Dampierre (-le-Château), who held the title castellan of Vitry until his departure on the Fourth Crusade in 1202 (Longnon, *Les compagnons de Villehardouin*, 60–3). Hugh of Vitry is here liquidating the debts he incurred before acquiring his inheritance.

2 See **3** n. 1.

3 The letters of Count Hugh II of Rethel (1198–1228) are in Saige, *Trésor des chartes du comté de Rethel*, 1: 42–98.

51

1209 May

Jean, lord of Montmirail and Oisy,[1] *and Helvide, lady of Montmirail and Oisy,*[2] *make known that Countess Blanche has agreed to warrant the 1300* l. *they owe the monks of Longpont. They permit the countess to seize their fief if they do not repay that debt within two years; and if they both die before redeeming it, neither their heirs nor any advocate for their heirs may hold their land until the debt is repaid.*

COPIES: CR 1, fol. 245v (>CR 6, fol. 201r–v).
EDITION: Chantereau-Lefebvre, *Traité des fiefs*, 2: 38 (from CR 6).
CALENDARED: AJ, no. 702.

Ego Joannes Montismirelli et Oisiaci dominus, ego Helvidis Montismirelli et Oisiaci domina, notum facimus universis presentes litteras inspecturis quod karissima domina nostra Blancha, illustris comitissa Trecensis, de mille et trecentis libris quas debemus domui et fratribus Longipontis, se ad preces nostras plegiam et responsalem pro nobis constituit erga domum et fratres predictos. Nos vero dicte domine nostre concessimus bona fide quod si prefatam pecuniam non reddiderimus terminis constitutis, videlicet ab instanti festo Sancti Remigii unum annum VI^c^ and L libras, et eodem termino anno revoluto alias VI^c^ et L libras, et domina comitissa super hoc dampnum aliquod incurrerit vel gravamen, inde se capiat sine contradictione aliqua et sine fidem suam mentiri ad omnia que de feodo suo tenemus. Si vero nos ambo, quod absit, decesserimus antequam prefata pecunia persolvatur vel quicquid de nobis contigat, volumus et statuimus ne alicui heredum nostrorm vel cuilibet alii pro ipsis nomine advocatis reddatur terra nostra donec prefata pecunia memoratis fratribus Longi Pontis in integrum fuerit persoluta. In cujus rei testimonium et confirmationem, presentes litteras fieri voluimus sigillorum nostrorum munimine roboratas. Actum incarnationis Dominice M ducentesimo nono, mense maio.

1 See **11** n. 1.
2 See **11** n. 2.

52

1206 August

Milo of Pougy[1] *pledges that if Norbert of Bessy flees the lands of Countess Blanche, Milo will pay her 200* l. *from Norbert's property.*

COPIES: CR 1, fol. 245v (>CR 6, fol. 201v).
CALENDARED: AJ, no. 657.

Ego Milo de Pogiaco notum facio omnibus ad quos littere iste pervenerint quod domine mee Blanche, illustris Campanie comitisse, redditor sum pro Norberto de Bessiaco de ducentis libris super res ipsius Norberti si contingerit quod idem Norbertus diffugiat terram domine comitisse; et si non diffugerit, ego exinde quitus ero. Actum anno Domini M CC VI, mense augusti.

53

1210 June

Guy II of Dampierre[1] *states that, with the consent of Countess Blanche, he holds the castle and castellany of Beaufort*[2] *in security for a debt of 829* l. *and will surrender possession twenty days after next Christmas.*

COPIES: CR 1, fol. 245v (>CR 6, fols. 201v). CR 3, fol. 71r. CR 4, fol. 104r.
TRANSLATION: Evergates, *Documents*, 83–4, no. 65B.
CALENDARED: AJ, no. 744.

Ego Guido de Dampetra notum facio universis quod ego habeo in vadio pro octigentis et XXIX libris Belfort castrum et totam castellania, laude karissime domine mee Blanche, comitisse Campanie, ita quod a XX diebus post natale Domini in antea, nichil potero clamare in illa terra. Quod ut ratum sit, sigillo meo feci confirmari. Actum anno Domini M CC X, mense junio.

---

1 Milo of Pougy (1186–1219) was the second of three sons of Renaud II, lord of Pougy (1163–1206). Milo became lord of Marolles-sur-Seine and Saint-Valérien (Roserot, *Diction-naire historique*, 2: 1184), and held one-third of the viscounty of Troyes in fief from the count (Longnon, *Documents*, 1: 72, no. 2008).

1 See **3** n. 1.

2 Felicity, heiress of Beaufort, became countess of Rethel by marriage (ca 1191) to Hugh II, count of Rethel (1198–1228). It appears that Beaufort was mortgaged in 1210 but that the debt was repaid, since Felicity held the castle as a widow in 1239 and allowed her eldest son, Hugh III of Rethel (1228–43), to dower his wife with it (Saige, Trésor des chartes du comté de *Rethel*, 1: 139–41, no. 86).

[quire 23: fols. 254r–255v]

54

1206 July

Abbot Louis and the community of Saint-Vanne of Verdun associate Countess Blanche in lordship over the village of Chaudefontaine,[1] *where they will share equally the revenues and administration.*[2] *Saint-Vanne will retain the head tax of residents, the ovens, mills, tithes,* corvées, *and carting service. All men of the village will owe the countess military service according to the custom of Sainte-Menehould. The provost of the monks and the count's provost of Sainte-Menehould together will select the mayor and local officials, who will exercise local justice except in cases involving judicial duels.*

ORIGINAL: AN, J 197, no. 6 (missing).
COPIES: CR 1, fol. 254r (second half of text continues from a folio now missing).[3] CR 8, fol. 345r.
EDITION: *Layettes*, 1: 305, no. 811 (from CR 8).
CALENDARED: AJ, no. 655.

Ego Ludovicus, Sancti Vitoni Virdunensis abbas, et totus ejusdem loci conventus, omnibus tam futuris quam presentibus, notum esse volumus quod nos, de communi assensu capituli nostri, associavimus venerabilem dominam nostram Blancham, comitissam Trecensem, et heredes suos dominos Campanie ad medietatem banni, justicie, et assisie ville que dicitur Calida Fontana, et ad medietatem terragiorum ubicumque ea habeamus in bosco vel in plano infra fines ville iam dicte, et ad medietatem censuum, preter XX^ti^ quatuor solidos quos nos prius capiemus. Retinuimus etiam capitagia hominum Sancti Vitoni

1 In 1206 Bertrand of Sainte-Menehould sold one-third of Chaudefontaine to Saint-Vanne and two-thirds to Countess Blanche (AN, J 197, no. 105, original letter of Bertrand done at Vitry, now missing; see notice in *Layettes*, 1: 567, no. 810bis). See also **67**.

2 Countess Blanche's own letter with the same text was preserved by the priory of Chaudefontaine (edited in Barthélemy, *Le prieuré de Saint-Laurent de Chaudefontaine*, 30–1). Those two letters of July 1206 are much more precise than the abbot's letter of December 1204 (**105**), which appears to have been a working draft or an initial proposal to the countess. See also Higounet, *Défrichements et villeneuves*, 166, 168.

3 The folio containing the first part of this text was already missing by 1232, when the duplicate CR 6 was made; the copyist of CR 6 skipped over this fragmentary text to begin his own quire with **55**.

qui nunc ibi sunt manentes vel de cetero sunt mansuri, et furnos, et molendina, decimas, altaria, prata, corveias, et aquas, et tria carrugia; sed plus quam tria carrugia non poterimus habere quin domina comitissa et heredes sui domini Campanie in illis habeant medietatem. In aquis vero piscari facient dicta comitissa et heredes sui quotienscumque erunt in patria. In aliis autem exitibus et redditibus quibus villa crescet in futurum, medietatem habebunt.

Sciendum etiam quod omnes homines ville cavalchiam[a] et exercitum comitisse et heredibus ejus dominis Campanie debent secundum usus et consuetudinem Sancte Manehuldis. Ad hoc autem adjecimus quod prepositus monacus[b] de Calida Fontana et prepositus[b] Sancte Manehuldis per communem assensum in villa Calide Fontane majorem constitutent et scabinos; et si de electione majoris non possent insimul convenire, per concordiam scabinorum de Calida Fontana in hoc se concordarent. Ista autem in quibus associata est, ipsa et heredes sui domini Campanie, nullo modo de manu sua alienare poterunt vel quomodolibet commutare, aut in feodum vel in elemosinam dare nisi ecclesie Sancti Vitoni. Omnia autem jura que in eadem villa evenient, deducentur in ipsa villa per majorem et justiciarios ejusdem ville, nisi talia esset illa jura que essent de vadio duelli, et tunc ducerentur jura duelli ad Sanctam Meneholdim,[c] salva in omnibus medietate monachorum. Et propter hec, jura nostra, ubicumque sint, dicta comitissa et heredes sui domini Campanie in posse tanquam sua propria custodire tenentur. Quod ut ratum permaneat et firmum,[d] sigillorum nostrorum testimonio confirmavimus. Actum anno Domini[d] M CC sexto, mense julio.

[a] *text in CR 1 begins here with* ...chiam. [b] monacus *through* prepositus *omitted in CR 1.* [c] Manehuldum *in CR 8 and Layettes.* [d] futurum *in CR 8 and Layettes.* [e] incarnationis Dominice *in CR 8 and Layettes.*

55

1205 December

Robert, bishop of Langres,[1] *confirms that in his presence the abbot and monks of La Crête quitclaimed their dispute with Countess Blanche over Lady Chaumonde's gift.*[2] *The countess assigned them a 10* l. *rent payable by the provost of Chaumont.*[3]

1 See **42** n. 1.

2 See **96** n. 2 for Lady Chaumonde of Chaumont.

3 Countess Blanche obtained this quitclaim at her Christmas court in December 1205 in the presence of all her barons (*me et omnes dominos Campanie*) and the bishop of Langres (AD Haute-Marne, 6 H 13, no. 54). She gave her letter to the monks and received this letter from the bishop as her record of the event. See also **10**, **96**.

COPIES: CR 1, fol. 254r (>CR 6, fol. 270v). CR 3, fol. 130r–v. CR 4, fols. 121v–122r. CR 8, fol. 200r–201v.
CALENDARED: AJ, no. 638.

Robertus, Dei gratia Lingonensis episcopus, omnibus Christiani fidelibus, in domino Jhesu Christo, salutem. Notum vobis facimus et testamur quod abbas et fratres de Crista, in mea presentia constituti, cognoverunt se nobili in Christo domine amice et fideli nostre Blanche, illustri Campanie comitisse, et heredibus Campanie, quitavisse omne jus et omnem querelam quam clamabant in quadam elemosina domine quondam Chaumonde. Et ipsa comitissa predictis fratribus decem libras annui redditus assignavit, quas in octabis Resurrectionis dominice reddet eis quicumque sit prepositus Calvimontis. Actum anno Domini M CC V, mense decembri.

56

1206 or 1207 (n.s.) March

The dean Hugh and the chapter of Châlons-sur-Marne ask Countess Blanche to protect their men at Saint-Julien-de-Courtisols from oppressors. They inform her that each household there by custom pays 12 d. *and one* mine *of oats annually, and they ask her for a letter promising not to increase that customary obligation.*

COPIES: CR 1, fol. 254r (>CR 6, fols. 270v–271r). CR 3, fol. 129r–v. CR 4, fol. 186r–v. CR 8, fol. 428v.
CALENDARED: AJ, no. 662.

Venerabili et karissime domine sue Blanche, comitisse Trecensis palatine, Hugo decanus totumque Cathalaunus ecclesie capitulum, salutem et sinceram in Domino karitatem. Vestre benignitati gratias referentes multimodis super hoc quod precibus nostris sepius acquievistis et peticiones nostras effectui mancipastis, rogamus quantum possumus affectuose sublimitatem vestram quatinus homines qui manent in terra nostra apud Sanctum Julianum de Cortisol contra omnes oppressores suos auxilium et deffensionem[a] fideliter exhibeatis. Sciatis enim quod nos, salvo jure nostro, ratam habemus costumiam quam idem homines promiserunt se nobis a singulis domibus in villa eadem annuatim reddituros, videlicet unam minam avene ad mensuram Cathalaunum et XII denarios in festo Sancti Remigii percipiendos sub hac tamen conditione, quod costumiam illam a predictis hominibus pro se tuendis constitutam, alteri[a] dare, vendere, commutare, pignori obligare vel aliquo modo a vestra et heredum vestrorum manu nobis et eisdem heredibus non licebit alienare. Volentes itaque ut hoc perpetue tradatur memorie, supplicamus nobis quatinus litteras vestras nobis mittatis, et has litteras nostras illamque costumiam nequid in futuro super addatur in litteris vestris contineri faciatis. Actum anno Domini M CC VI, mense martio.

[a] deffensionem *in CR 1 and CR 8*, defensionem *in CR 3 and CR 4*. [b] Alii *in CR 3, CR 4, and CR 8.*

57

1205 May

The prior Erard and community of Cluny, in recognition of Countess Blanche's devotion, receive her as a sister in the order of Cluny and grant her Cluny's spiritual benefits, including prayers for her before and after her death and the inscription of her name in the mortuary roll that is circulated among Cluniac monasteries.

COPIES: CR 1, fol. 254r–v (>CR 6, fol. 271r–v).
CALENDARED: AJ, no. 617.

Illustri comitisse Campanie, karissime domine nostre, frater Airardus prior Cluniacensis et ejusdem loci conventus, eternum in Domino salutem. Cum erga Cluniacensem ecclesiam dilectionis plurimum in natura vobis pietatem evidenter habere cognoverimus, vobis vices quas possumus in hoc referre volumus et tenemur. Inde est quod in recompensatione devotionis vestre, vos in sororem Cluniacensis ordinis recipimus, facientes participem et consororem omnium beneficiorum que de cetero fient in ecclesia Cluniacensis et in omnibus menbris ejus sive pro vitiis sive pro defunctis agantur. Concedimus etiam vobis quod cum de transitu vestro Cluniacensis ecclesie per presentes litteras innotuerit pro vobis in ecclesia Cluniacensis solempne officium cum missis et aliis beneficiis fiet, sicut si in aliquo monasteriorum nostrorum consororibus nostris contingeret vos obisse. Tricenarium etiam fiet in conventu pro vobis et nomen vestrum scribetur in brevibus que per domos congregationis nostre ex consuetudine transmituntur ut ubique in locis nostris pro nobis fiat officium et consueta beneficia paschiantur. Insuper scribetur in cathalono defunctorum nomen vestrum in regula. In die anniversarii vestri singulis annis perpetuo in capitulo recitandum ut pro vobis fiat officium et anima vestra absolutionem et debitta beneficia consequatur. Rogamus autem delectionem vestram et monemus in Domino ut interim dum in hac luce fueretis. In qua per domum gratie Dei longo tempore nos esse cupimus et oramus ecclesiam Cluniacensis et omnia loca ad eam pertinentia. Et fratres tocius congregationis sicut soror Cluniacensis ordinis affectuose diligere et eorum negotia cum vobis occurrerint curetis secundum Deum liberaliter promovere. Actum anno Domini M CC V, mense maio.

58

1208 August, Pont-sur-Seine

Manasses, abbot of Saint-Loup of Troyes, exchanges dependent men and women with Countess Blanche.

COPIES: CR 1, fol. 254v (>CR 6, fol. 271v). CR 3, fol. 114v–115r. CR 4, fol. 157r–v. CR 8, fol. 307r.
CALENDARED: AJ, no. 687bis.

Ego frater Manasserus dictus abbas totusque conventus Beati Lupi Trecensis notum facimus tam presentibus quam futuris quod karissime domine nostre Blanche, illustri comitisse Trecensis, Giboinum Audefredum et uxorem suam et Elisabeth de Faiel et familias eorum in excambium dedimus pro Savina, filia Dominici Divitis de Trecis, ita quod Savina de cetero erit femina ecclesie nostre et predicti homines cum familiis suis erunt domine comitisse. Quod ut notum permaneat et ratum teneatur, litteris annotatum sigillorum nostrorum munimine fecimus roborari. Actum apud Pontes, anno incarnati Verbi[a] M CC VIII, mense augusto.

[a] anno Domini *in CR* 1.

59

[1198–1201]

Hugh, abbot of Essômmes, thanks Count Thibaut III for giving their canons residing at Tréfols the right to collect dead wood in the forest del Gaut. *In appreciation, the monks promise to celebrate three Masses weekly for Thibaut, both before and after his death, as well as a solemn annual Mass on the anniversary of his death.*

COPIES: CR 1, fol. 254v (>CR 6, fol. 272r).
EDITION: *Gallia Christiana*, 10: *instr.*, 131, no. 52.
CALENDARED: AJ, no. 452.

Devotioni vestre dilectissime princeps Theobalde, quam bone indolis judicium commendat et prohibet magis ac magis flagratura, ego Hugo, Sosmensis ecclesie Dei permissione dictus abbas, et totus ejusdem conventus humilis, pro modulo nostro gratias referimus quod ecclesie de Trefollis et canonicis nostris ibidem demorantibus usuarium de mortuo in nemore vestro *del Gaut* in perpetuo habendum concessistis. Inde et aliunde est hoc enim non sufficit. Porro unum est necessarium quod vobis concedimus ob salutem et remedium anime vestre: tres missas de Spiritu Sancto ante decessum vestrum, et post totidem, pro fidelibus defunctis in eadem ecclesia de Trefollis singulis septimanis fore celebrandas, et diem obitus vestri sollempni officio annuatim recolendum.

60

[1201–11][1]

The prior of Saint-Martin-des-Champs seeks Countess Blanche's advice regarding an order from Etienne of Hautvillers, the royal bailiff, to remove the toll at Cannes, which had existed for over forty years. The prior will not proceed without Blanche's directive, since the village and water of Cannes are under her protection. He has already notified her provost of Montereau and her bailiff, Simon of Courpalay (the prior's brother).

COPIES: CR 1, fol. 254v–255r (>CR 6, fol. 272r–v).
CALENDARED: AJ, no. 1418.

Excellentissime et illustri domine Blanche, comitisse Trecensis palatina, frater E., humilis prior Sancti Martini de Campis, camerarius domini abbatis in Francia, salutem et devotas orationes in Christo. Excellencie vestre notum fieri volumus quod Stephanus de Altovillari, ballivus domini regis, accessit ad nos apud Conam ex parte domini regis nobis percipiens ut conductum aque de Cona, qui ibi per XL annos et eo amplius sine aliqua contraditione fuit, commutari faceremus et alibi facere perciperemus. Cum enim villa de Cona cum aqua et alia que ibi habemus et alii habent sub custodia et protectione vestra sint, hoc mandatum sine consilio vestro et voluntate facere non possumus nec debemus. Et sciatis quod si hoc fieri contigerit non sine magno prejudicio vestro et heredum vestrorum fiet. Et hoc inde vestro preposito Musterollii et ballivo vestro, domino Symon de Corpalai, fratri nostro,

1 This letter must be dated before October 1211, as it appears in a quire that was completed by that date.

significavimus. Super hoc voluntatem vestram nobis rescribere dignemini quia terminus tollendi conductum est ad octabas Pentecostes nec prolixiores inducias habere potuimus.

*61

1210 November 22, Lateran

Pope Innocent III, in a letter to Countess Blanche, confirms her treaty with King Philip II as described in the king's letter that Blanche sent him.[1] *The pope specifically mentions Blanche's custody over her son and the king's promise to receive Thibaut's homage.*

ORIGINAL: AN, J 198, no. 133 (missing pendant seal).
COPIES: CR 1, fol. 255r (>CR 6, fol. 272v).
EDITIONS: Chantereau-Lefebvre, *Traité des fiefs*, 2: 97 (from CR 6). *PL*, 267: 350, no. 180 (incomplete). *RHF*, 19: 536. *Layettes*, 1: 359, no. 945.
CALENDARED: AJ, no. 752. Barbiche, *Les actes pontificaux*, 39–40, no. 91.

Innocentius episcopus, servus servorum Dei, dilecte in Christo filie nobili mulieri Blanche, comitisse Campanie, salutem et apostolicam benedictionem. Justis petentium desideriis dignum est, nos facilem prebere consensum et vota, que a rationis tramite non discordant, effectu prosequente complere. Eapropter, dilecta in Christo filia, tuis justis postulationibus grato concurrentes assensu, compositionem inter te ac carissimum in Christo filium nostrum Philippum, regem Francorum illustrem, super custodia nati tui, et ab ipso nato eidem regi hominio faciendo, et quibusdam aliis articulis initam, sicut provide facta est, et ab utraque parte sponte recepta et juramento firmata, et in autenticis exinde confectis plenius continetur,[2] auctoritate apostolica confirmamus et presentis scripti patrocinio communimus. Nulli ergo omnino[a] hominum liceat hanc paginam nostre confirmationis infringere vel ei ausu temerario contraire. Si quis autem hoc attemptare presumpserit, indignationem omnipotentis Dei et beatorum Petri et Pauli apostolorum ejus se noverit incursurum. Datum Laterani, X kalendas decembris, pontificatus nostri anno tercio decimo.

[a] omnino *omitted in CR 1*, omnium *in Layettes*.

1 **App. 2**. See also **38**, **48**, **65**, ***120**.
2 See **38** n. 2.

*62

1213 November [21], Compiègne

King Philip II announces the agreement he concluded with Countess Blanche regarding her son Thibaut. She swore on holy objects that Thibaut will not do homage for any of his lands until he reaches twenty-one, and she promised not to fortify the towns of Meaux, Lagny, Provins, and Coulommiers until that time. The king will occupy the castles of Bray-sur-Seine and Montereau-faut-Yonne until Thibaut does homage for his inheritance. Ten barons of Champagne will swear to abide by this agreement and will give the king their sealed letters affirming their oaths. The knights and townsmen of Meaux, Château-Thierry, Lagny, Provins, and Coulommiers also will swear to uphold this agreement. The king reiterates that he will not hear any case against Blanche or Thibaut until the latter completes twenty-one years, at which time the king will receive his homage.[1]

ORIGINAL: AN, J 1035, no. 6 (heavily damaged; missing pendant seal).
COPIES: CR 1, fol. 255v.[2] CR 4, fol. 7v–8r. CR 7.1, fol. 7r–8r.
EDITIONS: Martène and Durand, *Veterum scriptorum ... amplissima collectio*, 1: 1125. *Layettes*, 5: 71–2, no. 199. *Recueil des actes de Philippe Auguste*, 3: 455–8, no. 1314.
CALENDARED: AJ, no. 835. Delisle, *Catalogue*, no. 1463.

Philippus, Dei gratia Francorum rex. Noverint universi presentes pariter et futuri quod hee sunt conventiones inter nos et dilectam et fidelem nostram Blancham, comitissam Trecensem, et Theobaldum filium ejus:

Comitissa juravit super sacrosancta quod nullo modo sustinebit quod Theobaldus filius ejus capiat aliqua hominagia de tota terra sua nec faciat alteri, nisi salvis conventionibus hic scriptis inter nos et ipsos.

Barones, milites, et homines villarum qui hic subscripti sunt, jurabunt super sacrosancta quod ipsi dicto Theobaldo non facient hominagium nec fidelitatem nisi salvis conventionibus subscriptis inter nos et ipsos; jurabunt etiam et inde dabunt litteras suas patentes quod si comitissa vel Theobaldus filius ejus non tenerent nobis conventiones nostras sicut hic continentur, quociens comitissa vel Theobaldus interciperent erga nos, ipsi cum feodis et domaniis suis se bona fide tenerent nobiscum donec nobis esset emendatum ad gratum nostrum.

1 This agreement extends the arrangements made in July 1209 (**App. 2**). In her side agreement (***121**), Countess Blanche referred to her own letter accepting the king's terms, but it has not survived.

2 It is not clear why the scribe of CR 6 skipped over this obvious addition on the verso of folio 255.

Tales sunt conventiones quod comitissa et Theobaldus filius ejus de cetero non deficient nobis de bono et legitimo servitio quamdiu vivent, contra omnes homines et feminas que possunt vivere vel mori. Talis etiam est conventio quod comitissa vel Theobaldus filius ejus non possunt firmare has quatuor villas, scilicet Meldis, Latiniacum, Pruvinum et Columbarias, nisi per gratum nostrum, donec dictus Theobaldus compleverit viginti et unum annum; et nos debemus tenere Braium et Mosterolium donec idem Theobaldus viginti et unum annum compleverit, per conventiones illas per quas nos easdem villas antea tenebamus, sicut scripte sunt in carta comitisse quam habemus.[3] Et nos non tenemur Theobaldum recipere in hominem donec viginti et unum annum compleverit, nisi per volutatem nostram. Cum autem idem Theobaldus viginti et unum annum compleverit, ipse jurabit super sacrosancta has conventiones nobis tenendas et inde dabit nobis litteras suas patentes et faciet renovari nobis juramenta et litteras patentes baronum, militum, et hominum villarum, sicut hic scripti sunt, super conventionibus istis tenendis. Cum vero nos dictum Theobaldum in hominem recipiemus, ipsum recipiemus in hominem salvo jure alieno, et cum Theobaldus has conventiones sicut hic scripte sunt impleverit, nos reddemus ei Braium et Mosterolium.

Has conventiones tenendas jurabunt et inde facient litteras suas patentes, sicut dictum est, isti qui subscribuntur: Guido de Dampetra,[4] comes Sancti Pauli, comes Blesensis,[5] comes Sacricesaris, comes Jovigniaci,[6] comes Grandisprati,[7] comes Registestis,[8] dominus Marigniaci, dominus Trianguli,[9] dominus Marrolarum, milites et homines de potestate Meldis, milites et homines de potestate Castri Theoderici, milites et homines de potestate Latigniaci, milites et homines de potestate Provini, milites et homines de potestate Columbariarum. Si vero aliquis istorum qui nominati sunt moreretur, predicti comitissa et Theobaldus facerent quod heres illius qui moreretur faciat nobis tale juramentum quale ille qui mortuus erit nobis facerat, et inde nobis litteras suas patentes exhiberet.

Sciendum est preterea quod nemo potest trahere in placitum dictum Theobaldum nec comitissam matrem ejus in curia nostram de re unde sit modo

3 This refers to Countess Blanche's letter of July 1209 (**App. 3**).

4 Letter of Guy II of Dampierre: AN, J 199, no. 7, November 1213, at Compiègne [= *Layettes*, 1: 395, no. 1055].

5 Letter of Thibaut VI, count of Blois: AN, J 199, no. 6, November 1213, at Chartres [= *Layettes*, 1: 394–5, no. 1054].

6 Letter of Guillaume I, count of Joigny: AN, J 199, no. 9, December 1213, at Provins.

7 Letter of Henri IV, count of Grandpré: AN, J 199, no. 8, December 1213, at Meaux

8 Letter of Hugh II, count of Rethel: AN, J 199, no. 11, December 1213, at Troyes.

9 Letter of Ida, guardian lord of Traînel for her minor son: AN, J 199, no. 10, December 1213, at Provins.

saisita, nec nos audiremus inde causem donec Theobaldus filius ejus viginti et unum annum compleverit. Omnes autem has conventiones supradictas comitissa faciet nos habere bona fide infra quindenam instantis Nativitatis Domini et, si aliquis de supranominatis nollet nobis assecurare dictas conventiones aliqua occasione, dicta comitissa super hoc se contineret ad laudem et voluntatem nostram. Quod ut firmum sit et stabile, litteris annotatum sigilli nostri munimine roboramus. Actum Compendii, anno Domini millesimo ducentesimo tertio decimo, mense novembri.

[quire 33: folios 256r–259v]

63

1203 July, Soissons

Abbot Raoul and the community of Saint-Jean-des-Vignes of Soissons exchange the revenues that Count Henry I granted them (in 1177) for celebrating an anniversary Mass for Levulf (an eleventh-century count of Oulchy) and his wife.[1] *Their canons at Oulchy henceforth will collect 60 s. from the tolls at Oulchy in lieu of the pasture rights they formerly had for this purpose. Countess Blanche, whose officials at Oulchy will pay the monks, consented to the exchange. If the payment is not made, the monks will resume their pasture rights according to the terms of Count Henry's charter.*

ORIGINAL: AN, J 197, no. 4 (missing pendant seal).
COPIES: CR 1, fol. 256r (>CR 6, fols. 272v–273r). CR 3, fol. 132r–v. CR 4, fol. 187r–v. CR 8, fol. 251r.
CALENDARED: AJ, no. 590. *Layettes*, 1: 242–3, no. 679.

Ego Radulphus, dictus abbas Sancti Johannis in vineis Suessionensis, totusque ejusdem ecclesie conventus, omnibus in perpetuum. Noverint universi quod de duobus pastibus qui continentur in quadam carta illustris comitis Henrici, quondam patris comitis Theobaldi, qui pro anniversario comitis Levulfi et uxoris sue Hildeardis annuatim reddi debent canonicis nostris de Ulcheio, de voluntate nostra istud cum domina nostra in Christo karissima Blancha, comitissa Trecensis palatina, ordinavimus: quod singulis annis octo diebus ante diem

1 Arbois de Jubainville, *Histoire*, 3: 467–8, no. 148, 1177 (act of Henry I for the canons of Oulchy). The anniversary was established in 1042 (Arbois de Jubainville, *Histoire*, 1: 481–3, no. 44).

anniversarii reddent prepositi et baillivi sui de Ulcheio canonicis nostris predictis per singulis pastuum triginta solidos pruvinensis monete qui capientur in thelonio Ulcheii; quos similiter triginta solidos pro singulis pastuum reddent similiter in futurum heredes ipsius comitisse ad terminum nominatum. Quod si non facient, licebit nobis ad cartam comitis Henrici reverti et secundum cartam jus nostrum requirere. Quod ut firmum sit, presentem paginam sigillo nostro fecimus confirmari. Actum apud Suessionem, anno Verbi incarnati, M CC tercio, mense julio. Datum per manum Petri, notarii mei.

64

1162, Dammartin

The dean Ibert and the chapter of Notre-Dame of Senlis notify Count Henry I that they have approved the resolution of a dispute with their bishop over the men of Saint-Gervais. The bishop will collect the head tax of residents there but will share equally the other personal tax revenues. The dean and twenty-two members of the chapter placed crosses on this document to mark their approval of the settlement.

COPIES: CR 1, fol. 256r (>CR 6, fol. 273r–v). CR 3, fol. 168v–169v. CR 4, fols. 180v–181r.
EDITIONS: Martène and Durand, *Veterum scriptorum ... amplissima collectio*, 1: 863. *Gallia Christiana*, 10: *instr.*, 214–15, no. 22 (omits several witnesses).
CALENDARED: AJ, no. 107.

Domino suo Henrico, Dei gratia Trecensi comiti egregio, Ibertus eadem gratia ecclesie Beate Maria Silvanectensis decanus, Stephanus precentor, Petrus archidiaconus totumque ejusdem ecclesie capitulum, salutem. Querelam que inter nos et dominum nostrum Silvanectensem episcopum, Amalaricum nomine, pro quibusdam hominibus Sancti Gervasii versabator, compositione quadam terminatam audivimus et gravisi sumus indeque vestri pietati grates referimus. Porro modum compositionis presentibus litteris inferere nostrique sigilli impressione atque capituli subscriptione munire curavimus.

Statutum inter nos ut annis singulis idem episcopus noster et successores ejus episcopi predictorum hominum capitalia libere et integre habeant; cetera vero, id est mortuam manum, licentiam matrimoniorum, et alegia inter nos equaliter dividatis, ita scilicet ut ipse episcopus et succesores ejus medietatem habeant, nos autem et heredes nostri aliam medietatem habeatis. Statutum est etiam ut super predictos homines episcopus et successores ejus unum de ipsis, quem voluerint, majorem constituant qui eis singulis annis capitalia et cetera que concessistis Silvanectum deferat; qui quandiu majoriam tenuerit, liber ab omni consuetudine erit; ipsi vero qui post ipsum jubentibus episcopis successerint, similiter liberi erunt. Pactus est enim nobis idem episcopus, assensu nostro et voluntate, quod nequaquam a nobis et heredibus nostris amplius aliquid exigeret quam id per quod inter nos et ipsum pax et concordia facta est. Nos igitur hujusmodi compositionem seu conventionem a nobis et ecclesie nostra perpetuo ratam illibatamque conservari decernimus. Signum[a] Iberti decani. Signum Stephani cantoris. Signum Petri archidiaconi. Signum Ebroini. Signum Johannis. Signum Giraudi, presbyterorum. Signum Giraudi. Signum Azanis. Signum Guidonis. Signum Nevelonis. Signum Balduinis, diaconorum. Signum Petri. Signum Guidonis. Signum Renaldi. Signum Johannis. Signum Stephani. Signum Bernardi. Signum Petri. Signum Odonis. Signum Willelmi. Signum Fulberti. Signum Matthei. Signum Petri. De nobilibus: Signum Galteris.[1] Odoni de Ponte. Actum apud Dammartinum, anno ab incarnatione Domini M centesimo sexagesimo secundo.

[a]*The first* 'Signum' *is written out: the rest are abbreviated* 'S.' *in all copies.*

65

1210 (n.s.) January

Guillaume of Joinville, bishop of Langres,[1] *approves King Philip II's treaty with Countess Blanche regarding her son Thibaut, specifically that no challenge may be made to his paternal inheritance until he completes his twenty-first year.*[2]

1 Probably Gautier II of Aulney-lès-Bondy, Seneschel of Dammartin (Newman, *Nesle*, 1:265 no. 2, 4).

1 Guillaume was the third son of Geoffroy IV of Joinville, seneschal of Champagne (1188–90), and Heloise of Dampierre. He entered Clairvaux, then become archdeacon of Châlons-sur-Marne, bishop of Langres (1208–19), and archbishop of Reims (1219–26). His brother, Simon, was seneschal of Champagne (1204–33). Within a few years of this letter, Guillaume had become an implacable opponent of Countess Blanche, in part because of his familial connections to the barons of south-eastern Champagne, who resented the increasing comital influence in the area. See Humblot, 'Guillaume II de Joinville' and Desportes, *Fasti Ecclesiae Gallicanae*, 158–60.

2 This letter, like the one sealed by Odo III, duke of Burgundy (**48**), refers to the king's *judicium* (see **App. 2**). Bishop Guillaume sent another, more detailed approval in the same month (***120**). See also **38**, ***61**.

COPIES: CR 1, fol. 256r (>CR 6, fol. 160r). CR 3, fol. 28r. CR 4, fol. 125v. CR 8, fol. 201r.
CALENDARED: AJ, no. 723.

Willelmus, miseratione divina Lingonensis episcopus, omnibus ad quos presentes littere pervenerint, salutem in Domino. Notum volumus fieri quod nos laudamus et approbamus judicium a domino Philippo rege factum de Theobaldo, filio dilecte nostre illustris domine Blanche, comitisse Campanie, videlicet quod ipse Theobaldus et dicta Blancha, comitissa mater ejus, non possunt nec debent trahi in causam de aliquo quod pater dicti Theobaldi teneret quando decessit, quoad usque dictus Theobaldus vicesimum primum compleverit annum. Actum anno Domini M CC IX, mense januario.

66

1210 November

Gautier of Vanault[1] *sells the viscounty of Cuis and the advocacy of the town of Cuis to Countess Blanche. But he retains the fiefs held from him and not attached to either the viscounty or the advocacy there.*

COPIES: CR 1, fol. 256v (>CR 6, fol. 160r–v). CR 7.3, fol. 156r–v.
EDITION: Chantereau-Lefebvre, *Traité des fiefs*, 2: 41 (from CR 7).
CALENDARED: AJ, no. 756.

Ego Galterus de Visnou notum facio tam presentibus quam futuris quod ego vendidi domine comitisse Blanche, Trecensi palatine, vicecomitatum de Cuis cum omnibus pertinentiis ad vicecomitatum, hoc excepto, quod si in allodio domini Anselli Bridaine quod est in eadem villa, latro captus fuerit, domine comitisse vel mandato ejus debet tradi totus nudus. Vendidi etiam eidem comitisse advocatiam ejusdem ville et quicquid habebam infra mesum demainum ipsius ville; illud autem mihi retinui quod si aliquis in eadem villa de me tenet feodum, dummodo non sit de vicecomitatu vel de advocatia, mihi liberum remanebit. Si vero in ipsa villa aliquis manserit qui teneat de terris pertinentibus ad territorium de Monte Felici vel ad territorium de Montejoy, meas consuetudines mihi solvet. De predicta autem venditione domine comitisse teneor

1 Gautier, lord of Vanault (1188/90–1212/19), and his brother Robert, lord of Pierrepont and Montaigu (1188/90–1209/11), divided their father Hugh's lands; see Bur, *Vestiges d'habitat seigneurial fortifié du Bas-Pays Argonnais*, 95–9.

legitimam ferre garantiam. In qua ferenda si deficerem, ipsa comitissa posset assignare ad feodum meum sine injuria mihi inferenda. In cujus rei testimonium presens scriptum fieri volui et sigilli mei munimine roborari. Actum anno gratie M CC X, mense novembri.

67

1209 June, Payns

Bertrand of Sainte-Menehould sells to Countess Blanche one-sixth of the woods of Verrières beyond the Aisne, except for the cleared land, rents, half of his rights in the woods of la Germenia, *and a fief held from him.*[1] *His wife and his brother consent to and warrant the sale.*

COPIES: CR 1, fol. 256v (>CR 6, fol. 160v). CR 7.3, fols. 161v–162r.
CALENDARED: AJ, no. 703.

Ego Bertrandus de Sancta Menoldi notum facio tam presentibus quam futuris quod ego sextam partem totius nemoris de Verrerus quod est ultra aquam que dicitur Aisna, et totam terram quam ibidem habebam exceptis exartis, censibus, et terragiis qua usque ad tempus venditionis possederam, et medietatem quam habebam in bosco de *la Germenia,* nec[a] non et feodum quod Clarinus de me tenebat in ipso bosco de *la Germenia,*[a] domine Blanche, comitisse Trecensi palatina et heredibus suis, vendidi ab omni jure et consuetudine libere perpetuo possidenda. Huic venditioni presentes fuerunt et eam laudaverunt dilecti mei Huardus, frater meus, et Sarrasina, uxor mea, et etiam ad preces meas plegios se constituerunt fiduciantes quod omni tempore domine comitisse et successoribus ejus libertatem ejusdem venditionis contra omnes homines, si aliquis in posterum ibi vel feodum vel domanium vel jus aliud querelaret, garantizabunt. Quod[b] ut notum et firmum permaneat, presentem cartam sigilli mei munimine roborari.[b] Actum anno gratie M CC IX, apud Paentium, mense junio.

[a] nec *through* Germania *omitted in CR 1.* [b] Quod ut ratum permaneat etc. *in CR 1.*

1 See also **54**.

68

1199 July, Provins

Guillaume, archbishop of Reims,[1] *announces that his sister Adele, dowager queen of France,*[2] *relinquished her wardship over the lands of her nephews Guillaume, count of Sancerre, and his brother Etienne.*[3] *In return, the archbishop gives her some of his rents and toll revenues in Provins for as long as Count Thibaut III retains wardship over the brothers.*[4]

COPIES: CR 1, fol. 256v (>CR 6, fol. 160v). CR 3, fol. 79v. CR 4, fol. 133r. CR 8, fol. 83r–v.
CALENDARED: AJ, no. 487.

Guillelmus, Dei gratia Remensis archiepiscopus, sancte Romane ecclesie titulus Sancte Sabina cardinalus, omnibus ad quos littere iste pervenerint, in Domino salutem. Noverit universitas vestra quod soror nostra Adela, Francorum regina, id quod clamabat in advocatia terre nepotum suorum et nostrorum Willelmus, comitis Sacricesaris,[a] et Stephanus, fratris ejusdem, totum quitavit et dimisit. Nos autem dedimus ei et assignavimus quicquid habebamus apud Pruvinum in theloneo et redditibus percipiendum ab ipsa quamdiu nepos noster Theobaldus, comes Trecensis palatinus, terram predictorum Willelmi et Stephani tenebit per advocatiam, et eundem comitem Trecensem, cujus assensu factum est hoc, constituimus fidejussorem portande garantie, salvo jure quod ecclesie Sancti Quiriaci et Sancti Aygulphi habent in domibus nostris apud Sanctum Aygulphum, que ad predictas ecclesias post decessum nostrum libere debent reverti. In cujus rei testimonium presentes litteras scribi et sigillo nostro fecimus communiri. Actum anno Verbi incarnati, M C nonagesimo IX. Datum per manum Mathei, cancellarii nostri, apud Pruvinum, mense julio.

[a] *CR 6 ends here with* et cetera, ista autem carta superius est notata; *the copyist apparently refers to a copy of the letter in a now-missing folio.*

1 Guillaume was the youngest brother of count Henry I. Born in 1135, he was elected bishop of Chartres and named papal legate (1165), then became archishop of Sens (1168–75) and Reims (1176–1202). See Desportes, 'Guillaume de Champagne,' in *Fasti Ecclesiae Gallicanae*, 151–4.

2 Adele was the youngest sister of Count Henry I. She became the third wife of King Louis VII in 1165 and gave birth to the future Philip in 1165. She was regent during Philip's absence on the Third Crusade but had little public role thereafter. She died in 1206.

3 Etienne I, count of Sancerre (1152–90), died on the Third Crusade, leaving his eldest son Guillaume as heir of his county (see **47**) and his younger son, Etienne, as lord of Saint-Brisson and Châtillon-sur-Loing.

4 See **93**.

69

1201 (n.s.) Feburary

Abbot Lambert and the chapter of Saint-Martin-ès-Aires of Troyes acknowledge that Count Thibaut III gave them the hospital of Saint-Abraham in Troyes.[1] *The count may recover it whenever he wishes to grant it to someone else.*

COPIES: CR 1, fol. 256v (>CR 6, fol. 161r). CR 3, fol. 84r. CR 4, fol. 184r–v. CR 8, fol. 311r.
CALENDARED: AJ, no. 534.

Ego Lambertus abbas totumque capitulum Beati Martini Trecensis, notum facimus omnibus presentes litteras inspecturis quod dominus Theobaldus, illustris comitis Campanie, domum de Sancto Abrahan Trecensis nobis commisit, quamdiu volueruit, conservandam. Cum autem ipse vel heredes sui voluerunt eandem domum cum appendiciis et pertinentiis suis dare aut conferre aliis, poterunt et inde suam per omnia facere voluntatem, ita quod nos in domo illa aut in pertinentiis nichil poterimus reclamare. Actum anno Domini M CC, mense februario.

70

1210 May

Henri of Sorcy[1] *gives Countess Blanche this sealed letter affirming that he has sold his village of Dormans and all its appurtenances to her.*

COPIES: CR 1, fols. 256v–257r (>CR 6, fol. 161r). CR 3, fol. 143r. CR 4, fol. 23r. CR 7.3, fol. 229v.
CALENDARED: AJ, no. 741.

Ego Henricus de Sorciaco notum facio universis presentibus pariter et futuris quod quidquid habebam in villa de Dormans et in ponte, et in aliis, et in omnibus commodis que in illa villa aliquo modo ad me pertinere, ego vendidi karissime domine mee Blanche, illustri Trecensis comitisse, et totum ei et

1 Count Henry I founded a commmunity of canons there in 1179 and endowed it with 60 *l.* annual revenue (Arbois de Jubainville, 'Etudes sur les documents,' 109–10, no. 19).

1 Henri of Sorcy owed three months castle-guard for his inherited fief of Dormans (Longnon, *Documents*, 1: 23, no. 699, ca 1190). An entry made in a feudal roll after this sale states: *Domina* [Countess Blanche] *emit de ipso pontem Domarcii de quo erat ligius* (ibid., 1: 122, no. 3302). See also **83**.

heredibus illius quito in perpetuum pacifice possidendum. In cujus rei memoriam, presentes litteras eidem tradidi[a] sigilli mei munimine roboratas. Actum anno gratie M CC X, mense maio.

[a] eidem tradidi *omitted in CR 1.*

71

1211

Guillaume, provost of Chablis, thanks Countess Blanche for permitting him to transfer the provostship of Chablis to Guillaume of La Chapelle for seven years.[1] He gives her this letter affirming that her rights and custody at Chablis are not infringed, and that the provostship will revert to him after the prescribed term of the contract.[2]

COPIES: CR 1, fol. 257r (>CR 6, fol. 161r–v). CR 3, fols. 82v–83r. CR 4, fol. 163r.

CALENDARED: AJ, no. 771bis.

Karissime domine sue Blanche, illustri comitisse Trecensis, suus in omnibus, Willelmus prepositus Chableiarum, salutem in salutis Auctore. Grates vobis referimus uberimas super eo quod ad preces nostras concessistis, ut ea que habemus in villa Chableiarum que est in custodia nostra ponantur in manu domini Willelmi de Capella usque ad terminum constitutum. Nolentes igitur quod vobis vel successoribus vestris dominis Campanie dampnum aut gravamen veniat in futurum ex eo, quod pro amore nostro et precibus tam benigne fecistis, presentibus litteris testificamus universis quod id fecistis salva predicta custodia vestra[a] et salvo gistio et omni jure vestro. Et firmiter concedimus quod post terminum illum nec dictus Willermus nec alius predicta tenere[b] possit nisi de assensu et voluntate vestra, scilicet omnia tunc redeant in manu nostra et in vestra sicut prius erant cum omnino jure vestro et custodia vestra, de qua predicta subtrahere non volumus nec possumus nec debemus. Actum anno gratie M CC XI.

[a] vestra *omitted in CR 1.* [b] tenere *omitted in CR 1.*

1 A royal letter of April 1211 explains that Guillaume of La Chapelle was a royal sergeant who, with Countess Blanche's approval, received the provostship of Chablis for seven years (CR 7.1, fol. 44r–v [= *Layettes*, 1: 366, no. 964 = *Receuil des actes de Philippe Auguste*, 3: 303–4, no. 1196]). See **36** for another example of a seven-year contract.

2 See also **23**, **104**.

72

1201

Pierre (of Corbeil), archbishop of Sens, announces that he has carefully examined the sealed letter by which Abbot Fulk and the monks of Saint-Remi of Sens owe 1400 l. *to two Jews of Countess Blanche, Manasses the Black and Valin.*[1] *The archbishop has decided, with the consent of Blanche and her Jews, that the abbot and monks will give him possession of property and revenues yielding 150* l. *annually, which will be deducted from their debt until it is fully repaid.*

COPIES: CR 1, fol. 257r (>CR 6, fols. 161v–162r).
CALENDARED: AJ, no. 560.

Petrus, Dei gratia Senonensis archiepiscopus, omnibus presentes litteras inspecturis, in Domino salutem. Notum facimus quod sicut ex autentico Fulconis abbatis et conventus Sancti Remigii Senonensis diligenter inspecta, didicimus idem abbas et conventus de mille et CCCC libris pruvinensis monete quas karissime in Christo filie Blanche, illustri comitisse Trecensis palatina, pro judeis suis, videlicet Manasse Nigro et Walino, debebant; de assensu ejusdem comitisse et ipsorum judeorum cum ea, composuerunt in hunc modo: videlicet quod idem abbas et conventus assignabunt ei apud vicum novum et apud Vallem Hedere tantum terre quod redditus et proventus illius terre valebunt comitisse singulis annis CL libris, que cadent de predicta summa debiti et computabuntur in solutione. Et hanc terram tam diu tenebit quod prefatum debitum ei ex integro persolvitur. Que terra, si valuerit per annum plusquam CL libris, abbas et conventus illud quod super fuerit recipient; si vero terra eadem non valuerit per annum CL libras, dicti abbas et monachi illud quod defunctum perficere tenebuntur. Et hec summa debiti usuris amodo cessantibus persolvetur. Quod ut ratum sit, presentes litteras ad petitione sepedictorum abbatis et conventus sigilli nostri munimine fecimus roborari. Actum anno gratie M CC primo.

73

1199 November

Michel, archbishop of Sens, makes known that Pierre Etienne quit Count Thibaut III of all the debts incurred by Count Henry II and Countess Marie.[1]

1 See **7** n. 2.

1 The archbishop sealed a virtually identical letter of the same date for Bernard *Scriptor* (CR 3, fol. 28v [= CR 8, fol. 123r]). See also **78**, **80**.

COPIES: CR 1, fol 257r (>CR 6, fol. 162r). CR 8, fol. 123r.
CALENDARED: AJ, no. 492.

Michael, Dei gratia Senonensis archiepiscopus, omnibus presentes litteras inspecturis, in Domino salutem. Notum facimus quod constitutus in presentia nostra Petrus Stephani quitavit omnino dilectum in Christo filium nostrum,[a] comitem Theobaldum, et terram suam et homines suos et omnes ipsius heredes in perpetuum et animam pie memorie Maria, quondam illustris Trecensis comitisse, et animam comitis Henrici, ejus filii, super omni debito quod eadem comitissa et comes Henricus tenebantur memorato Petro. Actum anno Domini M C XC nono, mense novembri.

[a] nostrum *omitted in CR 1.*

74

1187, Sézanne

Abbot Bernard and the community of Saint-Oyand (Saint-Claude of Lyon) grant their community's rights of justice and ban at Sermaize to Count Henry II, who will found a new village there.[1] *The monks will have half of the market taxes and will retain their banal ovens and mills, as well as their land and crop rents.*[2]

---

1 In 1094 Count Hugh of Troyes, his brother Philippe, bishop-elect of Châlons-sur-Marne, and their mother Adelaide, countess of Bar-sur-Aube, gave the allod of Sermaize to the monks of Saint-Claude for building a priory (Lesort, 'Les chartes de fondation du prieuré de Sermaize').

2 The chancery retained a copy of Count Henry's own sealed letter describing the transaction and later copied it into the cartulary of 1271 (see below). In 1187 the scribes copied one letter from the other, making the appropriate shifts in pronouns, with two significant changes: where Abbot Bernard's letter concedes to Henry the *bannum et justiciam* of Sermaize, Count Henry's letter refers to a concession of *totum dominium et justiciam*; Bernard's letter also omits the count's gift:

Ego Henricus, Trecensis comes palatinus, notum facio presentibus et futuris, Bernardum Sancti Eugendi priorem totumque ejusdem ecclesie conventum, totum dominium et justiciam ville de Sarmasio mihi concessisse. Ego vero novam* villam ibidem faciam, in cujus foro unam medietatem Sancti Eugendi conventus habebit,* altera vero mea erit; furni autem et molendina, census et terragia cum decimis et pratis suis in manu sua absque participatione mea monachi retinuerunt. Nullique ibidem furnos aut molendina preterquam monachis facere licebit. Et quicumque apud predictam villam novam mansurus venerit, predictis monachis sex denarios, mihi vero nonam minam avene, annuatim persolvet. Concessi etiam quod nec ego nec heres meus quod ibi mihi concessum est absque eorum consensu a manu nostra non alienabimus. Predictis preterea monachis in perpetuam elemosinam dedi viginti sextarios melioris avene que in terragio de Cheminum invenientur annuatim recipiendos. Quod ut notum pemaneat, litteris annotatum sigillo meo confirmavi. Actum Sezannia, anno Verbi incarnati MCLXXXVII. Data per manum Guidonis, cancellarii (CR 7.3, fols. 245v–246r: * *novam* through *habebit* omitted in CR 7.3; missing words furnished by BNF, Lat. 2452, fol. 612r, a seventeenth-century copy).

ORIGINAL: AN, J 197, no. 1 (two missing pendant seals).
COPIES: CR 1, fol. 257r (>CR 6, fol. 162v–163r). CR 3, fols. 165v–166r.
CALENDARED: AJ, no. 357. *Layettes*, 1: 148, no. 347.

Ego Bernardus,[a] Dei gratia Sancto Eugendi abbas, totusque eidem ecclesie conventus notum facimus, presentibus et futuris, nos Henrico, illustri Trecensis comiti palatino, bannum et justiciam de Sarmaise concessisse. Ipse vero novum villam ibidem faciet[b] et medietas fori quod ibidem erit ad nos pertinebit. Altera vero domini comitis erit. Furnos autem et molendina nostra et census et terragia cum decimis nostris et pratis in manu nostra absque predicti comitis participatione retinuimus. Nullique molendina et furnos nisi nobis ibidem facere licebit. Hoc autem conditione factum est ita, quod predictus comes vel heres ejus hoc quod ei ibi concessimus absque consensu nostro a manu sua alienare non poterit. Concessum est etiam quod quicunque apud predictam villam mansurus venerit domui de Sarmasia, VI denarios domino vero comiti [et] unam minam avene annuatim persolvet. Quod[c] ut ratum inviolatumque permaneat, litteris annotatum sigillo nostro confirmavimus. Actum Sezannie, anno Verbi incarnatio M C LXXX septimo.[c]

[a] Renaudus *in CR* 1. [b] ibi facerit *in CR 1.* [c] Quod ut ratum et cetera. Anno Domini M C LXXX VII *in CR 1.*

75

1211 October

The dean Nicholas and chapter of Saint-Pierre of Troyes announce an exchange of dependent women with Countess Blanche.

COPIES: CR 1, fol. 257v (>CR 6, fols. 162v). CR 3, fol. 160v. CR 8, fol. 421v.
CALENDARED: AJ, no. 781.

Nicholaus decanus et capitulum Beati Petri Trecensis omnibus ad quos littere iste pervenerint, in Domino salutem. Notum vobis facimus et testificamus quod cum karissime domine nostre Blanche, illustri Campanie comitisse, in excambium Badon, uxoris Guioti Alemanni, et Resennete de Barro,[1] duas feminas deberemus. Reddidimus ei pro illis duabus filiam Cortois de Pontallia et filiam Nicholai de Lustria. Actum anno Domini M CC XI, mense octobri.

1 She may be Ressana, widow of Giles *Pennelarius* of Bar-sur-Aube, who in May 1205 gave her dower lands to Saint-Maclou of Bar-sur-Aube (BNF, nouv. acq. Lat. 110, Cartulary of Saint-Maclou of Bar-sur-Aube, fol. 13r).

76

1205 July, [Sézanne]

The dean Geoffroy and chapter of Saint-Quiriace of Provins announce the resolution of their dispute with the taverners of Provins that was settled in the presence of Countess Blanche. The chapter agreed not to tax wine imported from this side of the Seine river, that is, from the lands and fiefs of Countess Blanche, but it will collect a tax of 12 d. *per cart from wine produced beyond the Seine and Yonne rivers, and 5* s. *per cart from wine produced in Auvergne.*[1] *This settlement modifies count Henry I's 'great charter' (of 1176), which the chapter still possesses.*[2]

ORIGINAL: AN, J 203, no. 7 (missing pendant seal).
COPIES: CR 1, fol. 257v (>CR 6, fols. 162v–163r). CR 3, fol. 134r. CR 4, fol. 188r–v. CR 8, fol. 435r.
CALENDARED: AJ, no. 623. *Layettes*, 1: 294, no. 777.

Ego Gaufridus, ecclesie Beati Quiriaci[a] decanus, totumque ejusdem ecclesie capitulum. Notum esse volumus presentibus ac futuris quod cum inter nos ex una parte et tabernarios de Pruvino ex altera conteintio[b] esset de rotagio vinorum. Tandem[c] in presentia domine et advocate nostre Blanche, illustris comitissime[d] Trecensium palatine, concordata[e] est in hunc modum, quod nos firmiter concessimus nichil omnino de tabernariis accipere pro rotagio citra aquam Senneam in locis que sunt de feodo et propria terra ipsius, preterquam apud territorium Cableiarum et apud territorium Joviniaci. In locis autem que

1 Countess Blanche sealed a similar letter, since the agreement was reached in her court:
Ego Blancha, comitissa Trecensis palatina, notum esse volo presentibus et futuris quod cum inter capitulum Sancti Quiriaci de Pruvino, ex una parte, et tabernarios ex altera, contentio esset de rotagio vinorum, tandem in nostra presentia concordia est in hunc modum, quod canonici de Sancto Quiriaco firmiter concesserunt nihil omnino de tabernariis accipere pro rotagio citra aquam Seneam in locis qui sunt de feodo et propria terra nostra, preterquam apud territorium Cableianum et apud territorium Jovigniaci. In locis autem que sunt de ultra Seneam et Yonam, rotagium habebunt de omnibus locis ex quibus vina venient apud Pruvinum, videlicet de unaquaque quadriga duodecim denaria, et de quadrigio de Averna veniente quinque solidos; et tali modo quod pro nullo puncto quod sit in majori carta capituli Sancti Quiriaci non capere vel exigere de rotagio aliquo modo nisi quod divisum est in presenti carta. Et id factum est ad voluntatem capituli et tabernariorum. Actum apud Sezannam, anno Domini MCCV, mense julio. Datum per manum Gauteri, cancellarii. Nota Johannis (Veissière, *Une communauté canoniale*, 293, no. 64, July 1205, from sixteenth- and seventeenth-century copies).

2 In his 'great charter' for Saint-Quiriace, Count Henry I confirmed the chapter's many possessions and revenues, including one-half of the tolls collected from imported wine (Veissière, *Une communauté canoniale*, 264–72, no. 33, 1176).

sunt de ultra Senneam et Yonam, rotagium habebimus ex omnibus locis ex quibus vina veniant apud Pruvinum, videlicet de unaquaque quadriga duodecim denarios, et de quadrigis de Averna venientibus, quinque solidos; et tali modo quod pro puncto quod sit in majori carta nostra non capiemus vel exigemus de rotagio aliquo modo nisi quod divisum est in presenti carta. Et id factum est ad voluntatem nostram et tabernariorum. Quod ut ratum habeatur, sigilli nostri fecimus munimine roborari. Actum anno Domini M CC quinto, mense julio.[f]

[a] Kiriaci *in CR 1.* [b] contentio *in CR 1.* [c] talem *in CR 1.* [d] comitisse *in CR 1.* [e] concordita *in CR 1.* [f] mense julio *omitted in CR 1.*

77

1203 (n.s.) January

The dean Nicholas and chapter of Bray-sur-Seine make known that they accede to Countess Blanche's right to name the treasurer and chanter of the chapter.[1]

ORIGINAL: AN, J 203, no. 4 (missing pendant seal).
COPIES: CR 1, fol. 257v.[2] CR 3, fol. 128r. CR 4, fol. 185v. CR 8, fol. 437r.
CALENDARED: AJ, no. 572.[3] *Layettes*, 1: 239–40, no. 661.[4]

Ego Nicholaus decanus et universum capitulum ecclesie Braiacensis. Notum facimus omnibus tam presentibus quam futuris quod cum inter nos et venerabilem comitissam Trecensem palatinam Blancham de donacione[a] personatuum ecclesie nostre, videlicet thesaurarie et cantorie, verteretur querela, tandem pacificata est in hunc modum, quod nos honori et amori[b] ejus cupientes deferre volumus et tam pacienter quam unanimiter sustinemus quod ipsa comitissa et heredes sui in perpetuum habeant donacionem[c] personantuum predictorum. Quod ut ratum sit[d] et firmum, sigilli nostri munimine roboramus.[d] Actum anno ab incarnacione Domini M CC secundo, mense januario.

[a] donatione *in CR 1.* [b] amori et honori *in CR 1.* [c] donationem *in CR 1.* [d] etc *in lieu of* sit *though* roboramus *in CR 1.*

1 See also **106**, **109**.
2 The copyist of CR 6 skipped this letter and continued with **78**.
3 AJ cites **77** and **106** as being identical documents.
4 The editors of the *Layettes* identify this letter as being identical to **106**.

78

1199 December, Dijon

The papal legate Pierre, cardinal-deacon of Santa Maria in Via Lata,[1] *announces that four men quit Count Thibaut III of the debts that Countess Marie had incurred on behalf of Count Henry II.*[2]

COPIES: CR 1, fol. 257v (>CR 6, fol. 163r). CR 3, fol. 118v. CR 4, fol. 121r.
CALENDARED: AJ, no. 496.

Petrus, Dei patientia Sancte Marie in via lata diaconus, cardinalis apostolice sedis legatus, omnibus presentes litteras inspecturis, in Domino salutem. Notum esse volumus universis quod de omni debito quod dilecta filia pie memorie Maria, comitissa Campanie, debebat pro filio suo comite Henrico defuncto, Bertrando de Lambes et Bernardo de Conchis et Bernardo Anfredi et Willelmo Giraudi, ipsi in presentia nostra constituti, quitaverunt principem Theobaldum comitem Campanie et omnes ejus heredes et terram et homines suos et animam comitisse predictem et animam memorati comitis Henrici. Quod ut firmum et stabile perseveret fideliter, hic inscribi et sigilli nostri appensione fecimus communiri. Actum Duyone, anno gratie M C XC none, mense decembri.

79

1210 September

Geoffroy, abbot of Saint-Pierre of Chézy, recognizes that he has no right to the woods located across the Marne River, but that Countess Blanche has allowed him to collect two carts of firewood there on two days each week.

ORIGINAL: AN, J 197, no. 8 (missing pendant seal).
COPIES: CR 1, fol. 257v (>CR 6, fol. 163r–v). CR 8, fol. 275v.
CALENDARED: AJ, no. 749. *Layettes*, 1: 357, no. 941.

Ego Gaufridus, dictus abbas Cheziaci, notum facio omnibus presentibus et futuris quod nos in nemoribus de ultra Maternam nullum usuarium reclamamus.

1 For Pierre's career, see Maleczeck, *Papst und Kardinalskolleg von 1191 bis 1216*, 117–22.

2 The comital archive held two related letters of quittance for the same debt: one from King Philip II (*Recueil des actes de Philippe Auguste*, 2: 141, no. 590, November 1198 [= CR 7.3, fol. 258v]), the other from the archbishop of Sens (CR 3, fol. 117r, November 1199 [= CR 4, fol. 120r = CR 8 fol. 123r]). See also **73**, **80**.

Sed karissima domina nostra Blancha, comitissa Campanie, nobis concessit quod in qualibet septimana duobus diebus cum duabus bigis possimus ire in nemoribus supradictis quamdiu ei placuerit per nostro ardere. Actum anno Domini M CC X, mense septembri.

80

[1199–1201]

Octavian, cardinal bishop of Ostia and papal legate,[1] *states that in his presence Count Thibaut III paid Pierre* Estrovat *160 marks after being presented with Count Henry II's letter of debt.*

COPIES: CR 1, fol. 257v (>CR 6, fol. 163v). CR 3, fol. 117v. CR 4, fol. 120r.
CALENDARED: AJ, no. 541.

Octavianus, Dei gratia Hostiensis et Velletrensis episcopus, apostolice sedis legatus, omnibus presentes litteras inspecturis, in Domino salutem. Noveritis quod super C LX marcis quas bone memorie comes Henricus Petro Estrovat[a] debebat, dominus Theobaldus illustris comes Campanie, mandato dicti Petri, in nostra presentia satisfecit adeo quod littere dicti comitis Henrici super eodem debito facte memorato, comiti Theobaldi in nostra fuerit presentia resignare. In cujus rei testimonium,[b] presentes fecimus litteras sigilli nostri munimine roborari.

[a] Espiovet *in CR 3 and CR 4.* [b] *Text in CR 1 ends here.*

81

1211 April

Milo of Nanteuil,[1] *provost of the cathedral chapter of Reims, makes known that his brother-in-law, Hugh of Pomponne,*[2] *gave him life use of the village of Saint-Germain in Brie, which Hugh holds in fief from Countess Blanche. The countess allowed it, providing that Hugh continues to render the feudal service owed for that village, on pain of confiscation.*

---

1 For Octavian's career, see Maleczeck, *Papst und Kardinalskolleg von 1191 bis 1216*, 80–3.

1 Milo of Nanteuil, fourth son of Gaucher I (of Châtillon) of Nanteuil-la-Fosse, was a canon (1206) then provost (1207–17) of the cathedral chapter of Reims, and finally bishop of Beauvais (1218–34); see Newman, *Les seigneurs de Nesle*, 1: 195; and Desportes, *Fasti Ecclesiae Gallicanae*, 3: 436, no. 1101.

2 For Hugh of Pomponne (1200–28), see Newman, *Les seigneurs de Nesle*, 1: 196–7.

COPIES: CR 1, fol. 258r (>CR 6, fols. 163v–164r).
EDITION: Chantereau-Lefebvre, *Traité des fiefs*, 2: 43 (from CR 7).
CALENDARED: AJ, no. 772.

Ego Milo de Nantolio, Remensis ecclesie prepositus, notum facio omnibus ad quos littere iste presentes pervenerint quod cum dilectus sororius meus, Hugo de Pompona, villam suam que appellatur Sanctus Germanus in Bria, mihi in presentia karissime domine Blanche, illustris Campanie comitisse, quoad vixerim, concessisset habendam, hoc modo, quod quicquid meliorationis et incrementi circa eandem villam fecero, Deo dante, post decessum meum tam ad ipsum Hugonem quam ad ejus heredes libere revertatur. Prefate comitisse Campanie, in cujus presentia facta fuit, hec recognovi et adhuc presentibus litteris recognosco quod si idem Hugo erga dictam comitissam aut de suo servitio aut de hoc quod debet ei pro prefata villa, que est de feodo comitisse, deficeret et ipsa propter hoc ad suum feodum assignaret vel illud saisiret, ego non possem contraire, neque per apostolicum archiepiscopum, episcopum vel ecclesiasticam personam, ipsam comitissam terram suam vel aliquem ex parte sua cogere vel in causam ponere quominus si hoc fieret, ad suum feodum manum mitteret. Quicquid non contingat dictus Hugo servicium faciet de ipso feodo. Quod ut ratum sit etc. Actum anno Domini M CC XI, mense aprili.

82

1177, Troyes

A notice states that Geoffroy of Mousson[1] *gave the Templars property located in the market of Ramerupt that he had mortgaged to Count Henry I for 100* l. *They may keep the property during Geoffroy's lifetime, but after his death the count may redeem it by paying the Templars 100* l. *This agreement was reached in Count Henry's chamber in Troyes.*

COPIES: CR 1, fol. 258r (>CR 6, fol. 164r). CR 3, fol. 12r. CR 4, fol. 151r. CR 6, fol. 164r, 179v–180r.
EDITION: Chantereau-Lefebvre, *Traité des fiefs*, 2: 6 (from CR 6).
CALENDARED: AJ, no. 278.

Notum sit universis tam presentibus quam futuris quod Gaufridus de Monchon concessit Deo et Beate Marie et domui Templi Salomonis in elemosinam

1 Geoffroy held a comital fief owing two months castle-guard in the castellany of Rosnay circa 1178 (Longnon, *Documents*, 1: 7, no. 193); he joined the Cistercians at Trois-Fontaines before 1189 (Denaix, *Chartes des Cistercians de Saint-Benôit-en-Woëvre*, 209).

vadium illud quod pignoraverat a comite Henrico pro C libris, tali videlicet conditione, quod quamdiu prelibatus Gaufridus vixerit, fratres milite Templi Salomonis elemosinam libere et quiete possidebunt. Gaufrido autem defuncto, si comes Henricus voluerit ad se pignus revocare vel heres ejus, fratribus Templi centum libras exsolvet. Et sciendum quod ista elemosina sita est in foro de Rameru. Actum in thalamo comitis Henrici apud Trecas, anno M C LXX VIII ab incarnatione Domini.

83

1208 May[1]

Abbot Hugh and the chapter of Saint-Martin of Epernay announce that they quit to Countess Blanche, in return for three modii *of grain annually, the mills of Aubérive that they acquired through gifts from former counts and through an exchange with Richilde of Dormans.*[2] *Neither Blanche nor her successors may alienate the mills or grant them in fief. Hugh describes the conditions under which Saint-Martin will continue to collect the grain in the event the mills are destroyed.*

ORIGINAL: AN, J 1035, no. 4 (heavily damaged; missing pendant seal).

COPIES: CR 1, fol. 258r–v, dated May 1208 (>CR 6, fols. 164r–166r). CR 8, fols. 276r–277v, dated May 1206.

EDITION: *Layettes*, 5: 58–9, no. 164, dated May 1206 (based on CR 8).

CALENDARED: AJ, no. 684 (CR 6), no. 653 (CR 8).

Ego Hugo, Dei patientia Sparnacensis ecclesie abbas, et capitulum nostrum notum facimus tam presentibus quam futuris quod quicquid habebamus in molendinis de Alba Ripa de dono et elemosina dominorum Campanie et de escambio domine Richoldis de Dormanz, communi voluntate et assensu concessimus et donavimus in perpetuum possidendum karissime domine et advocate nostre Blanche, illustri Trecensis comitisse palatine, et omnibus dominis Campanie, tali modo quod in eisdem molendinis habebimus annuatim tres modios frumenti de admodiatione ad mensuram Sparnaci; quos videlicet

1 The date of the original document cannot be read. The two copies give different dates: May 1208 (CR 1) and May 1206 (CR 8, which gives a slightly different ending). The editors of the *Layettes* chose 1206, but 1208 is preferable for two reasons: CR 1 was made within five years of the original letter and its text is entirely unproblematic; and 1208 is closer to a related act of 1210 dealing with property at Dormans (**70**).

2 See also **70**.

tres modios frumenti recipiemus de cetero annuatim a proximo ventura festivitate Sancti Remigii et ultra, tali modo quod statim post idem festum Sancti Remigii quod est in capite octobris, nullus de proventibus molendinorum molentium aliquid levabit donec illos tres modios frumenti integre habuerimus, tale scilicet frumentum quale molendina supradicta lucrabuntur vel equivalens. Et si proventus molendinorum a predicta festivitate Sancti Remigii usque ad festum Sancti Johannis Baptiste tres modios frumenti non valerent, ex tunc pro defectu trium modiorum nos teneremur ad exitus omnium molendinorum, tam mollentium quam fullentium, et ad exitus piscature usque dum totam admodiationem haberemus. Preterea cum hiis tribus modiis frumenti habebimus annuatim quinque solidos pruvinensium censuales in predicto festo Sancti Remigii persolvendos. Habebimus etiam medietatem totius piscature in omnibus commodis sine aliqua operis expensa et impensa.

Quotienscumque vero servientes molendinorum mutabuntur, totiens data cautione juratoria facient fidelitatem abbati et ecclesie nostre de medietate piscature et de admodiatione, sicut prescriptum est abbati et ecclesie nostre legitime persolvenda. Si quos autem sumptus in neccesariis piscature pro defectu vel negligentia servientium apposuimus,[a] comitissa vel heredes Campanie de proventibus piscatura nichil percipiet quoadusque sumptus appositi nobis fuerint restituti. Sciendum est etiam quod ipsa comitissa vel heredes Campanie molendina supradicta in alterius manu quam in nostra ponere non poterit, nec aliquid in elemosinam vel feodum exinde dare alicui nisi nobis et ecclesie Sparnacensis. Et si forte molendina ista corruerent vel aliquo modo deficerent et comitissa vel heres de Campanie ad requisitionem nostram dicta molendina nolle reficere nec debitam ecclesie nostre admodiationem nostram persolvere, nobis et posteris nostris ex tunc liceret, sine aliqua interceptione erga eos, quod molendina illa reficeremus et in manu nostra teneremus cum tali banno et justicia quali comitissa vel heredes Campanie ea tenebat, tam molentia[b] quam fullentia, usque dum haberemus sumptus facture, et necessarias molendinorum expensas et impensas cum debitis nobis ad commaditionibus[c] cum autem sumptus facture cum necessarias molendinorum expensis et impensis et debitis nobis admodiationibus receperimus. Ex tunc comitissa Campanie vel heres Campanie molendina illa, si voluerit, poterit rehabere[d] et eodem modo quod prenotatum est obtinere. Quod ut ratum firmumque permaneat, presens scriptum emisimus sigilli capituli nostri munimine confirmatum. Actum anno ab incarnatione Domini M CC VI mense maio, littera dominicali A.[e]

[a] apposuerimus *in CR 8 and Layettes.* [b] molendina *in CR 8 and Layettes.*
[c] admodiationibus *in CR 8 and Layettes.* [d] potuerit retrahere *in Layettes.*
[e] *CR 1 ends with* Quod ut ratum permaneat et ceterea. Actum anno gratie M CC VIII, mense maio.

84

1205

Renaud, dean of the chapter of Villemaur, grants Countess Blanche half of the revenues from the taille *and justice of his inherited villages of Dierrey and Moirey.*[1]

COPIES: CR 1, fol. 258v (>CR 6, fol. 165r). CR 3, fol. 83v. CR 8, fol. 485r.
CALENDARED: AJ, no. 644

Ego Renaudus, decanus Ville Mauri, notum esse volo presentes litteras inspecturis quod in illa terra quam habeo de heredibus Villemauri apud Morriacum et Derriacum, associavi karissimam dominam meam Blancham, illustrem comitissam Campanie, ad medietatem tallie hominum et justicie predictarum villarum, tali modo quod ipsa id in quo eam associavi de manu sua alienare non poterit ullo modo. Ego vero omne quod est residuum, exceptis supradictis, in supradicta terra michi retinui. Actum anno Domini M CC V.

85

1207 December

The dean Iter and chapter of Saint-Etienne of Troyes make known that Countess Blanche has lent the chapter a certain Herbert, exempt from all taxes, military obligations, and justice – except in cases of bloodshed, larceny, rape, murder, and false measure – for as long as she wishes.

COPIES: CR 1, fol. 258v (>CR 6, fol. 165v). CR 3, fol. 25r. CR 8, fol. 430v.
CALENDARED: AJ, no. 673.

Iterus decanus universumque capitulum Beati Stephani Trecensis, omnibus ad quos littere iste pervenerint, in Domino salutem. Notum vobis facimus quod karissima domina et advocata nostra Blanche, illustris Campanie comitissa, domui Dei Beati Stephani Herbertum de Horrido Monte accomodavit, quamdiu ipsa voluerit, liberum et quietum ab omni tallia et exactione, ab omni expeditione et exercitu, et ab omni justicia, preterquam a sanguinis effusione, a latrocinio, et raptu et multro et falsa mensura. Nos vero veritati testimonii perhibentes, litteras presentes nostro sigillo munitas fecimus. Anno incarnati Verbi, M CC VII, mense decembri.

1 See Roserot, *Dictionnaire historique*, 1: 498–9; 2: 914.

86

1202

Odo of Sully, bishop of Paris,[1] *quits to Countess Blanche the 120* l. *rent that Count Thibaut II had granted in fief to his father, Archambaud I of Sully, who had mortgaged it to Count Henry I for 550* l., *money of Provins and Meaux.*[2]

COPIES: CR 1, fol. 258v (>CR 6, fol. 165v). CR 3, fol. 81r. CR 4, fol. 134v. CR 8, fol. 194r.
CALENDARED: AJ, no. 579.

Odo, Dei gratia Parisiensis episcopus, omnibus presens scriptum inspecturis, in Domino salutem.[a] Notum facimus quod nos quitavimus in perpetuum et concedimus illustri domine Blanche, comitisse Trecensis, et heredibus suis VI[xx] libras pruviniensis monete quas bone memorie Theobaldus, quondam comes Blesensis, dedit in feodum Erchambaldo, quondam domino Soilliaci,[b] patri meo et nepoti suo, quas etiam dictus Erchambaldus postmodum comiti Henrico, consanguineo suo, pro[c] quingentis quinquaginta libris pruviniensis et meldensis monete pignori obligavit. In hujus autem quitationis, testimonium presentes litteras fieri fecimus et sigilli nostri impressione muniri. Actum anno incarnati Verbi M CC secundo.

[a] in Domino salutem *omitted in CR 1.* [b] Soliaci *in CR 3.* [c] pro *omitted in CR 1.*

*87

1205 June

Anselm, bishop of Meaux, makes known that Raoul of Montguichet[1] *sold his rights in the forest of Mans to Countess Blanche for 400* l. *The countess allows his settlers at Montguichet to continue to collect firewood and wood for building houses, and she allows Raoul the right to clear eighty arpents of the forest.*

ORIGINAL: AN, J 203, no. 6 (missing pendant seal).
COPIES: CR 1, fol. 259r.[2] CR 3, fol. 118r. CR 4, fol. 120v. CR 8, fol. 184r.
CALENDARED: AJ, no. 619. *Layettes*, 1: 293, no. 769.

1 Odo, bishop of Paris (1196–1208), was the youngest son of Archaumbaud I of Sully; see Devailly, *Le Berry*, 486–7.

2 See also **34**, **46**.

1 Raoul of Montguichet held a fief at Montguichet and Mans circa 1178 (Longnon, *Documents*, 1: 48, no. 1238). See Bur, 'Le défrichement et le partage de la forêt du Mans près de Meaux (1150–1250),' 97.

2 The copyist of CR 6 skipped this text and ***88**.

Anselmus, Dei gratia Meldensis episcopus, omnibus presentibus et futuris, in Domino salutem. Notum vobis facimus et testamur dilectum in Christo, Radulphum de Moncuichet, karissime in Christo amice nobili mulieri Blanche, illustri comitisse Campanie, laude et assensu liberorum suorum et omnium ad quos pertinebat, vendidisse grueriam quam habebat in foresta de Mant pro quadringentis libris, et cum grueria quicquid habebat juris in eadem foresta. Ipsa vero comitissa concessit eidem Radulpho quod hospites sui de Moncuichet et ipse et heredes ejus qui manebunt apud Moncuichet in eadem foresta habeant usuarium suum, scilicet nemus mortuum ad ardendum et vivuum ad herbergandum. Concessit etiam comitissa eidem Radulpho quod in eadem foresta possit octaginta arpenta nemoris extirpare. Nos vero ad petitionem ipsius Radulphus et comitisse simul, presentem cartam fieri precepimus in testimonium veritatis. Actum anno Domini M CC V, mense junio.

*88

1214 July, Compiègne

King Philip II notifies Guillaume of Chartres, master of the Templars,[1] *that the ancient custom in France is that no one may be challenged as to his paternal inheritance before he is twenty-one. The king states that he and Prince Louis affirmed in the presence of Jean of Brienne, king of Jerusalem,*[2] *that they will not hear any case brought against Thibaut by Count Henry II's daughter or by anyone else until Thibaut reaches twenty-one, especially since the king has heard the testimony of many credible noble men that Henry II, when he left for Jerusalem (in 1190), transferred all his lands to his brother Thibaut III in the event he did not return. The king also prohibits the marriage of Erard of Ramerupt*[3] *with Count Henry II's daughter because he has heard that the couple was consanguineously related and therefore not able to be legitimately married.*

COPY: CR 1, fol. 259r.[4]

EDITION: *Recueil des actes de Philippe Auguste*, 3: 478–9, no. 1338 (from CR 1).

CALENDARED: Delisle, *Catalogue des actes de Philippe Auguste*, no. 1502.

1 A brief biography of Guillaume of Chartres, master of the Templars (1210–19) is in Bulst-Thiele, *Sacrae Domus Militiae Templi Hierosolymitani Magistri*, 159–69.

2 See **22** n. 1.

3 Erard 'of Brienne,' lord of Ramerupt (1203–43), was the younger son of André II (of Brienne), lord of Ramerupt, and nephew of Erard II, count of Brienne (1143–91). Erard of Ramerupt married Count Henry II's daughter Philippa in 1213 in order to claim the county of Champagne as her inheritance. Erard's challenge to Thibaut IV's succession dominated Countess Blanche's regency. See above, introduction, n. 68; Roserot, *Dictionnaire historique*, 3: 1228; and Arbois de Jubainville, *Histoire*, 3: 101–97, and 'Les premiers seigneurs de Ramerupt,' 447–51.

4 See ***87** n. 2.

Philippus, Dei gratia Francorum rex, dilecto[a] suis fratri Willelmo de Carnoto, magistro, et universis fratribus domus milicie Templi, salutem et dilectionem. Scire vos volumus quod consuetudo antiqua et per jus approbata talis est in regno Francie, quod nullus ante viginti et unum annos potest vel debet trahi in causam de re quam pater ejus teneret sine placito cum decessit. Hujus igitur ratione consuetudinis, nos et karissimus filius noster Ludovicus statuimus et concessimus dilecte et fideli nostre comitisse Trecensi et Theobaldo filio ejus, presente et audiente dilecto nostro Johanne, rege Jerosolime, quod si filie comitis Henrici vel aliquis pro ipsis vellent predictum Theobaldum vel matrem ejus in causam trahere de terra quam pater ejus tenuit, nos non audiremus inde verbum donec idem Theobaldus haberet viginti et unum annos, nec ipsum vel matrem ejus antea in causam trahi permitteremus, precipue cum, de testimonio multorum nobilium virorum quibus fidem bene adhibere debemus, bene constet quod karissimus quondam nepos noster comes Henricus, cum vellet Jherosolimam proficisci, totam terram suam dimisit et dedit Theobaldo fratri suo, quondam comiti Trecensi, si ipsum comitem Henricum de transmarinis partibus contingeret non redire. Ad hec nullo modo volumus quod Erardus de Rameruco filiam comitis Henrici habeat in uxorem, sed id fieri modis omnibus prohibemus quia, si fieret, contra nos fieret, nec est conveniens quod tam nobilis domicella habeat talem virum, et preterea dictum est nobis quod in eo gradu consanguinitatis sese attingunt quod non possunt nec debent legitime copulari. Actum Compendii, anno Domini M CC XIIII, mense julio.

[a] dilectis *in Recueil.*

*89

1205 October 20

Pope Innocent III orders all prelates to prohibit the taxing of the Templars' men and goods, on pain of excommunication and interdict.

COPIES: CR 1, fol. 259r–v (>CR 6, fols. 165v–166r).
CALENDARED: AJ, no. 633.

Innocentus, episcopus servus servorum Dei, venerabilibus fratribus, archiepiscopis, episcopis, et dilectis filiis abbatibus, prioribus et aliis ecclesiarum prelatis ad quos littere iste pervenerint, salutem et apostolicam benedictionem. Religiosos viros fratres ordine Templi domus pro religione et honestate sua tanto propensius a malignorum incursibus protegere volumus et tueri, quanto puriorem devotionem cura nos et Romanam ecclesiam exibere noscuntur. Inde est quod per apostolica scripta percipendo mandamus quatinus universis parrochianis vestris, sub interminatione anathematis, prohibere curetis ne a prefatis fratribus vel eorum hominibus de victualibus, vestimentis, pecudibus seu de aliis rebus eorumdem fratrem usibus deputatis, passagium, vendam, pedagium, cautagium seu aliam quamlibet consuetudinem exigere vel extorquere presumant. Si qui autem contra prohibitionem vestram venire presunpserint, eos a prescriptione sua non differatis per excommunicationis sentenciam cohercere, et in terris eorum si quas habent omnia divina, preter baptisma parvulorum et penitencias morientium, prohibeatis officia celebrari. Ad hec qua, sicut predicti fratres asserunt, quidam presbiteri et alii clerici vestre jurisdictionis in ecclesiis illis que per excessibus in domum predictorum fratrum commissis sub interdicto tenetur divina celebrant presumerunt, si res ita se habet a sue presumptionis audacia per suspensionis et excommunicationis sententiam compescatis. Datum Romam apud Sanctum Petrum, XIII kalendas novembris, pontificatus nostri anno octavo.

*90

1205 July

Anselm III of Traînel recognizes that he holds the fortified residence at Villeneuve-aux-Riches-Hommes as a liege fief from Countess Blanche. He promises that if he ever is unable to warrant it, he will dismantle it at her will.

COPY: CR 1, fol. 259bis (one-half of a loose folio).

[same as **15**]

*91

1205 July, Troyes

Hermesend (of Bar-sur-Seine), lady of Traînel,[1] *affirms that she holds her (dower) residence of Villeneuve-aux-Riches-Hommes as a liege fief from Countess Blanche. She promises that if ever she is unable to warrant it, she will dismantle it at the will of the countess.*[2]

1 Hermesend was the widow of Anselm II of Traînel, butler of Champagne, 1152–84 (see **45** n. 3). She remarried in 1189 to Thibaut of Briey, who became count of Bar-le-Duc (1192–1214), but after having three more children she was divorced in 1196. She returned to Traînel, outlived her son Anselm III (d. 1210), and died in 1211. A brief biography is in Evergates, 'Aristocratic Women in the County of Champagne,' 99–101, and Poull, *La maison souveraine et ducale de Bar*, 150. See also ***117**.

2 Her son Anselm III sealed an almost identical letter at the same time (**15**).

ORIGINAL: AN, J 196, no. 2 (missing pendant seal).[3]
COPIES: CR 1, fol. 259bis. CR 3, fols. 93v–94r. CR 4, fol. 102v. CR 6, fol. 223r.
EDITION: Chantereau-Lefebvre, *Traité des fiefs*, 2: 29 (from CR 6).
CALENDARED: AJ, no. 626. *Layettes*, 1: 567, no. 777ter.

Ego Hermesendis, domina de Trianguli, notum esse volo presentibus et futuris, et animo bono cognosco, domum meam de Villa Nova Parva Divitum Hominum esse de feodo ligio karissime domine mee ligie Blanche, illustris Campanie comitisse, et heredum suorum tali modo, quod de quacumque hora verbum inde veniret per quod domus illa esse posset de alterius feodo quam de feodo domine comitisse, et ego domum hanc, quam recognosco esse de feodo ligio comitisse et heredum suorum, non possem garantire, creanto ei tamquam domine mee et promitto, supra omne quod de illa teneo, quod domum ipsam diruam ad voluntatem comitisse vel illius quem ad id faciendum mitteret. Quod si non facerem, ex tunc volo quod domina comitissa licenter se capiat ad me et ad feodum quod de illa teneo, usque dum id fiat et hoc poterit facere, salva fide sua erga me. Actum Trecis, anno gratie M CC quinto, mense julio.

[quire 34: fols. 260r–266v]

92

1198

The dean Jean and chapter of Saint-Pierre of Troyes acknowledge the arbitration by Michel, archbishop of Sens, and Geoffroy of Villehardouin, marshal of Champagne,[1] in resolving the question of the chapter's jurisdiction within its cloister.[2] The chapter's cloister will be absolutely immune from the count's provost, and three of the chapter's officials will be exempt from the count's justice, except if caught in flagrante delicto. The chapter's men are liable for military service when the count summons them in person or sends a letter or credible representative.

3 This is the earliest extant sealed letter from a woman in the chancery archive (see also **20**, **21**). The earliest extant letter from a baron is from 1199 (**14**).

1 See Longnon, *Recherches sur la vie de Geoffroy de Villehardouin*, 45–110.

2 Count Thibaut III sealed a similar letter (AD Aube, G 2608, 1198 [= *Gallia Christiana*, 12: *instr.*, 282, no. 53]).

ORIGINAL: AN, J 195, no. 2 (missing pendant seal)
COPIES: CR 1, fol. 260r (>CR 6, fol. 274r–v). CR 3, fol. 111r–v. CR 4, fol. 152r–v. CR 8, fol. 420v.
EDITIONS: Lalore, *Cartulaire de Saint-Pierre de Troyes*, 93–5, no. 87. *Layettes*, 1: 198–9, no. 484.
CALENDARED: AJ, no. 470.

Johannes, ecclesie Beati Petri Trecensis decanus, totumque ejusdem ecclesie capitulum, omnibus presentes litteras inspecturis, in Domino salutem. Noverit universitas vestra quod discordia que inter nos et nobilem Campanie comitem Theobaldum vertebatur super justicia hominum nostrorum, compromissione facta a nobis et ab ipso comite in dominum Senonensem Mychaelem archiepiscopum et in Gaufridum marescallum Campanie, receptis ex utraque parte testibus, terminata est in hunc modum: Si aliquis conqueritur de aliquo hominum nostrorum qui non sit de liberis servientibus nostris, ipse homo debet ire ad citationem prepositi comitis. Sed si de aliqua querela agatur contra eum, non respondebit ibi nec remanebit, sed in curia nostra querela audietur et terminabitur; et de omnibus querelis et admissionibus homines nostri non nisi coram nobis respondebunt. Si comes iturus est in exercitum vel in expeditionem in propria persona pro negotio proprio, per litteras suas vel per credibilem nuntium nobis mandabit ut homines nostros submoneamus, et hoc fecimus et ad nostram submonitionem ibunt homines nostri, et aliter non, et eunte ipso comite.

Diffinitum est etiam quod hec est libertas claustri nostri et domorum in quibuscumque manemus, sive in claustro sive extra claustrum: quod nec furem nec falsam mensuram nec aliquam rem aliam poterit prepositus comitis vel aliquis alius capere in eis, nec aliquid justicie habebit in eis, nec aliquis ex parte comitis. Omnes etiam servientes nostri qui de bonis nostris vivunt in domibus nostris liberi sunt ab omnibus consuetudinibus et clamoribus et ab omnibus servitiis, et hanc libertatem habent tres servientes nostri, scilicet granetarius, cellerarius, et major noster. Si quis autem omnium istorum in justicia comitis captus fuerit vel deprehensus ad presens et cognitum delictum, justicia erit comitis. Si vero delictum negetur, comes vel sui recredent hominem captum et delictum probabunt in curia nostra, et probata veritate, comes justiciam obtinebit. Quod ut ratum et inconcussum permaneat, litteris annotatum sigilli nostri testimonio roboravimus. Actum anno incarnati Verbi millesimo centesimo nonagesimo octavo.

93

1199 December, Provins

Guillaume, archbishop of Reims and cardinal,[1] *announces that he has granted his nephew, Count Thibaut III, for the next three years the revenues from the tolls in Provins that Guillaume had received from his father, Thibaut II, and his brother, Henry I.*[2] *Guillaume also gave his nephew three years' worth of revenues from certain houses in Provins and some allods in Troyes.*

COPIES: CR 1, fol. 260r.[3] CR 3, fols. 111v–112r (dated 1190). CR 4, fols. 182v–183r (dated 1190). CR 8, fol. 83r.

EDITION: Chantereau-Lefebvre, *Traité des fiefs*, 2: 10 (from CR 3).

CALENDARED: AJ, no. 497.

Willelmus, Dei gratia Remensis archiepiscopus, Sancte Romane ecclesie titulus Sancte Sabina cardinalis, omnibus ad quos littere iste pervenerint, in Domine salutem. Noverint presentes pariter et futuris quod nos karissimo nepoti nostro Theobaldo, comiti Trecensis palatino, quitum clamavimus et dimisimus in perpetuum quicquid ex dono patris nostri Theobaldi et ex dono fratris nostri Henrici, patris predicte Theobaldi, habebamus in theloneo Pruvini, et insuper dimisimus ei a proximo sabbato ante natale Domini usque ad instans festum Omnium Sanctorum, et ab eodem festo Omnium Sanctorum usque ad tres annos completos precipiendum, id quod habebamus in quibusdam domibus apud Sanctum Aygulphum. Elapsis vero illis tribus annis, ad nos revertetur. Si vero decesserimus, ad Sancti Quiriaci et Sancti Aygulphi ecclesias revertetur. Ad illas enim post decessum nostrum debet reverti.

Similiter dimisimus eidem nepoti nostro ab eodem festo Omnium Sanctorum in tres annis completos Trecensium allodii quem ab ecclesia Sancti Aygulphi tenebamus. Elapsis vero hiis tribus annis, ad nos revertetur. Si vero decesserimus, ad ecclesiam Sancti Aygulphi revertetur, ad quam post decessum nostrum debet reverti. Nos igitur in hujus rei testimonium, presentes litteras scribi et sigillo nostro fecimus roborari. Actum Pruvinum, anno incarnationis Domini M C nonagesimo nono,[a] mense decembri. Datum per manum Mathei, cancellarii nostri.

[a] nono *omitted in CR 3 and CR 4.*

1 See **68** n. 1.

2 Guillaume probably received the toll revenues in 1150 or 1151, when he was about fifteen and in search of a prebend. This grant of December 1199 appears to have been in support of the Fourth Crusade.

3 Perhaps by oversight, this text was not copied into CR 6.

94

1206

Abbot Milo and the chapter of Saint-Remi of Reims announce their association with Countess Blanche to found a new village, Villiers-en-Argonne, where they will share the lordship and revenues.[1] *The monks will retain their banal mills, tithes, and churches. The mayor and village officials will be selected by the two provosts representing the countess and the monks.*

ORIGINAL: AN, J 197, no. 7 (two missing pendant seals).
COPIES: CR 1, fol. 260v (>CR 6, fols. 274v–275r). CR 3, fols. 112r–113r. CR 4, fol. 152v–153v. CR 8, fol. 245.
EDITION: *Layettes*, 1: 307–8, no. 817.
CALENDARED: AJ, no. 664.

Milo, Dei permissione Sancti Remigii Remensis abbas, totumque loci ipsius capitulum, omnibus ad quos littere iste pervenerint, in Domino salutem. Noverit universitas vestra quod nos pari voluntate associamus karissimam in Christo dominam et amicam nostram Blancham, illustrem Campanie comitissam, et venturos Campanie heredes ad faciendam novam villam in nemoribus nostris Sancti Remigii juxta Villare tali modo, quod ipsa comitissa et omnes Campanie heredes nobiscum partientur in eadem villa in omnibus modis et commodis, videlicet in omni banno et justicia et bosco et plano et assisia. Retinemus tamen nobis furnos bannales, molendinos et piscariam et decimas et altaria et cetera spiritualia sine parte comitisse. Nemus etiam nostrum de Moissones remanet nobis quitum ad faciendam volutatem nostram in omnibus modis et commodis. Et notandum quod prepositus monachus noster qui in eadem villa manebit pro nobis et prepositus comitisse majorem et scabinos eligent per commune; et major et scabini fidelitatem facient monacho nostro pro nobis et preposito comitisse pro comitissa. Ceterum omnia carrucagia et veteres census et prata et terre et alia domania que apud Braux et apud Villare antequam carta hec fieret habebamus,[2] nobis remanent omnino libera et quita in custodia comitisse.

Due partes nemoris nostri quod est inter Altam Ripam et Villare ille exartabuntur pro nova villa facienda; tercia autem pars ejusdem nemoris erit

1 Countess Blanche's letter on the same matter was preserved in the monastery's own archives and later copied into its cartulary (AD Marne, 56 H 1031, fol. 606r–v). See also Bur, 'Le défrichement,' 97, and Higounet, *Défrichements et villeneuves*, 168.

2 The reference may be to Count Henry I's charter of 1153 in which he renewed his father's custody over the land and men of Saint-Remi (AD Marne, 56 H 1029, fol. 65r; extract published in Varin, *Archives administratives de la ville de Reims*, 1: 328).

monachi et in advocatione solummodo comitisse. Sed de forifactis ejusdem nemoris, medietas erit nostra, medietas erit comitisse, si ballivi ejus ad forisfactum sint vocati. Domus nostre de Curtesor et de Braux et villa de Braux usuarium suum in illa tercia parte nemoris habebunt. Et ad habendum usuarium dabit comitissa, si necesse est, salvum eundo et redeundo conductum. Omnes servientes monachi manentes in villa liberi erunt. Nullus poterit tenere terram in villa nisi mansionarius sit in illa. Homines Sancti Remigii qui sint apud Curtesor, in illa villa mansuri venire non poterunt. Comitissa guarantizabit et defendet per rectum domum nostram de Braux et jura ad eam pertinentia. Sciendum etiam quod in eadem villa nova comitissa vel ejus ballivi nullam talliam, nullum gistum, nullam procurationem habebunt.

Nos autem associationem hanc concedimus comitisse et heredibus Campanie ea conditione, quod illa que ipsis in hac associatione concedimus de manu sua aliquo modo tollere non poterunt vel in feodum vel in elemosinam dare. Quod ut ratum permaneat, paginam nostram sigillorum nostrum appensione munitam, ipsi comitisse et heredibus Campanie dedimus in testimonium hujus associationis. Actum anno Dominice incarnationis millesimo ducentesimo[a] sexto, regnante glorioso et victorioso Francorum rege Philippo.

[a] M CC *in CR 1.*

95

1203 (n.s.) February

Ebles, abbot of Saint-Jean of Laon, makes known that he has been granted life use of Marmoutier's priory of Ventelay, free from the count's advocacy, unless he abuses his right.

COPIES: CR 1, fol. 260v–261r (>CR 6, fol. 275v). CR 3, fol. 39v. CR 4, fol. 160v. CR 8, fol. 381r.
CALENDARED: AJ, no. 576.

Ego Ebalus, Dei patientia Sancti Johannis Laudunensis dictus abbas, omnibus ad quos littere presentes pervenerint. Notum fieri volo me libenti animo et voluntate spontanea concessisse quod de prioratu de Ventelaio, quem abbas et conventus Majoris Monasterii mihi quamdiu viverem concesserunt habendum, et de pertinentiis ejusdem prioratus, nullum advocatum vel defensorem secularem requiram, nec dominam comitissam Campanie vel ejus heredes ad quos advocatio[a] dicti prioratus dignoscitur pertinere. Et si hoc aliquo malo consilio facere presumerem, concessi quod eadem comitissa vel ejus heredes ad dictum prioratum et ad ejus pertinentias libere et sine contradictione aliqua inde se vertent, nulla injuria super hoc michi facta. In cujus rei testimonium, presentem paginam fieri volui sigilli mei appensione munitam. Actum anno incarnationi Verbi M CC secundo, mense februario.

[a] advocatia *in CR 3 and CR 4.*

96

1205 December

Robert, bishop of Langres,[1] *announces the resolution of a dispute between Countess Blanche and Josbert of Chaumont over the property that Josbert claimed by collateral inheritance from Lady Chaumonde (of Chaumont).*[2] *Josbert and his heirs quitclaimed the inheritance and all property they might have in Chaumont, in fief and domain, in return for 200* l. *and property at Ageville, for which he will be Blanche's liegeman and owe one month castle-guard annually at Chaumont. The countess will not allow any men who live in Aubepierre or Ageville to establish residence in her towns of Bar-sur-Aube, Laferté-sur-Aube, and Chaumont or within their castellanies.*[3]

COPIES: CR 1, fol. 261r (>CR 6, fols. 275v–276r). CR 3, fols. 129v–130r. CR 4, fol. 121r–v. CR 8, fol. 200r.
CALENDARED: AJ, no. 636.

Robertus, Dei gratia Lingonensis episcopus, omnibus ad quos littere iste pervenerint, in Domino salutem. Notum facimus vobis et testamus quod cum inter dilectam nostram Blancham, illustrem comitissam Campanie, et dominum Joibertum de Calvo Monte discordia esset de caduco domine Chaumonde, quam ipse Joibertus ad se debere venire dicebat et comitissa id ei non cognoscebat, tandem in hunc modo pacem composuerunt: quod tam ipse dominus Joibertus quam heredes sui comitisse et filio ejus Theobaldo et

1 See **42** n. 1.

2 Chaumonde was the widow of Milo, lord of Chaumont, who died on the Fourth Crusade (Longnon, *Les compagnons de Villehardouin*, 76; Dessargues, 'Notes d'histoire généalogique,' 9–11, 13, genealogical table). Since Milo had mortgaged his castle to Count Thibaut III in order to finance his journey, Countess Blanche continued to hold the castle, against the objections of Josbert of Chaumont, Milo's older half-brother, who claimed the castle through collateral inheritance (*de caduco*). Here the countess buys off Josbert's claim with a new fief and 200 *l.* in cash.

3 See also **10**, **55**.

omnibus heredibus Campanie quitaverunt omne illud jus quod habere poterant in hoc caduco, si quod jus in illo habebant. Quitaverunt etiam quicquid clamare poterant in Calvo Monte et in pertinentiis ejus, tam in feodis quam in dominiis, et preterea quitaverunt quicquid habebant apud alteram villam de qua comitissa dicebat quod dominus vir ejus, illustris comes quondam Theobaldus, eam comparaverat et ipse dominus Joibertus hoc negabat. Et propter has quitationes dedit comitissa eidem domino Joiberto ducentas libras pruviniensium et preterea dedit comitissa dicto domino Joiberto et heredibus suis quicquid habebat apud Agivillam, salvo jure hominium comitisse militum, et partem comitisse de furno et de molendino Albe Petre. Voluit etiam Joibertus quod feoda de Nuilliaco et de Marsoil remanerent Renero de Nogento, exceptis centum viginti libris que sunt de vadio apud Nuilliacum. Et quicquid teneat ea que eis donavit inde comitisse et dominorum Campanie, ligius homo erit et debebit custodiam uno mense in anno apud Calvum Montem. Et comitissa pro custodia hac facienda, concessit domino Joiberto et heredibus suis quod domum suam de Calvo Monte possent redimere, domum videlict illam quam Girardus Borgenon habebat in vadio. Et sciendum quod comitissa apud Barrum vel apud Firmitatem vel apud Calvum Montem vel in castellaria eorum nullum hominem poterit retinere qui sit de Alba Petra vel de Agivilla vel de excambio isto. Ex hiis autem omnibus que fecit Joibertus, debet comitisse et heredibus Campanie garantiam firmam portare et hec omnia fide et juramento dato firmavit. Quod ut ratum et firmum premaneat in futurum, presentem cartam sigilli nostri fecimus appensione munimine. Actum anno gratie M CC V, mense decembri.

97

1210

The prior Geoffroy[1] *and community of La Charité-sur-Loire make known that they sold to Countess Blanche for 500* l. *all the men and women in Sézanne and within its castellany who belong to Saint-Julien of Sézanne.*

COPIES: CR 1, fol. 261r (>CR 6, fol. 276v). CR 8, fol. 397r.
CALENDARED: AJ, no. 770.

1 Prior Geoffroy (1209–12), the younger brother of Hervé IV of Donzy, count of Nevers, was excommunicated and deposed for malfeasance and violent conduct in 1212 (*PL*, 126: 662–7, *ep*. 144, 28 June 1212, letter of Innocent III describing the deposition by Cluny's chapter general and ordering the bishops of Troyes and Meaux and the abbot of Lagny to excommunicate Geoffroy).

Ego frater Gaufridus prior et conventus de Caritate notum facimus presentibus et futuris quod nos vendimus et quittamus in perpetuum domine Blanche, illustri comitisse Trecensis, omnes homines et feminas Sancti Juliani de Sezannia quos et quas idem prioratus habebat et habere debebat in castro de Sezannia et in tota potestate ipsius castri, exceptis illis hominibus et feminis quos et quas vendidimus fratribus militie Templi et domino Ogerio de Sancto Cherione. Et ipsa domina comitissa pro ipsa venditione dedit nobis quingentas libras pruviniensis. Hanc autem venditionem et quitationem fecimus eidem domine comitisse de consilio et assensu monachorum nostrorum de Sezannia eo tempore quo ipsam prioratum tenebamus in manu nostra. Et eadem venditionem et quitationem sigillis ipsius confirmamus. Actum anno gratie M CC X.

98

1207 September

Abbot Amalvin and the chapter of La Sauve Majeure associate Countess Blanche in joint lordship over a new village (La Neuville-aux-Larris) that they wish to found in the forest of Belval.[1] *The prior of Belval will appoint the mayor, but the countess retains jurisdiction over murder, rape, and theft, and the men of the village owe her military service. Current tenants of Belval and of fiefs held from the countess may not settle here; any dependent of a knight or religious institution who does so may be expelled after a judicial finding on the oaths of three knights and three other worthy men.*

COPIES: CR 1, fol. 261v (>CR 6, fols. 276v–277v). CR 3, fols. 164r–165v. CR 8, fol. 363r–v.

EDITION: Not in Higounet and Higounet-Nadal, *Grand Cartulaire de la Sauve Majeur.*

CALENDARED: AJ, no. 670.

Ego Amalvinus, Dei permissione Silve Majoris dictus abbas, totusque eisdem ecclesie conventus. Notum facimus presentibus et futuris quod ad nemus nostrum juxta Bellam Vallem situm quod dicitur de Larriz, nobilem mulierem Blancham, comitissam Trecensem palatinam, tali conditione associavimus: quod nos insimul faciemus ibi villam novam in qua nos et ecclesia Belle Vallis

1 The priory retained a virtually identical letter sealed by Countess Blanche and Abbot Amalvin (AD Marne, 27 H 8, no. 1, 1207 [= Martène and Durand, *Thesaurus novus anecdotorum*, 1: 828–31]). See also Higounet, *Défrichements et villeneuves*, 192–3 (with a topographical photograph of the village).

habebit altare et decimam liberam et quietam. Omnes alios redditus et proventus ejusdem ville inter nos equaliter partiemus. Comitissa tamen in manu sua habebit multrum, raptum, et latronem, ita quod de corpore sua erit justicia, sed res deprehensi in aliquo predictorum erunt sue communiter et prioris Belle Vallis. Preterea nec prior Belle Vallis nec comitissa aliquid poterunt adquirere vel capere aliquo modo in jamdicta villa quod non sit inter eos commune, excepto quod si aliquis de villa sub testimonio capellani et duorum hominun ejusdem ville aliquod mobile priori ecclesie Belle Vallis in elemosinam legaverit, prior illud per se habebit. Si vero domus vel alia hereditas priori legaretur, ultra annum et unum diem non teneret nisi de voluntate domini Campanie. Concessum est etiam quod prior Belle Vallis habebit duo arpenta terre in eadem villa nova ab omni exactione et tallia libera et quieta pro suo herbergagio faciendo, et comitissa similter habebit unum arpentum terre pro sua grangia facienda.

Prior autem Belle Vallis in eadem villa majorem ponet et deponet ad suam voluntatem, et major jurabit quod bona fide tam comitis quam prioris Belle Vallis redditus recipiet et servabit. Et si major domino Campanie displicuerit, prior Belle Vallis completo anno illum amovebit et alium substituet. Et si major aliquod servitium fecit pro majoria, dominus Campanie inde habebit medietatem. Si forte contigerit quod villa destruatur vel alio modo deficiat, fundus ecclesie Belle Vallis in integrum remanebit. Dominus Campanie villa extra manum suam mittere non poterit nec aliquo modo a manu sua alienare. Si quis vero comitus Campanie has conventiones non tenuerit, tam villa quam fundus ecclesie Belle Valis remanebit. Homines siquidem ville ibunt in expeditionem et exercitum pro proprio negotio domini Campanie, si ipse presens fuerit vel aliquis de domo sua. Si autem homines ejusdem ville extra metas ipsius ville aliquid acquisierint in territorio priori Belle Vallis, prior per se habebit terragium et consutudinem inde sibi debitam. Similiter si aliquid acquisierint in territorio comitis Campanie, comes per se habebit terragium et consuetudinem inde sibi debitam.

Ceterum in predicta villa nullus hominum comitis Campanie nec alius de feodis suis nec de custodia suo nec etiam aliquis hominum priori Belle Vallis nec aliquis eorum qui manent in ejus potestate recipietur pro remanentia facienda. Et si quis de feodo comitis Campanie vel de custodia sua venit in villam illam qui sit homo de corpore alicujus militis vel aliqui ecclesie aut cujuslibet alterius persone, et dominus hominis illius juramento trium militum et trium aliorum proborum hominum probaverit quod ille sit homo suus de corpore et quod eum pro voluntate sua sicut hominem de corpore talliabat, dominus ille hoc probato hominem suum rehabebit sive vadio duelli dando et sine omni alio impedimento, salvo tamen conductu XV dieorum debito hominibus dicte ville. Quod ut ratum permaneat et firmum, presentem cartam fieri volumus sigilli nostri munimine roboratam. Actum anno incarnati Verbi M CC septimo, mense septembri.

99

1205

Abbot Aubry and the community of Saint-Médard of Soissons announce the resolution of a dispute between their monastery and the knights of Villegruis over lands and taxes there. In Countess Blanche's court it was decided that the knights, who initially denied the obligation, must pay the monks 40 s. *and 1* d. *of gold annually.*

ORIGINAL: AN, J 197, no. 5 (two missing pendant seals).
COPIES: CR 1, fol. 262r (>CR 6, fols. 277v–278r). CR 3, fol. 84v. CR 8, fol. 251r.
CALENDARED: AJ. no. 645. *Layettes*, 1: 300, no. 794.

Ego Aubricus, Sancti Medardi Suessionensis minister, ejusdemque loci conventus, omnibus in perpetuum. Noverint presentes pariter et futuri quod cum inter nos, ex parte una, et Henricum de Crochet[1] et Johannem Pigace[2] et Hugonem de Bosco[3] et alios milites de Vilegruis, ex alia, discordia esset de terris, bosco, plano et cavagiis hominum de Vilegruis, tandem sopita est in hunc modum: dicti milites et eorum heredes in perpetuum ecclesie nostre singulis annis in festo Sancte Remigii apud Sanctum Medardum XL solidos pruviniensem monete et unum denarium auri reddent; de quibus coram domina Blancha, comitissa Trecensis, recognitum fuit quod XX solidi et denarius auri ecclesie nostre debebantur de consuetudine, et alii XX solidi dati fuerint a militibus et concessi pro pace facienda super cavagiis hominum de Vilegruis, que ecclesia nostra requirebat, sed milites ea nobis deberi non cognoscebant. Si vero isti XL solidi et denarius auri die Sancti Remigii apud Sanctum Medardum non redderentur, memorata domina Blancha comitissa ex inde requisita, eos facere reddi teneretur cum emenda, sicut in litteris suis patentibus ex eo nobis indultis continetur. Nos autem in supradictis nichil possumus reclamare preter id quod nobis concessum est pro pace ista. Residuum enim totum quod milites tenent est de feodo domine comitisse, eo excepto quod sex arpennos terre liberos et

1 He is listed as a knight in the feudal roll for Provins, circa 1204 (Longnon, *Documents*, 1: 117, no. 3122). In September 1205 Henry gave the Paraclete his rents at Villegruis as an entry gift for his daughter Isabelle (Lalore, *Cartulaire de l'abbaye du Paraclet*, 142, no. 129, letter of countess Blanche at Pont-sur-Seine).

2 He is listed as a knight in the feudal rolls for Sézanne circa 1190 and circa 1201 (Longnon, *Documents*, 1: 65, no. 1814; 1: 94, no. 2497).

3 He is perhaps the Hugh of Villegruis who is listed as a knight in the feudal roll of Provins ca 1204 (Longnon, *Documents*, 1: 117, no. 3091).

quittos in nemore ville de Villegruis proximo habere debemus pro grangia, si volumus facienda. Illud vero preterundum non est quod supradicti milites coram domina comitissa se ubique ad expensas tamen nostras testificaturos promiserunt quod omnes decime ecclesie nostre esse debent undecumque veniant, tam de veteribus quam de novis essartis, ad territorium sepedicte ville et adjacentium villarum appendentibus. Quod ut futuris temporibus stabile esset et inconcussum, presentem paginam exinde conscriptam sigillorum nostrorum appensione roboravimus. Actum anno Dominice incarnationis M CC quinto.

100

1200 October

Milo, abbot of Châtrices, gives notice that the monks of Moiremont granted Count Thibaut III the use of half of certain forests and a hill outside Sainte-Menehould for the foundation of a new village (La Neuville-au-Pont).[1] *The monks of Moirement and the count will share the lordship and revenues of the place. Since neither the abbot nor the chapter of Moiremont possessed a seal, they asked Abbot Milo of Châtrices to seal this document.*

ORIGINAL: AN, J 197, no. 104 (in poor condition and missing a pendant seal).
COPIES: CR 1, fol. 262r–v.[2] CR 8, fols. 348r–349v.
EDITION: Robert, 'La ville neuve de La Neuville-au-Pont,' 142–3, no. 1.
CALENDARED: AJ, no. 522 (with an erroneous identification of monastery). *Layettes*, 1: 222, no. 600 (with erroneous identifications of abbot and monastery).

Ego Milonis, Dei gratia Castriciensis ecclesie dictus abbas, universis tam presentibus quam futuris, salutem in perpetuum. Noverint universi qui presentem inspexerint paginam quod monachi Maurimontensis medietatem omnium nemorum suorum domino Theobaldo, illustri comiti Campanie, dederunt, ita tamen quod in omnibus nemoribus illis usuarium suum et ad edificandum et ad comburendum ad usus proprios monachi habebunt, et dominus comes similiter suum. Si vero idem monachi medietatem suam vendere voluerint aut dominus comes suam, dominus comes monachos nec monachi dominum comitem poterunt

1 The count's similar letter on the same matter (***115**) includes the land granted by the monks of Châtrices (**43**). In the same month the count granted a community franchise to all residents of the new village he founded on these lands (***114**).
2 The copyist of CR 6 omitted this and the next two texts.

impedire. Si autem nemora illa fuerint extirpata vel ibi ville facte fuerint, monachi totam decimam tam grossam quam minutam habebunt, et medietatem censum et terragii, et dominus comes reliquam. Furnus bannalis monachorum erit. Totum residuum dominus comes habebit. Similiter apud montem ultra Aysniam ante Sanctam Menehildym, quem idem monachi domino comiti dederunt, inter ipsum comitem et monachos sunt eadem pactiones, si forte ibi villa fuerit constituta. Dominus autem comes, nolens a manu sua vel heredum suorum alienari, dictis monachis concessit quod omnia predicta nullo modo poterunt alienari a manu heredis sui qui Vitriacum tenebit. Quia vero sepedicti monachi tunc temporis nec abbatem nec sigillum capituli habebant, ad petitionem ipsorum, cartam presentem sigilli nostri testimonio confirmavimus. Actum anno Domini M CC, mense octobri.

101

1208 (n.s.) January

Etienne, master of the Hospitallers in the diocese of Langres, grants Countess Blanche half of all their rights and revenues in Esnouveaux, except their own house there, the village church, the lands they cultivate themselves, and their tithes, oven, and mill.[1] *The two parties will jointly select the mayor of the village. The countess may not alienate her half of the village.*

ORIGINAL: AN, J 201, no. 2 (missing pendant seal).

COPIES: CR 1, fol. 262v.[2] CR 3, fols. 26v–27r. CR 4, fol. 177v.

EDITION: Delaville le Roulx, *Cartulaire général de l'ordre des Hospitaliers*, 2: 82–3, no. 1286.

CALENDARED: AJ, no. 676. *Layettes*, 1: 313, no. 837.

Stephanus, humilis magister Hospitalis in diocesi Lingonensi, omnibus presentem cartam inspecturis, salutem in Domino. Noverit universitas vestra quod nos carissime domine nostre Blanche, illustri comitisse Campanie, et heredibus suis dominis Campanie dedimus in perpetuum et concessimus medietatem omnium que Hospitale habebat apud Novax et in finagio, in redditibus et exitibus, et in omnibus proficuis, tam in nemoribus quam in terra plana, in aquis et in pratis, in omni justitia et in banno, et in omnibus aliis rebus, exceptis domo nostra quam habemus apud Novax cum omni porprisio et ecclesia ejusdem

1 In 1187 Simon of Clefmont gave the village of Esnouveaux to the Hospitallers (Jolibois, *La Haute-Marne*, 207, and Higounet, *Défrichements et villeneuves*, 133).

2 See **100** n. 2.

ville, et decimis, et furnis et molendinis, et exceptis illis pratis et terris arabilibus que tenueramus et colueramus usque modo. Nullus apud Novax vel in finagio nisi per nos furnum facere poterit vel molendinum. Major in predicta villa assensu nostro et comitis Campanie communiter eligetur, et tam nobis quam ipsis faciet fidelitatem quod jus utriusque servabit integrum et illesum. Et si major nobis vel comiti Campanie fecerit forisfactum, emenda communiter erit nostra. Comes Campanie in predicta villa non poterit aliquam vim facere sine nobis, nec nos sine ipso. Hanc autem villam comes Campanie nullo modo a manu sua poterit alienare; et si forte faceret, omnia supradicta ad Novax et finagium pertinentia ad nos absque diminutione aliqua redirent. Domina siquidem comitissa hoc donum recepit, salvo jure omnium eorum qui aliquod jus habent ibidem. Quod ut ratum sit et firmum in posternum perseveret, presentem cartam fieri voluimus et sigilli nostri munimine roborari. Actum anno ab incarnatione Domini M ducentisimo septimo, mense januario.

102

1209 July

In a chirograph, Simon of Passavant and his brother Guichard make peace with Countess Blanche over their claim to the village of Montigny by quitclaiming all their rights there. Simon did homage to Blanche for Montreuil, just as his father had done homage to Count Henry I, and in return Blanche gave Simon 200 l. *to fortify Montreuil. Odo II of Grancey*[1] *will hold the money until the work has been completed. Simon promised to render the fortress whenever ordered to do so, and Blanche promised to return it in its former state within forty days.*[2] *This chirograph is sealed by Guillaume of Joinville, bishop-elect of Langres,*[3] *by Countess Blanche, and by Simon.*[4]

COPIES: CR 1, fol. 262v–263r.[5] CR 3, fol. 53v–54r. CR 4, fol. 103 r–v. CR 8, fol. 201r–v.

1 For Odo II of Grancey (1191–ca 1229), see Bouchard, *Sword*, 332–4.

2 In 1216 Simon recognized that he had received the 200 *l.* and a 30 *l.* rent for becoming a liegeman (*homo ligius*) of the countess (CR 6, fols. 125v, 207v–208r [= Chantereau-Lefebvre, *Traité des fiefs*, 2: 61], and CR 7.3, fols. 92v–93r).

3 See **65** n. 1.

4 This is the only chirograph in the cartulary. It is unusual in that each of the two parts of the document was sealed by bishop Guillaume of Joinville as well as by the parties to the dispute. The bishop's good offices may have been invoked because the agreement provided for the future payment of 200 *l.*, contingent upon the completion of the fortification at Montreuil.

5 See **100** n. 2.

EDITION: Chantereau-Lefebvre, *Traité des fiefs*, 2: 38–9 (from CR 6).
CALENDARED: AJ, no. 706.

Noverint omnes presentes cyrographi inspectores quod cum inter mulierem nobilem Blancham, comitissam Campanie, ex una parte et Symonem, dominum de Passavant ex altera, super villa que dicitur Montigniacum discordia verteretur, tandem pax et concordia inter eos facta est in hunc modum: videlicet quod predictus Symon et Wischardus, frater ejus, quitaverunt dicte comitisse et heredibus suis dominis Campanie in perpetuum quicquid juris habebant in prefacta villa. De Musteriolo vero et de omni finagio Musteriolii fecit idem Simon hominium comitisse eo modo quo Wischardus, pater ejus, fecit comiti Henrici patri. Comitissa autem dedit ei ducentas libras pro Musteriolo firmando, quos Odo de Granciaco debet tenere in manu sua donec Simon illas expendat ad firmitatem Musteriolii faciendam. Juravit siquidem dictus Simon quod Musteriolium bona fide pro posse suo firmabit et quod illud reddet comitisse et successoribus suis vel eorum mandato ad magnam vim et ad parvam quandocumque opus fuerit. Comitisse vero jurare fecit super animam suam quod ipsa et sucessores sui domini Campanie, infra quadraginta dies postquam ab exonio suo fuerint expediti, reddent Simoni vel heredibus suis Musteriolium in eo statu in quo eos illud constiterit accepisse. Si quis vero contradixerit, ne Musteriolium firmetur et per vim operarios amoverit; si Simon ad vim illam repellendam indiguerit auxilio comitisse, requiret auxilium illius. Et si comitissa non fuerit aaisita de eo juvando eumque non juvaverit infra XL dies postquam ad ipso fuerit requisita, ex tunc Simon habebit predictus ducentas libras sine aliqua contradictione. Ut autem hac omnia nota permaneant et rata teneantur, ego Willelmus Dei gratia Lingonensis electus, ego Blancha comitissa Trecensis palatina, et ego Simon de Passavant utramque partem presentis cyrographi sigillorum nostrorum munimine voluimus roborari. Actum anno gratie M CC IX, mense julio.

103

1210 (n.s.) January

The abbess of Fontevraud[1] *makes known that Countess Blanche lent 500* l. *to the priory of Foissy for the payment of its debts and therefore will enjoy that priory's revenues at Bar-sur-Aube until the debt has been repaid.*

1 The abbess was Alix of Blois (1209–18), daughter of Thibaut V, count of Blois (1152–90), and Alix of France (*Histoire de l'Ordre de Fontevrault*, 2: 89–99).

COPIES: CR 1, fol. 263r (>CR 6, fols. 278r–v). CR 3, fols. 163v–164r. CR 4, fol. 193r. CR 8, fol. 390r.
CALENDARED: AJ, no. 724.[2]

Ego ..[a] humilis abbatissa and conventus Fontis Ebris. Notum facimus universis ad quos littere iste pervenerint et testamur quod cum karissima domina Blancha, illustris Campanie comitissa, ad sublevandas sarcinas debitorum domus de Fossiaco quingentas libras pruvinensis monete ipsius domus nostris sororibus mutuasset, dicte sorores de mandato et conscientia nostra, manu domine comitisse obligate, miserunt omnia que apud Barrum super Albam habebant, tam in domibus quam in vineis et rebus aliis quibuscumque, que videlicet ipsa comitissa vel ejus mandatum percipiet usque dum ei sit de mutuo prefate pecunie satisfactum. Dicte vero sorores de Fossiaco in propriis sumptibus et expensis vineas excolent et aliis rebus necessaria ministrabunt, et comitissa percipiet fructus et omnes redditus et proventus, ita tamen quod cum ei fuerit de quingentis libris plenarie satisfactum, scilicet de proventibus, ad sorores prefatas omnia que comitisse obligata sunt libere tenerentur. Quod ut ratum habeatur et firmum, presentem paginam sigilli nostri munimine fecimus roborari. Actum anno incarnati Verbi M ducentesimo nono, mense januario.

[a] *The scribe made two dots to indicate the absence of a name for the abbess of Fontevraud.*

104

[1209–1210][1]

Stephen Langton, archbishop of Canterbury,[2] and Jean, archbishop of Tours, seal a verbatim copy of Count Henry I's letter of 1152 (n.s.) regarding his custody over Chablis.[3] The provost of Chablis and master Absolon of Saint-Martin of Tours vehemently protested when the count gave the revenues from

2 AJ cites AN, J 196, no. 64 as the original document.

1 Major, *Acta Stephani Langton*, 153, observes that this *vidimus* was probably drawn up by the episcopal chancery of Tours sometime before 1223. But its inclusion in the cartulary of 1211 requires an earlier date. Since the duke of Burgundy's letter on the same subject is dated 1209 (**23**), this letter most likely belongs to the fall of 1209 (ibid., 164, Itinerary of Langton), probably in October before Langton traveled from France to Dover or after his return to France. He must have passed through Tours, where the monks of Saint-Martin of Tours presented him count Henry's act for confirmation.

2 See Powicke, *Stephen Langton*.

3 Henry's original letter (AD Yonne, G 2311) was retained at Chablis.

his custodial right there to Anseric II of Montréal.[4] *But in his letter, the count maintained that he had granted only the revenues, not the right of custody itself, which he said he would never alienate.*[5]

COPIES: CR 1, fol. 263r (>CR 6, fols. 278v–279r). CR 3, fols. 81v–82r. CR 4, fol. 135r–v. CR 8, fol. 83v.

EDITIONS: Chantereau-Lefebvre, *Traité des fiefs*, 2: 3–4 (from CR 6). Brussel, *Nouvel examen*, 771 note a (from CR 8, fol. 83v). *RHF*, 16: 101 note (from Brussel). Quantin, *Cartulaire général*, 1: 481–2, no. 329 (from Chantereau-Lefebvre). *Layettes*, 1: 68, no. 118 (from AN, J 254, no. 44, part 4, copy made 13 June 1299 *ex Registris chartarum Campaniae* [= CR 8] and sealed by the chapter of Saint-Etienne of Troyes).

CALENDARED: AJ, no. 1. Major, *Acta Stephani Langton*, 153, no. 139.

Stephanus, Dei gratia Cantuariensis archiepiscopus totius Anglie primas, Sancte Romane ecclesie cardinalis, et Joannes eadem gratia archiepiscopus Turonensis, omnibus Christi fidelibus, salutem in vero salutari. Noverit universitas vestra nos vidisse litteras sigillatas sigillo Henrici bone memorie, quondam comitis Trecensis palatini, in quibus hec continebantur:

Quoniam preteritarum rerum memoria facile labitur et transit, ego Henricus, Trecensis comes palatinus, ad presentium et futurorum noticiam volo pervenire quod cum redditus meos quos in villa Chableie pro custodia ab ecclesia Beati Martini Turonensis habeo, Anserico de Monte Regali, nobili viro, contulissem, Mauricius, tunc prepositus Chableie, et magister Absalon[a] et Robertus de Vernevelis, ex parte capituli Beati Martini Turonensis, meam presentiam adierunt. Audierant enim quod quicquid habebam apud Chableiam predicto contuleram Anserico, et ut factum meam revocarem, vehementer institerunt. Ego autem respondi eis quod custodiam predicte ville et procurationem semel in anno michi persolvendam, et hominum fidelitatem[6] Anserico de Monte Regali non contuli nec alicui conferam, cum eandem custodiam extra manum meam ponere non possim nec debeam. Et ut hoc ratum permaneat et firmum, per presentem paginam sigilli mei impressione munitam, omnium memorie commendare curavi. Hujus rei testes sunt: Theobaldus, comes Blesensis; Guillermus,[b] comes Nivernensis; Odo, constabularius; Guillermus[b] de Dono[c] Petro; Anselmus de Traginello[d]; ex parte ecclesie: Guillermus,[b] Senonensis archidiaconus; Landricus de Traci; Mauricius, prepositus Chableie; Absalon,[a] Sancti Martini canonicus; Robertus de Vernevelis, canonicus Sancti Martini;

4 See **23** n. 2.

5 See **23**, **71**.

6 See the oath of fidelity taken by the men of Chablis (**23** n. 3).

Johannes, major de Chableia; Raembaudus, Milo, servientes Sancti Martini de Chableia. Actum est hoc anno dominice Incarnationis M C LI,[7] Eugenio papa, Laudovico rege Francorum.[e]

Nos vero, ad petitionem capituli Beati Martini, presens rescriptum nostris sigillis fecimus sigillari.

[a] Asalon *in the original* (*see note 3*). [b] Willermus *in the original.* [c] Domno *in the original.* [d] Aserinus de Triagnello *in the original.* [e] Ludovico Francorum rege *in the original.*

105

1204 December

Abbot Louis and the community of Saint-Vanne of Verdun associate Countess Blanche in the lordship over their village of Chaudefontaine, excepting only their banal ovens and mills, tithes, crop rents, and carting service. This document appears to have been a preliminary text of the agreement of July 1206 establishing a shared lordship over the village.[1]

COPY: CR 1, fol. 263v [crossed out].[2]

In nomine sancte et individue Trinitatis, amen. Ego Ludovicus abbas totusque conventus Sancti Vitoni Verdunensis. Notum facimus presentibus et futuris nos de communi consilio et voluntate totius capituli nostri associavisse venerabilem in Christo dominam et amicam nostram Blancham, illustrem Campanie comitissam, et heredes ejus ad medietatem totius justicie et totius banni ville et hominum nostrorum de Calida Fontana qui ad presens ibi manent vel mansi advenerint in futurum, unumcumque homines veniant et qualescumque sint, ita quo comitissa et ejus heredes nobiscum partientur per medium omnes exitus justicie et banni quomodocumque proveniant, excepto quod cavagia nostra, decime, terragia, furni, molendina et alia jura que in villa antea habebamus, nobis sine parte remanent quitta.

Ad hoc autem addicimus quod prepositus noster monachus de Calida Fontana et prepositus Sancte Menoldis per communem consensum in eadem villa majorem constituent et scabinos, ita quod si in hoc non possunt convenire, per

7 The date would be 1152 n.s., after 10 January (death of Count Thibaut II) and before 30 March 1152 (Easter).

1 **54**.

2 This document may have been discarded by the chancery after 1211 (it was superseded by **54**), as it was not copied into any later cartulary; even the copyist of CR 6 skipped over it.

assensum IIII^{orum} legitimorum hominum de Calida Fontana in hoc se concordarent. Concedimus preterea ipsi comitisse et heredibus suis quod singuli hominum de Calida Fontana et de locis ad eam pertinentibus annuatim et in perpetuum reddent comitisse et suis heredibus duos solidos et unum sextarium avene de commandisa. Illi homines reddent commandisam qui terras colunt ex animali trahente. Qui vero terras non colunt ex animali trahente, duos solidos tamen reddent et avenam non. Et propter hoc ipsi homines quitti erunt ab omni alia exactione. Et si homines de Calida Fontana aut de locis ad ea pertinentibus volentes effugere dominum Calida Fontana mansuri venirent ad castrum Sancte Menoldis, illuc non reciperentur. Item quotiens necesse fuerit operari ab castri Sancte Menoldis, homines illuc ibunt operari semel in anno tribus diebus in septimana, et hoc facient sine occasione et rachato. Item cavalchiam et exercitum Sancte Menoldis ibunt dum tam eos ire non conveniat ultra Marnam. Ipsa vero comitissa et heredes ejus propter hanc associationem et commandisiam quam illis concedimus, omnia jura nostra ubicumque sint in posse suo nobis fideliter custodire tenentur tamquam sua. Propter videlicet commandisiam et associationem, nullo modo possunt de manu sua alienare aut in feodum dare aut quomodolibet commutare; quod si fierent, et associationem perderent et commandisam. Ut autem hac omnia firma et inconcussa permaneant in futurum, tam sigillo abbatis quam nostri capituli fecimus roborari. Actum anno Domini M CC IIII, mense decembri.

106

1202

The dean Nicholas and chapter of Bray-sur-Seine make known that they have resolved their dispute with Countess Blanche over the appointment of the treasurer and chanter.[1]

ORIGINAL: AN, J 203, no. 3 (missing pendant seal).
COPIES: CR 1, fol. 263v (> CR 6, fol. 279r). CR 8, fol. 437v.
CALENDARED: AJ, no. 572.[2] *Layettes*, 1: 239–40, no. 661.[3]

Ego Nicholas, Braiacensis ecclesie decanus, et universum ejusdem ecclesie capitulum. Notum facimus tam presentibus quam futuris quod cum querela inter nos et venerabilem comitissam palatinam, videlicet Blancham, de

1 See also **77**, **109**.
2 AJ cites **77** and **106** as identical documents.
3 The editors of the *Layettes* identify this letter as identical to **77**.

donacione[a] personatuum ecclesie nostre, scilicet thesaurarie et cantorie, verteretur, sic tandem pacificata est, quod nos honori et amori ejus deferentes volumus et pacienter[b] sustinemus, ut ipsa et heredes sui donationem prefatorum personatuum habeant. Quod ut ratum sit et firmum, sigilli nostri munimine roboramus. Actum anno ab incarnacione[c] Domini M CC secundo.

[a] donatione *in CR 1.* [b] patienter *in CR 1.* [c] incarnatione *in CR 1.*

107

[ca 1194][1]

Simon, bishop of Meaux, makes known that Count Henry II gave him life use of the justice over Etrépilly.[2]

ORIGINAL: AN, J 203, no. 98 (missing pendant seal).
COPIES: CR 1, fols. 263v–264r (> CR 6, fol. 279v). CR 3, fol. 114r. CR 4, fol. 193r.
CALENDARED: *Layettes*, 1: 179–80, no. 422.

Ego Simon, Dei gratia Meldensis ecclesie minister humilis, presentibus et futuris notum fieri volo quod dominus noster comes Henricus partem quam habebat in[a] viaria de Strepilliaco mihi concessit, sic tamen quod, cum Deo volente, decessero vel quacumque ex causa episcopatum resignavero, in manum ejus et heredum suorum revertetur.

[a] in *omitted CR 1.*

108

[1198–1201]

Guillaume (of Champagne), archbishop of Reims and cardinal,[1] *reaffirms to Count Thibaut III that the nuns of Avenay may not elect an abbess without the count's license. Nevertheless, he has confirmed the election of Guillemette,*[2]

1 The editors of the *Layettes* follow the *Gallia Christiana* in placing this letter at the extreme end of the bishop's episcopacy and in identifying the count as Henry II, rather than Henry I.
2 On the meaning of *viaria* as rights of justice, see Bur, *La formation du comté de Champagne*, 334–6.
1 See **68** n. 1.
2 Guillemette of Joinville, abbess of Avenay (1197–1202); see Paris, *Histoire de l'abbaye d'Avenay*, 1: 82–90.

paternal aunt of the seneschal Geoffroy V of Joinville,[3] *as abbess because he has assumed fiduciary responsibility for the indebted convent.*[4] *He asks the count's forgiveness.*

COPIES: CR 1, fol. 264r (>CR 6, fol. 279v).
EDITIONS: *Gallia Christiana*, 10: *instr.*, 51, no. 54. Paris, *Avenay*, 86–7, n. 1.
CALENDARED: AJ, no. 451. Delaborde, *Jean de Joinville*, no. 125

Willelmus, Dei gratia Remensis archiepiscopus, sancte Romane ecclesie titulus sancte Sabina cardinalis, karissimo nepoti suo, Theobaldi comiti Trecensi palatino, salutem et sincere dilectionis affectum. Scimus et testamur quod ecclesia de Avenaio, quando abbatissam non habet, a comite Trecensis requirere debet licentiam eligendi; nec eligere debet aut potest donec a comite Trecensis licentiam requisierit, nec ab archiepiscopo vel ecclesie Remensis licentiam eligendi requirere tenetur. Quod autem de matertera fidelis nostri Gaufridi de Jonisvilla fecimus, propter necessitatem de Jothro et de Avenaio ecclesiarum fecimus, et de dilectione vestra fiduciam assumpsimus faciendi. Rogamus igitur vos et cum affectu requirimus ut propter honorem nostrum et amorem ecclesie et abbatisse de Avenaio, nostrum remittatis offensam.

109

1203 (n.s.) March, Paris

The bishops of Beauvais (Philippe of Dreux)[1] *and Meaux (Anselm) and the abbot of Sainte-Geneviève of Paris (Jean of Tocy) confirm the resolution of a dispute between Countess Blanche and the chapter of Bray over the selection of the chapter's treasurer and chanter. They seal a verbatim copy of the letter of Nicholas, dean of Bray, describing the settlement.*[2]

ORIGINAL: AN, J 203, no. 5 (three missing pendant seals).
COPIES: CR 1, fol. 264r (>CR 6, fols. 279v–280r). CR 3, fol. 54r–v.
CALENDARED: AJ, no. 577. *Layettes*, 1: 240, no. 665.

---

3 See **8** n. 1.

4 In 1201 the archbishop reduced the number of nuns there to forty (Paris, *Histoire de l'abbaye d'Avenay*, 2: 94, no. 34).

1 For the episcopacy of Philippe of Dreux (1175–1217), see Guyotjeannin, *Episcopus et comes*, 133–6.

2 See also **106**.

Philippus Dei gratia Belvacensis et Anselmus Meldensis episcopi et Johannis Sancte Genovese Parisiensis abbas, omnibus ad quos littere presentes pervenerint, in Domino salutem. Noveritis quod cum dudum suscepissemus causam terminandam auctoritate Romane sedis que inter nobilem mulierem Blancham, illustrem comitissam Trecensem, ex una parte, et canonicos Braii ex altera, versabatur, tandem in hanc formam pacis convenerunt, sicut per litteras eorum patentes huic rescripto insertas inspeximus:

[text of **77**]

Quam quidem compositionem ratam habemus et gratam, et sigillis nostris munitam approbamus. Actum Parisius, anno Domini M CC secundo, mense marcio.

110

1208 October, Nogent-sur-Seine

Geoffroy, bishop-elect of Meaux, makes a contract with Countess Blanche over the minting of coins of Troyes, Provins, and Meaux: the countess will collect two-thirds and the bishop one-third of the fees paid by the minters.[1]

COPIES: CR 1, fol. 264r (>CR 6, fol. 280r). CR 3, fols. 28v–29r. CR 4, fol. 126r. CR 8, fols. 184r–185v.

EDITIONS: Brussel, *Nouvel examen*, 195 note a (from CR 3, fol. 28). *Gallia Christiana*, 8: *instr.*, 558, no. 10.

CALENDARED: AJ, no. 695.

Ego Galfridus, Dei permissione Meldensis electus. Noverint universi presentes litteras inspecturis quod nos cum domina Blancha, comitissa Trecensis, super moneta Trecis, Pruvini, et Meldis, cum locus fuerit fabricanda, societatem inivimus ab instanti festo Beati Martini usque ad tres annos completos, tali modo scilicet, quod ubicumque fuerit fabricatum, sive Trecis sive Pruvini sive Meldis, dicta comitissa de omni monetagio et de servicio quod fiet pro moneta et de omnibus proventibus qui inde provenient quocumque modo proveniant, duas partes habebit et nos tertiam habebimus. In cujus rei testimonium presentes litteras fecimus sigilli nostri appensione munitas. Actum Nogenti, anno incarnati Verbi, M CC VIII, mense octobri.

1 Bisson, *Conservation of Coinage*, 126–35, analyzes this and other documents relating to coinage in Champagne.

111

1203 November

The dean Jean and chapter of Saint-Pierre of Troyes make known that Countess Blanche has given them her dependent woman, Margaret, who is married to the chapter's man, Robert of Poilly. In the future the chapter will give the countess a woman of equal value who marries one of her men.

COPIES: CR 1, fol. 264r–v (>CR 6, fol. 280r). CR 3, fol. 86r–v. CR 4, fol. 166v. CR 8, fol. 420r.
CALENDARED: AJ, no. 594.

Ego Johannes decanus Beati Petri Trecensis totumque capitulum ejusdem ecclesie notum facimus, tam presentibus quam futuris, quod nos venerabili domine Blanche, illustri comitisse Trecensis, concessimus ut pro Margarita, femina sua, uxore Roberti de Poilli, hominis nostri, quam ipsa nobis dedit, reddatur eidem comitisse rationabile excambium ad valentiam dicte Margarite quandocumque aliquem de hominibus comitisse alicui feminarum nostrarum contigerit per matrimonium copulari. Actum anno Domini M ducentesimo tercio, mense novembri.

*112

1212 (n.s.) February

Abbot Henri and the chapter of Saint-Denis make known that they have exchanged the blacksmith André for Countess Blanche's man, Hermand of Saint-Pierre.

COPIES: CR 1, fol. 264v (>CR 6, fol. 280v). CR 3, fol. 23r. CR 8, fol. 237v.
CALENDARED: AJ, no. 787.

Henricus, Dei gratia Beati Dionisii abbas, et capitulum omnibus presentes litteras inspecturis, salutem.[a] Universitati vestre notum facimus quod nos de communi excambivimus cum nobili Blancha, comitissa Campanie, Andream fabrum, hominem Beati Dionisii, pro Hermando de Sancti Petro, homine ejusdem domine comitisse Campanie. Et eundem Andream ipsi domine comitisse et suis heredibus omnino quitamus et in perpetum habendum concedimus. Quod[b] ut ratum sit et in posternum obtineat firmitatem, paginam hanc sigillis nostris munivimus.[b] Actum anno Domini[c] M CC XI, mense februario.

[a] omnibus *through* salutem *omitted in CR 1.* [b] Quod *through* munivimus *omitted CR 1.* [c] Domini *omitted in CR 1.*

*113

1212 (n.s.) February

Abbot Henri and the chapter of Saint-Denis announce the settlement reached by Geoffroy, bishop of Meaux, regarding their dispute with Countess Blanche over her actions at Nogent-sur-Seine. She had created a protected forest there, complained the abbot, built a mill to the prejudice of the abbey, prohibited the monks from collecting wood while licensing someone else to clear the forest, and did not allow the abbot to fish there. The countess, for her part, complained that the oven at Nogent was inadequate for the town and wanted the monks to enlarge it or build another one.[1] *The bishop found for the monks on all counts and decided that one oven was sufficient for Nogent.*

COPIES: CR 1, fols. 264v–265r (>CR 6, fols. 280v–281v). CR 8, fols. 236r–237v.
CALENDARED: AJ, no. 789.

Henricus Dei gratia Beati Dionisii abbas et capitulum, universis presentibus[a] et futuris, salutem. Notum facimus quod nos ex una parte et nobilis Blancha, comitissa Campanie ex altera, compromisimus in venerabilem Gaufridum, Meldensis episcopum, sub pena centum librarum pruvinensis, de querelis que inter nos et ipsam comitissam vertebantur, motis super rebus quas ipsa comitissa tempore suo cepit facere et super rebus quas nos tempore eisdem comitisse facere ceperamus, concedentes ex utraque parte quod dictum ejusdem episcopi sive per pacem sive per judicium observaremus.

Querele autem tales erant: Nos conquerebamur quod comitissa volebat facere forestam in aqua de Nogento, et quod construxerat molendina in aqua et fundo Beati Dionisii et inde dampna nobis evenerant; et quod non permittebat nos capere de nemore Nogenti ad omnia nostra necessaria sicut facere solebamus; et quod in illo nemore contulerat aliquibus licentiam extirpandi, et nobis abstulerat potestatem conferendi licentiam extirpandi. Conquerebamur etiam quod comitissa redegerat ad pratum pascua que solebant hominibus esse

1 The castellany Nogent-sur-Seine had been a fief held by its lords from the abbot of Saint-Denis. Elizabeth of Nogent became heiress in 1147, but after her three sons died without heirs in the 1180s, she retired to the Paraclete and later (ca 1198) sold Nogent to Count Thibaut III. Thibaut made Nogent part of Countess Blanche's dower (1199), and thus the changes she instituted there – especially the creation of a protected forest – infringed on the customary rights of Saint-Denis. The 'forest' of Nogent became a comital preserve where future counts allowed some clearing for arable but prohibited the construction of buildings, as Count Thibaut IV later explained in his grant to the Hospitallers (Delaville le Roulx, *Cartulaire général de l'ordre des Hospitaliers*, 2: 588–9, no. 1969, October 1230).

communia, unde ipsi homines nobis corveias persolvebant; et quod non permittebat abbatem Beati Dionisii piscari in stagno quod est apud Nogenti quando abbas ad partes illas accedebat; et quod stagnum ampliaverat per quam ampliationem nos amittebamus censum nostrum. Conquerebamur quoque nos amittere censum de veteri mercato in quo censum habebamus antequam mercatum ibi esset. Comitissa autem conquerebatur de furno Nogenti quod erat insufficiens ville et petebat pro hominibus quod nos faceremus illum sufficientem aut cum illo alium faceremus.

Super hiis vero prefatus episcopus dictum suum protulit et dixit: quod dominus Nogenti non potest facere forestam in aqua de Nogento; de nemore dixit quod nos habemus usuarium per totum nemus in quo habere solebamus, videlicet in nemore quod vocatur nemus Sancti Dionisii, et in foresta et extra forestam, tam in vivo quam in mortuo ad ardendum et edificandum et omnia necessaria ad domum nostram que est apud Nogenti que dicitur domus de Alna. In nemoribus autem que sunt propria comitissa, videlicet Illarem et Draese et Fraete, nos nichil habebimus, et comitissa et dominus Nogenti post comitissa habebunt in perpetuum potestatem dandi licentiam extirpandi, salvo censu quem solvemus habere quando nemus reducitur ad terram, scilicet quatuor denarius de arpento extirpando. De pascuis dixit quod comitissa vel dominus Nogenti non possit illa ad pratum redigere, et si aliqua redacta sunt tempore comitisse fient inde pascua et erunt hominibus communia et nos habebimus corveias sicut solemus. De stagno dixit scilicet de piscatione stagni quod abbas Beati Dionisii ibi potest facere piscari quando venit apud Nogentum. Ad domum suam de Alna ad opus suum et eorum quos tunc habebit secum et comitissa vel dominus Nogenti non possunt admensurare piscationem abbatis. De ampliatione stagni dixit quod non debebat ampliari in censiva Beati Dionisii sine nostro consensu. De veteri mercato ubi due domus, scilicet Galterii et Thome, facte sunt tempore comitisse, dixit quod nos non debemus habere censum inde. De furno dixit quod fiat unus furnus sufficiens ad totam villam et in loco competendi. De Ficha aque dixit quod debet requiri licentia a domino Nogenti et monachi Sancti Dionisii qui tenebit domum de Alna prius ab illo qui prius invenietur sine domino Nogenti sive monacho Sancti Dionisii, et postea ab alio. De molendinis que comitissa fecit Nogenti, dixit quod remaneant quita comitisse et domino Nogenti et propter dampnum quod inde patiebamur in nostris molendinis de Nueilli et stagno et in Lenatis de tribus gorgis avulsis per comitissam et pro dampno si quod habebamus pro ampliatione stagni que nunc facta est. Dixit comitissam et post comitissa dominus Nogenti debent reddere nobis singulis annis tres modios molturengie in perpetuum in festo Sancti Martini hiemalis ad mensuram de Nogento, et nos nichil habebimus deinceps in illis duobus molendinis, scilicet de stagno et de Nuelli; sed quod in illis habebamus, comitissa et dominus Nogenti habebunt in perpetuum. Hoc autem[b] dictum concedimus nos in perpetuum inviolabiliter observaturos. Quod[c] ut ratum permaneat et inconcussum, presentes litteras notari fecimus et sigillorum nostrorum munimine roborari.[c] Actum anno gratie M CC XI, mense februario.

[a] presentibus *through* salutem *omitted in CR 1.* [b] autem *omitted in CR 1.*
[c] Quod *though* roborari *omitted in CR 1.*

*114

1200 October, Troyes

Count Thibaut III announces that he has granted a charter of liberties to a new village (La Neuville-au-Pont) that he has founded on the hill beyond the Aisne river in front of Sainte-Menehould.[1] *Those who plow with their own animals will pay 2* s. *and 1* sextarium *of oats annually, and those who work with their hands will pay 2* s. *Each person will do castle work one week annually, and the count may claim military service up to the Marne river. Four sworn men will administer the village for the count, but he reserves jurisdiction over theft, rape, manslaughter, and murder. Residents may sell or lease their houses and may leave the village under the count's fifteen-day safe-conduct.*

COPIES: CR 1, fol. 265r (>CR 6, fol. 44r).
CALENDARED: AJ, no. 523.

Ego Theobaldus, comes Trecensis palatinus, notum facio tam presentibus quam futuris quod omnibus[a] apud montem ultra Ahismam manentibus et mansuris hanc concessi in posterum libertatem que in presenti carta plenissime contenetur. Quicumque excolet terram proprio animali, duos solidos et unum sextarium avene annuatim michi solvet in festo Sancti Remigii. Qui vero propriis manibus tantum duos solidos. Pro simplici emendi XII denarios; pro sanguine quindecim solidos; furtum, raptum, homicidium et multrum in manu mea reservo. Pro

1 The land for this new village was provided by the neighboring monasteries of Châtrices (**43**) and Moiremont (**100**, ***115**). Countess Blanche continued oversight of the new village (see ***118**), but none of her letters is included in the extant folios of this cartulary; see the analysis with edited texts in Robert, 'Le ville neuve de La Neuville-au-Pont,' and Higounet, *Défrichements et villeneuves*, 166–8. Comital interest in this region began with Count Thibaut III's acquisition of the castellany of Sainte-Menehould in September 1200 from Hugh, count of Rethel, whose letter (AN J 193, no. 2; tr. in Evergates, *Documents*, 3, no. 2A) might well have been included in the missing folios of the cartulary.

duello firmato uterque duodecim, et si sanguis fuerit fusus duodecim solidos. Si duellum victum fuerit, victus solvet novem libras. Unusquisque operabitur una septimana in anno sine redemptione ad firmitatem castelli. Exercitum et calvagiam meam michi facient, si ego vel aliquis de domo mea presens fuerit, ita tamen quod Maternam non transient. Quatuor jurati in villa erunt qui mea jura et ville conservabunt. Si miscla in villa forte facta fuerit, qui inde accusabitur, se tercio se purgabit; et si unus juratorum misclam inderit, reus non poterit se pignare. Quicumque domum ibi fecerit, eam vendere poterit sine destructione. Si vero eam locare voluerit, eam locare poterit. Si eam manutenuerit, licet alibi maneat. Quicumque ibidem mansurus advenerit et illinc recedere voluerit, conductum habebit per XV dies. Ut autem hec libertas et consutudines in[b] posterum firmiter observentur, in confirmationem consuetudines predictorum, presentem cartam fieri volui et sigilli mei munimine roborari.[b] Actum Trecis, anno gratie M CC, mense octobris. Datum per manum Galterii, cancellarii. Nota Alermi.

[a] hominibus *in lieu of* omnibus apud montem *in CR 6.* [b] in *through* roborari *omitted in CR 6.*

*115

1200 October, Marigny

Count Thibaut III states that the monks of Moiremont have given him half of their woods, as well as the hill beyond the Aisne river in front of Sainte-Menehould, for the founding of a new village (La Neuville-au-Pont).[1]

COPIES: CR 1, fol. 265v (>CR 6, fol. 44v).
CALENDARED: AJ, no. 520.[2]

Ego Theobaldus, Trecensis comes palatinus, notum facio omnibus tam presentibus quam futuris quod monachi de Morimont medietatem omnium nemorum suorum michi dederunt, ita tamen quod in omnibus nemoribus illis usuarium suum et ad edificandum et ad comburendum ad usos proprios habebunt, et ego similter meum. Si vero medietatem suam vendere voluerint aut ego meam, nec ipsi michi possent contradicere, nec ego eos in parte sua vendenda possem aliquatenus impedire. Si autem nemora illa fuerint extirpata vel ibi ville facte fuerint, ipsi totam decimam, tam grossam quam minutam, habebunt, et

1 This letter is the counterpart of the monks' letter (**100**). The count also obtained land here from Châtrices (**43**). See also **114**, ***118**.
2 AJ erroneously cites AN, J 197, no. 104 (the text of **100**).

medietatem censuum et terragii, et ego reliquam. Furnus bannalis monachorum erit. Totum residuum meum erit.

Similter apud montem ultra Aisniam ante Sanctam Menoldun, quem idem monachi michi dederunt, inter me et ipsos eadem sunt pactiones, si forte villa fuerit ibi constituta. Ego autem predicta, nolens a manu mea vel successores meorum alienari, dictis monachis concessi quod omnia predicta nullo modo poterunt alienari a manu heredis mei qui Vitriacum tenebit. Ut autem hec rata permaneat et in posterum teneatur, presentem cartam in testimonium fieri volui et sigilli mei munimine roborari.[a] Actum anno Domini M CC apud Marigniacum, mense octobri.

[a] Ut autem et cetera *in CR 6.*

*116

1212 October 1, Sainte-Menehould

Countess Blanche makes known that Ade of Avesne, widowed countess of Grandpré,[1] *brought a case against her stepson, Henry IV, count of Grandpré (1212–31), over the division of the community property she had with her husband, Count Henry III, and over her daughter's dowry. Her stepson then accused Ade of improperly increasing her dower. Blanche ordered that no changes were to be made until both parties appeared at her court in November.*[2]

COPIES: CR 1, fol. 265v (>CR 6, fols. 44v–45r).
EDITION: Lemaire, 'Les origines de la communauté de biens entre époux,' 608 note 1 (from CR 1 and CR 6).
CALENDARED: AJ, no. 798.

Ego Blancha, comitissa Trecensis palatina, notum facio universis presentes litteras inspecturis quod cum Ade, quondam comitissa Grandis Prati, se

1 Ade, daughter of Jacques of Avesnes, became the second wife of Henri III, count of Grandpré (1190–1211), who dowered her with the castle and castellany of Hans, which seems to have been at issue here. Ade retained her dower after remarrying, to Raoul, count of Soissons (1180–1235). In 1238 Ade allowed her eldest son, Jacques of Grandpré, to dower his wife with one half of the castle and castellany of Hans and to retain the entire residence there; Ade retained for herself only the 'new house' in the tower (Bur, *Vestiges d'habitat seigneurial fortifié du Bas-Pays Angonnais*, 59). She died after 1249 (Newman, *Nesle*, 1: 67, no. 28).

2 There is no evidence of any other hearing. Lemaire suggests ('Les origines,' 609) that Ade subsequently appealed to the king, and that this case might have prompted the (lost) royal ennactment of 1214 establishing the half-dower as the general custom of the realm (as reported by Beaumanoir in *Les coutumes de Beauvaisis*, 1: 212, par. 445).

clamavisset ad me de comite Grandis Prati, privigno suo, qui ei injuriosus existebat de conquerementis que pater ipsius fecerat cum predicta comitissa et de divisione quam fecerat in maritagio filie sue, et clamor iste factus fuisset infra annum post decessum comitis Grandis Prati, tandem cum inde litigatum fuisset coram me apud Sanctam Menoldim in festo sancti Remigii, tam comes quam comitissa diem pacis ceperunt videlicet in crastinum Omnium Sanctorum apud Viane. Et res remansit in eo ponto et statu in quo erat tempore illo quo pedicta comitissa se clamavit. Post ea comes dixit quod comitissa ei injuriam faciebat super eo quod quedam adiciebat in dotalicio suo que non erant de dotalicio suo. Et de hoc non se clamavit comes, sed monstrando hoc dixit. Et querela ista comitis remansit similiter in eo ponto et statu in quo erat in festo sancti Remigii. Actum apud Sanctam Menoldim, anno gratie M CC XII, in festo sancti Remigii.

*117

[ca 1211][1]

A notice lists the debts of Hermesend of Bar-sur-Seine, lady of Traînel.[2]

COPY: CR 1, fol. 265v.[3]

Hermansandis, domina Trianguli, debet per Bedino de Trecis VII^{c} libras. Per Manasses de Braio et fratre suo VIII^{xx} XIII libras. Per Cresselino de Pruvino[4] VIII^{xx} V libras. Per uxore Gargedele VIII^{xx} libras. Per Cressaito de Villemauri LX libras. Per Lemoine de Sezanna XLV libras. Per Moise de Nogent XL libras.

Summa: XIII^{c} XX III libras.[5]

Item, debet per Auberto de Veteri Castello C libras. Per Angelino de Sancto Justo CC libras. Per Sason de Dompetra CCC X libras XIII solidos.

Summa totius: XIX^{c} XXX IIII libras XIII solidas.[6]

Inde recepta sint XXIX^{xx} IX libras. Remanent XIII^{c} XLV libras XIII solidos. In manu fratris Haimon super pedagium ..., super portam Pruvinum, super Meilliacum et Bordenaium.

1 Hermesend died in 1211 (*Obituaires*, 4: 392).

2 See ***91** n. 1.

3 The copyist of CR 6 skipped over this outdated item.

4 A Jew of Troyes; see Arbois de Jubainville, *Histoire*, 4: 829–30.

5 The actual sum is 1343 *l.* 13 *s.* rather than 1323 *l.* 13 *s.*

6 This total (1934 *l.* 13 *s.*) is accurate: the scribe who calculated it counted all the individual amounts instead of adding the second group of debts to the first (incorrect) summation.

*118

1212 October

The provost, Milo of Nanteuil,[1] *the dean Etienne,*[2] *and the chanter Fulk*[3] *of the cathedral chapter of Reims announce the resolution of their dispute with Countess Blanche over rights and revenues at La Neuville-au-Pont.*[4]

ORIGINAL: AN, J 197, no. 10 (missing pendant seal).
COPIES: CR 1, fols. 265v–266r (>CR 6, fol. 51r–v). CR 8, fol. 444r.
EDITION: *Layettes*, 1: 383, no. 1024.
CALENDARED: AJ, no. 800.

Milo prepositus, Stephanus decanus, Fulco cantor ceterique Remensis ecclesie fratres, omnibus ad quos littere iste pervenerint, in Domino salutem. Notum facimus universis quod talis pax facta est inter nos et dominam Blancham, comitissam Campanie, de villa de Ponte, videlicet quod de exartis que homines in terra nostra fecerunt aut facient usque ad metas quas dilecti nostri Odo, marescallus Campanie, et Guido Pes Lupi, concanonicus noster, ponent, qui ex hoc sunt dictores: habebimus duodecimam garbam pro terragio, et illud terragium ducent homines intra villam de Ponte ad grangiam quam ibi habebimus, si voluerimus, nec extra villam ducere tenebuntur. In eadem villa habebimus unum servientem liberum ab exercitu, tallia, tolta, et chavalcheia, et ille serviens custodiet res nostras in omnibus in quibus jus habemus vel habebimus. Preterea prata que debent nobis costumam, que homines de imperio solent tenere, tenebunt homines de potestate et qui erunt extra imperium qui reddent nobis consuetudines et debitum terre. Quilibet mansionarius ejusdem ville qui habebit focum et locum reddet nobis ad festum Sancti Martini, nomine costume pro aisantiis boscorum et aquarum nostrarum, unum bichetum avene ad mensuram ad quam homines Maurimontis reddunt costumas suas, et unum caponem, et nichil ultra ab eis exigi poterit pro aisantiis memoratis. Nos vero habebimus in nostro domanio terras nostras arabiles, prata, aquas et nemora sicut hactenus dinoscimur habuisse, hoc excepto, quod in illis nemoribus habebunt homines ejusdem ville usuarium suum ad comburendum et edificandum, sicut ibi habent

1 See **81** n. 1.
2 Etienne, dean of the chapter (1212–16), became chancellor of the cathedral chapter of Notre-Dame of Paris (1215–18); see Desportes, *Fasti Ecclesiae Gallicanae*, 3: 528, no. 1113.
3 Fulk, chanter of the chapter (1207–16) until his resignation; see Desportes, *Fasti Ecclesiae Gallicanae*, 3: 268, no. 1265.
4 A similar letter from Countess Blanche was retained in the chapter's archive (Robert, 'La ville neuve de La Neuville-au-Pont,' 148–9, no. 6, October 1212). See also *__115__.

homines Maurimontis; et preterea habebunt ibi exarta sua que fecerunt et facient usque ad metas quas ibi ponent prefacti dictores, Odo marescallus et Guido. Et si ipsi dictores deficerent vel decederent, loco eorum unum eligeremus et predicta comitissa alium, ad ponendum predictas metas. Quod ut ratum permaneat et stabile, presentes litteras scribi et sigilli nostri appensione fecimus roborari. Actum anno gratie M CC[a] duodecimo, mense octobri.

[a] millesimo ducentesimo *in CR 1.*

*119

1213 (n.s.) January

Pierre, abbot of Saint-Remi of Reims, announces the agreement he made with countess Blanche to share equally the marriage and death taxes of the residents of Lavilleneuve-aux-Frênes.[1]

ORIGINAL: AN, J 197, no. 9 (missing pendant seal).
COPIES: CR 1, fol. 266r (>CR 6, fols. 45v). CR 3, fol. 23r–v.[2] CR 4, fol. 175r–v.
CALENDARED: AJ, no. 805. *Layettes*, 1: 387–8, no. 1034.

Petrus,[a] Dei permissione Sancti Remigii Remensis abbas, omnibus litteras istas visuris, salutem in Domino. Noverit universitas vestra quod inter nos et karissimam dominam nostram Blancham, comitissam Trecensis, talis compositio facta fuit, quod homines Beati Remigii Remensis manentes apud villam novam que Fraxinus dicitur, si decesserint vel se forismaritaverint, prepositus comitisse mortuam manum vel forismaritagium finare vel levare non poterit sine preposito Sancti Remigii de Cortisor.[b] Similiter nec prepositus de Cortisor[b] sine propositi comitisse mortuam manum aut forismaritagium finare poterit aut levare; et tunc ex eo quod inde pervenerit nos unam medietatem habebimus et comitissam aliam medietatem habebit. In cujus rei testimonium[c] presentes litteras sigilli nostri appensione roboravimus. Actum anno dominice incarnationis Domini millesimo ducentesimo duo decimo,[d] mense januario.

[a] Ego Petrus *in CR 1.* [b] Cortisol *in CR 1.* [c] In cujus rei testimonium etc *in CR 1.* [d] Actum anno Domini M CC XII *in CR 1.*

1 Saint-Remi had Countess Blanche's letter on the same subject (AD Marne, 56 H 1031, fols. 637v–638r). See also Higounet, *Défrichements et villeneuves*, 132, 143.
2 CR 3, fols. 128v–129r copies a variant (perhaps a preparatory draft) of this letter dated 1212.

*120

1210 (n.s.) January

Guillaume of Joinville, bishop of Langres,[1] *approves and confirms the decision contained in King Philip II's letter*[2] *not to hear any challenge to Thibaut IV's right to succeed his father until Thibaut is twenty-one, for according to the custom in France, which the king promised to enforce, no one should have to answer for his inheritance before attaining that age.*[3] *The bishop promises not to hear any challenge regarding the fief that Thibaut's father held from the bishop of Langres until Thibaut completes his twenty-first year; at that time the bishop will receive Thibaut's homage.*[4]

ORIGINAL: AN, J 198, no. 9 (missing pendant seal).[5]
COPY: CR 1, fol. 266v (>CR 6, fol. 46r). CR 3, fol. 5r. CR 4, fol. 140r. CR 8, fol. 201r.
CALENDARED: AJ, no. 723. *Layettes*, 1: 345, no. 911.

Ego Willelmus, Dei gratia Lingonensis episcopus, notum facimus presentibus et futuris quod nos laudamus, approbamus et concedimus illud quod karissimus dominus noster Philippus, rex Francorum, fecit erga Theobaldum, filium dilecte et fidelis noster Blanche, comitisse Trecensis, et erga ipsam Blancham, sicut in carta ipsius regis continetur, videlicet quod dictus Theobaldus et Blanche comitissa, mater ejus, non debent nec possunt trahi in causam de aliquo quod pater ipsius Theobaldi teneret quando decessit, quoadusque dictus Theobaldus vicesimum primum compleverit annum; quia usus et consuetudo talis est in regno Francie,[a] et justum est, quod nullus respondere debet infra vicesimum primum annum etatis sue de aliquo quod pater ejus teneret sine placito cum decessit. Quam igitur illud laudamus et approbamus, concedimus prefatis Theobaldo et Blanche mater ejus quod si aliquis velit eos trahere in causam de aliquo quod ad feodum nostrum pertineat, nos non audiremus inde verbum nec aliquis ex parte nostra donec sepedictus Theobaldus vicesimum primum compleverit annum. Immo ipsos inde in omnibus juraremus. Postquam vero dictus Theobaldus vicesimum primum compleverit annum vel etiam ante, si dicte

1 See **65** n. 1.
2 **App. 2**. See also **38**, **48**.
3 The bishop sent a shorter version of this letter in the same month (**65**).
4 Otto III, duke of Burgundy, sealed a similar letter in the same month (AN, J 198, no. 10 [= *Layettes*, 1: 344–5, no. 910]).
5 The chancery had another, slightly different version of the letter dated 1210 (AN, J 198, no. 19 [= CR 3, fol. 5r], calendared in *Layettes*, 1: 345, no. 911).

matri ejus Blanche placuerit, nos recipiemus eum in hominem de omnibus que pater ejus, comes Theobaldus, tenuit de predecessore nostro episcopo Lingonensis, et que Blancha, comitissa Trecensis[b] mater ejus, de nobis tenet. Quod ut ratum habeatur[c] et firmum, presentem paginam sigilli nostri fecimus munimine roborari. Actum anno Domini[d] M CC IX, mense januario.

[a] Francorum *in CR 1.* [b] comitissa Trecensis *omitted in CR 1.* [c] Quod ut ratum etc. *in CR 1.* [d] Anno gratie *in CR 1.*

*121

1213 November

Countess Blanche declares that she must pay King Philip II 20,000 l., *money of Paris, as agreed at Compiègne on 21 November.*[1] *If she fails to make the payment, Philip may seize and hold her lands until she does pay. She names Guy II of Dampierre*[2] *and Gaucher III of Châtillon, count of Saint-Pol,*[3] *as her sureties.*

COPIES: CR 1, fol. 266v (>CR 6, fol. 46r–v).
CALENDARED: AJ, no. 838.

Ego Blancha, comitissa Trecensis, notum facio universis presentes litteras inspecturis quod ego me obligavi erga dominum regum Francie de XX[m] libras parisiensis, tali modo, quod nisi tenerem ei has conventiones ultimas que continentur in carta mea facta Compendi die martis post octabas Sancti Martini,[4] et eadem conventiones infra quindenam nativitatis instantis non compleverim sicut continetur in carta mea, dominus rex sine forifacere alicui ex inde[a] se posset capere ad totam terram meam et eam in manu sua tenere donec dictas XX[m] libras ei reddiderim. Super hoc eidem domino regi fidejussores consitui Guidonum de Dampetri et comitem Sancti Pauli. Et dominus rex similiter se posset capere ad totas terras et ad feoda ipsorum nisi dictas conventiones ei tenerem. Actum et cetera. Anno gratie M CC tercio decimo, mense novembri.

[a] ex inde *omitted in CR 6.*

1 ***62**. In 1209 she paid Philip 15,000 l. (**App. 2**).
2 See **3** n. 1.
3 See **33** n. 2.
4 Blanche's letter, the counterpart of Philip II's letter (***62**), does not survive.

*122

1198

Count Thibaut III grants Vandières in fief to Raoul Plunquet.[1]

COPIES: CR 1, fol. 266v (>CR 6, fol. 46v).
EDITION: Brussel, *Nouvel examen*, 833 note a (from CR 6).
CALENDARED: AJ, no. 468.

Ego Theobaldus, Trecensis comes palatinus, notum facio tam presentibus quam futuris quod ego dedi domino Radulpho, cognomine Plunquet, villam que dicitur Venderie, que est prope Castellionem, in feodo et casamento, sibi et heredibus suis, cum nemore quod dicitur de Loco Martini cum omnibus proventibus et utilitatibus quas ibi habebam, excepto nemore de Ropeis,[a] quod detinui ex parte Castellionis in manu mea. Quod ut ratum et[b] firmum teneatur, litteris annotatum sigilli mei impressione firmavi. Cujus rei testes fuerunt: Galcherus de Castellione, Galterus comes Brene, Guillelmus et Johannes fratres ejus, Gaufridus marescallus, Guido de Cappis, Hugo de Sancto Mauricio, Ansellus Bridaine. Actum anno incarnationis Domini[c] M C nonagesimo octavo. Nota Petri.

[a] Forerio *in CR 6.* [b] et cetera *for rest of sentence in CR 6.* [c] incarnati Verbi *in CR 6.*

1 The feudal roll for Châtillon, circa 1201, lists Raoul as liege for Vandières and owing two months castle-guard (Longnon, *Documents*, 1: 83, no. 2274: *Radulphus Ploquet, ligius de Venderiis, salva ligeitate regis Francorum, et duos menses custodie*). Raoul is also listed in the royal Register A (ca 1205) among the king's *vavassores* (*Les registres de Philippe Auguste*, 1: 334).

APPENDIX

1

1198 April

Count Thibaut III announces that he did liege homage to King Philip II and that eleven named barons of Champagne swore to his observance of that homage. The king in turn swore by his own hand to accept the count as his liegeman and had eleven of his barons swear that they wished the king to keep his good faith to the count. If either the count or king is deficient in this matter, the barons who swore on his behalf will place themselves in captivity in Paris or Troyes, respectively, and will remain there every night until the matter is resolved. If the count leaves his barons captive more than one month, the prelates of Champagne may interdict his lands. The count concludes this letter by stating that it follows the format of the king's own sealed letter.[1]

ORIGINAL: AN, J 199, no. 2 (missing pendant seal).[2]
EDITION: Longnon, *Documents*, 1: 468, no. 4.
CALENDARED: AJ, no. 453. *Layettes*, 1: 196, no. 474. Delisle, *Catalogue*, no. 534.

Ego Theobaldus, Trecensis comes palatinus, notum facio presentibus et futuris quod domino et avunculo meo karissimo Philipo, regi Francorum illustrissimo, ligium hominium feci contra omnem creaturam que vivere possit aut mori de

1 The king's letter, *mutatis mutandis*, is identical (AN, J 198, no. 4 [= Longnon, *Documents*, 1: 467–8, no. 3 = *Layettes*, 1: 195–6, no. 473]).

2 This letter was not copied into any of Philip II's registers, perhaps because it had been superseded by Countess Blanche's own homage of May 1201, but the letter itself was retained in the royal chancery archive and copied into King Louis IX's cartulary of circa 1269 (AN, JJ 31, fol. 67v) under the rubric *Littere ducum, comitum et aliorum baronum Francie*.

tota terra quam pater meus comes Henricus tenuit a patre suo, rege Ludovico, et frater meus ab ipso rege Philipo. Juravi etiam domino regi super sacratissimum corpus Domini et super sancta Evangelia quod eum bona fide jurabo contra omnem creaturam que possit vivere aut mori, sicut dominum meum ligium. Meo autem mandato, juraverunt Guido de Dampetra, Galcherus de Castellione, Gaufridus marescallus, Galterus cancellarius, Robertus de Milliaco, Willelmus de Brena, Guido de Capis, Ugo de Sancto Maurithio, Milo de Pruvino, Petrus de Tosquino, Aubertus de Latiniaco quod de bona fide illud vellent et laudarent michi quod id tenerem. Si autem de hoc deficerem, infra mensem postquam id scirent, si non esset emendatum, aut prius si bona fide id scire possent, in captionem domini regis Parisius se mitterent et ibi essent usque dum esset emendatum, et quotienscunque ego inde deficerem predicti similiter facerent.

Dominus autem rex michi propria manu juravit quod me contra omnem creaturam que vivere possit aut mori tanquam hominem suum ligium jurabit. De mandato vero ipsius juraverunt comes Nivernis, Drogo de Melloto, Willelmus de Gallanda, Galterus camerarius, Bartholomeus de Roya, Philippus de Liviis, Ursus camerarius, Galterus juvenis, Galcherus de Jovigniaco, Willelmus de Alneto, Philippus de Nantolio quod hoc bona fide volent et laudabunt domino regi, ut id teneat. Si autem de hoc deficeret, et non esset emendatum, infra mensem postquam id scirent aut prius bona fide mitterent se in captionem meam apud Trecas usque dum esset emendatum, et ita facerent quotiens dominus rex inde deficeret. Ostagii vero qui captionem tenebunt hinc inde, tota die poterunt exire de villa in qua tenebunt captionem, dum tamen per suum sacramentum in villa jaceant ubi captio eis est statuta. Dominus autem rex bona fide faciet comitem Robertum, Gaufridum comitem Pertici et Guillelmum de Barris in eundem modum quo predicti juraverunt jurare. Ego vero bona fide faciam domino rege Johannem de Montemirabili, Garnerum de Triangulo et Ansellum de Triangulo eodem modo quo predicti juraverunt ex parte mea jurare.

Dominus autem rex concessit karissimo patruo meo Willelmo, Remensi archiepiscopo, et Cathalaunensi et Meldensi episcopis quod si ab his deficeret, quotiens deficeret, terram suam que sub eis est supponerent interdicto, nisi infra mensem postquam ostagii in captionem se dedissent esset emendatum. Si vero ego hoc deficerem, quotiens deficerem, predicti archiepiscopus et episcopi terram meam supponerent interdicto, si non esset ut predictum est emendatum. Ut[a] autem hoc ratum et inconcussum teneatur, sigilli mei caractere presentem feci paginam insigniri in hujus testimonium sub eadem forma domini regis autenticum accepturus.[a] Actum anno Verbi incarnati M C nonagesimo octavo, mense aprili.[b] Datum per manum Galteri cancellarii. Nota Petri.

[a] *entire sentence omitted in the king's letter (see n. 1).* [b] *the king's letter (see n. 1) ends here.*

2

July 1209, Paris

King Philip II makes known his agreement with Countess Blanche.[1] *Her son Thibaut will remain with him for four years from next February, after which she may have him whenever she wishes. Bray and Montereau castles will remain in royal hands until Thibaut's majority at twenty-one, when the king will receive Thibaut's homage. Thibaut will not be allowed to do homage before that time if Blanche is alive, except with her permission. Nor will the king consider any challenge to Thibaut's succession by the daughter of Count Henry II before Thibaut's majority. For this agreement, Blanche will pay the king 15,000* l. *over six terms.*[2]

COPY: CR 7.1, fols. 42v–44r.[3]
EDITION: *Recueil des actes de Philippe Auguste*, 3: 171–2, no. 1088.
CALENDARED: AJ, no. 707.

Philippus, Dei gratia Francorum rex, universis ad quos presentes littere pervenerint, [salutem. Noveritis] quod [hee] sunt conventiones inter nos et dilectam nostram Blancham[a], comitissam Campanie, scilicet quod nos Theobaldum filium ejus tenebimus ab instanti festo Purificationis beate Marie usque ad quatuor annos, et ex tunc in antea habebit dictum filium Theobaldum quantumcumque voluerit. Nos autem Braium et Monsterolium tenebimus sicut modo tenemus et per eas conventiones quibus nunc tenemus usque dum[b] dictus Theobaldus habeat viginti unum annos, et juramenta baronum et civitatum[c] castrorum et terre sue nobis facta volumus nobis teneri quousque dictus Theobaldus filius comitisse habeat viginti unum annos. Quando vero dicta comitissa ad predictum terminum voluerit habere filium suum, si nos voluerimus habere amplius de juramentis terre illius, quod tam ipsa quam Theobaldus filius ejus erunt fideliter ad servitium nostrum, ipsi amplius juramenta nos habere facient. Cum autem dictus Theobaldus impleverit viginti unum annos, nos

1 See countess Blanche's identical letter, *mutatis mutandis* (**App. 3**). See also confirmations of this agreement by the overlords of Champagne (**38**, **48**, **65**, and ***120**) and the pope (***61**).

2 She paid it in full by December 1210 (*Recueil des actes de Philippe Auguste*, 3: 252, no. 1154).

3 It is curious that such an important letter does not appear in any of the earlier comital cartularies. It is highly likely that it was copied into the now-missing folios containing royal letters in CR 1 (see Introduction, n. 77), but it is not clear why it was not copied into CR 3 or CR 4 of 1222, both of which contain comprehensive selections of letters pertaining to Thibaut's succession. The original letter disappeared after it was copied into CR 7 (the *Liber Principum*) in 1271.

recipiemus eum in hominem ligium de terra de qua pater ejus tenens erat quando decessit, salvo alterius jure; nec ante ipsum exinde in hominem recipiemus, sicut dictum est, quamdiu eadem comitissa vixerit, nisi per ipsam comitissam. Et si filie Henrici comitis quondam, nepotis nostri, vel aliquis alius eundem Theobaldum vel comitissam traherent in causam de comitatu Campanie priusquam Theobaldus viginti unum annos implevisset, dictus Theobaldus vel comitissa non tenerentur exinde respondere infra predictum terminum quandiu idem Theobaldus viveret, nec nos audiremus inde causam, quia usus et consuetudo Francie talis est, quod nullus infra vicessimum[d] primum annum respondere debet super hereditate de qua pater ejus tenens esset sine placito cum decederet.

Propter supradictas conventiones tenendas, dicta comitissa nobis debet dare quindecim millia librarum parisiensium his terminis: in instanti festo Beati Andree, duo millia et quingentas libras; ad Purificationem Beate Marie proximo subsequentem, duo millia et quingentas libras; ad octavam Pasche subsequentis, duo millia et quingentas libras; in[e] octabis Beate Marie Magdalene subsequentibus, duo milia et quingentas libras;[e] in octava Sancti Remigii subsequentis, duo millia et quingentas libras; in[f] festivitate Sancte Andree subsequenti, duo milia et quingentas libras.[f] Si vero, quod absit, dictus Theobaldus moreretur infra terminum qui est ab instanti Purificatione Beate Marie in quatuor annos, si nos teneremus comitatum Campanie in manu nostra, dicte comitisse gratum suum faceremus infra unum annum de predictis quindecim millibus libris. Et si comitatum Campanie alii tradere vellemus, nullum de eo saisiremus quousque dictam comitissam ad gratum suum securam fecissemus de predictis quindecim millibus libris ei reddendis infra annum, et de prenominato termino qui est ab instanti Purificatione Beate Marie in quatuor annos in antea, nec nos nec alii qui tenerent comitatum Campanie teneremus reddere dictas quindecim mille libras.

Omnes istas conventiones assecuravimus et in animam nostram jurari fecimus dicte comitisse et Theobaldo filio ejus bona fide tenendas, et ipsa nobis, et eis volumus similiter facere assecurari filio nostro.[4] Actum Parisius, anno Domini M CC IX, mense julio.

[a] Beatam *in CR 7.1.* [b] dum *in CR 7.1 and in Countess Blanche's letter* (*App. 3*), *corrected to* iam *in Recueil.* [c] civitatum *in Countess Blanche's letter* (*App. 3*), comitatum *in CR 7.1 corrected to* comitem *in Recueil.* [d] vigesimum *in CR 7.1.* [e] *clause in Countess Blanche's letter* (*App. 3*), *missing from CR 7.1 and Recueil.* [f] *clause in Countess Blanche's letter (App. 3), missing from CR 7.1 and Recueil.*

4 Prince Louis sealed two identical letters (AN, J 198, nos. 12–13, August 1209 [= Martène and Durand, *Thesaurus novus anecdotorum*, 1: 816–17]).

3

July 1209, Paris

Countess Blanche makes known her agreement with king Philip II.[1] *Her son Thibaut will remain with him for four years from next February, after which she may have him whenever she wishes. Bray and Montereau castles will remain in the king's hand until Thibaut's majority at twenty-one, when the king will receive Thibaut's homage. Thibaut will not be allowed to do homage before that time if Blanche is alive, except with her permission. Nor will the king consider any challenge to Thibaut's succession by the daughter of Count Henry II before Thibaut's majority. For this agreement, Blanche will pay the king 15,000* l. *in six terms.*

ORIGINAL: AN, J 198, no. 11 (missing pendant seal).
COPY: Vatican Ottoboni, lat. 2796 (royal Register A), fol. 73r (dated August); photograph in Delisle, *Le premier registre de Philippe Auguste*.
EDITIONS: Martène and Durand, *Veterum scriptorum ... amplissima collectio*, 1: 1094. RHF, 19: 536. *Layettes*, 1: 332–3, no. 878.
CALENDARED: AJ, no. 708. Delisle, *Catalogue*, no. 1141 (dated August 1209).

Ego Blancha, comitssa Trecensis palatina, notum facio universis presentes litteras inspecturis quod hee sunt conventiones inter me et karissimum dominum meum Philippum, illustrem Francorum regem, scilicet quod ipse Theobaldum filium meum tenebit ab instanti festo Purificationis beate Marie usque ad quatuor annos, et ex tunc in antea habebo dictum filium meum quandocumque voluero. Dominus rex autem tenebit Braium et Musterolium sicut modo tenet et per eas conventiones quibus nunc tenet usque dum Theobaldus filius meus habeat viginti et unum annos, et juramenta baronum et civitatum castrorum et terre mee domino regi facta volo ei teneri quousque dictus filius meus habeat viginti et unum annos. Quando vero ego ad dictum terminum voluero habere filium meum, si dominus rex voluerit habere amplius securitates terre mee, quod tam ego quam filius meus erimus fideliter ad servicium suum, nos amplius securitates eum habere faciemus. Cum autem dictus filius meus impleverit viginti et unum annos, dominus rex recipiet eum in hominem ligium de terra de qua pater ejus tenens erat quando decessit, salvo alterius jure; nec ante ipsum exinde in hominem recipiet, sicut dictum est, quamdiu ego vixero, nisi per me ipsam. Et si filie comitis Henrici vel aliquis alius dictum filium meum vel me ipsam traherent in causam de comitatu Campanie priusquam filius meus viginti

1 See the king's identical letter, *mutatis mutandis* (**App. 2**).

et unum annos complesset, filius meus vel ego non teneremur exinde respondere infra predictum terminum quamdiu idem filius meus viveret, nec dominus rex audiret inde causam, quia usus et consuetudo Francie talis est, quod nullus ante vicessimum primum annum respondere debet super hereditate de qua pater ejus tenens esset sine placito cum decederet.

Propter conventiones supradictas tenendas, debeo dare domino regi quindecim milia librarum parisiensium his terminis: in instanti festo Sancti Andree, duo milia et quingentas libras; ad Purificationem beate Marie proximo subsequentem, duo milia et quingentas libras; ad octabas Pasche subsequentis, duo milia et quingentas libras; in octabis Beate Marie Magdalene subsequentibus, duo milia et quingentas libras; in octabis Sancti Remigii subsequentis, duo milia et quingentas libras; in festivitate Sancti Andree subsequenti, duo milia et quingentas libras. Si vero, quod absit, dictus filius meus moreretur infra terminum qui est ab hac instanti Purificatione Beate Marie in quatuor annos, si dominus rex comitatum Campanie teneret in manu sua, ipse mihi gratum meam faceret de predictis quindecim milibus libris infra unum annum. Et si comitatum Campanie alii tradere vellet, nullum de eo saisiret quousque me securam ad gratum meum fecisset de predictis quindecim milibus libris mihi infra annum reddendis, et de prenominato termino qui est ab instanti Purificatione Beate Marie in quatuor annos in antea, nec dominus rex nec alii qui tenerent comitatum Campanie tenerentur reddere dictas quindecim milia libras.

Omnes istas conventiones assecuravi domino regi tenendas, et ipse mihi, et eas debet facere assecurari a domino Ludovico filio suo.[2] Actum[a] Parisius, anno Domini MCC nono, mense julio.[a]

[a] *the copy in the royal register reads instead*: Anno Domini MCCVIII [*crossed out and corrected to* MCCIX] mense Augusto, S[ignum] filio suo.

2 See **App. 2** n. 4.

CHRONOLOGICAL TABLE OF THE LETTERS

Date	Author	Subject	Number[†]
Count Henry I, 1152–81			
1158	Count Henry I	Archambaud of Sully's fief	46
1160	Robert I, count of Dreux	fortress of Savignies	1
1162	dean of chapter at Senlis	notification to Henry I	64
1165	Count Henry I	Jouy forest regulations	32
1165	Count Henry I	Sourdun forest regulations	**39**
1177	Count Henry I	a mortaged fief	82
1179	Count Henry I	purchase of fiefs	45
Countess Marie, 1181–87			
1186	Countess Marie	*mouvance* of La Ferté-Louptière	**37**
Count Henry II, 1187–90			
1187	Count Henry II	dispute over dependents	44
1187	Bernard, abbot of St-Oyand	*pariage* over Sermaise	**74**
Countess Marie, 1190–98			
[ca 1194]	Simon, bishop of Meaux	Henry II's gift	**107**
Count Thibaut III, 1198–1201			
1198 April	Count Thibaut III	homage to the king	**App. 1**
[1198–1201]	Hugh, abbot of Essômmes	thanks for a grant	59
[1198–1201]	Guillaume, archbishop of Reims	Avenay's license to elect	108
1198	dean of St-Pierre of Troyes	cloister's immunity	**92**
1198	Count Thibaut III	fief to Raoul Plumquet	*122
[1199–1201]	Guillaume, count of Vienne, Mâcon	payment of fief-rent	49

[†]A bold edition number indicates an extant original document. An asterisk indicates a text added to a completed quire after October 1211.

Date	Author	Subject	Number
[1199–1201]	Octavian, papal legate	Henry II's debts	80
1199 July	Geoffroy V of Joinville	restrictions on tenants	**14**
1199 July	Guillaume, archbishop of Reims	Queen Adele's wardship	68
1199 November	Michel, archbishop of Sens	Henry II's debt	73
1199 December	Pierre, papal legate	Marie's debts	78
1199 December	Guillaume, archbishop of Reims	exchange of revenues	93
1200	Odo III, duke of Burgundy	Thibaut III's homage	**6**
1200 February	Gautier III, count of Brienne	exchange of villages	18
1200 May	Jean I of Montmirail	wife's new dower	11
1200 October	Milo, abbot of Châtrices	forests to Thibaut III	43
1200 October	Milo, abbot of Châtrices	forests to Thibaut III	**100**
1200 October	Count Thibaut III	Neuville-au-Pont franchise	*114
1200 October	Count Thibaut III	Neuville-au-Pont *pariage*	*115
1201 January	Count Thibaut III	grants Gillancourt in fief	12
1201 February	abbot of St-Martin of Troyes	hospital of St-Abraham	69
1201 March	Jean I of Brienne	village of Fontaine-Mâcon	29
Countess Blanche, 1201–22			
[1201–1211]	prior of St-Martin-des-Champs	response to a royal order	60
1201	Pierre, archbishop of Sens	debts owed Blanche's Jews	72
1201 August	Geoffroy V of Joinville	Thibaut III's bequest	8
1202	Archambaud II of Sully	grandfather's fief-rent	34
1202	Odo, bishop of Paris	father's fief-rent	86
1202	Nicholas, dean of Bray	Blanche's prebends	**106**
1202 December	abbot of St-Martin of Epernay	sale of a woman	**40**
1203 January	Nicholas, dean of Bray	Blanche's prebends	**77**
1203 February	abbot of Saint-Jean of Laon	advocacy of Ventelay priory	95
1203 March	bishops of Beauvais and Meaux	Blanche's prebends at Bray	**109**
1203 June	Countess Blanche	tax rights at Baudement	36
1203 July	abbot of St-Jean-des-Vignes	exchange of revenue	**63**
1203 September	Henry III of Grandpré	*mouvance* of St-Jean-sur-Tourbe	**13**
1203 November	dean of St-Pierre of Troyes	exchange of dependent women	111
1204	dean of St-Pierre of Troyes	resolution of dispute	**35**
1204 January	Hugh, castellan of Vitry	pledge for a debt	50
1204 March	Pierre, count of Auxerre	arbitration of safeconduct	28
1204 November	Odo III, duke of Burgundy	a confiscated fief-rent	27
1204 December	abbot of St-Vanne of Verdun	*pariage* over Chaudefontaine	105
1205	Pierre, count of Auxerre	safeconduct	30
1205	Simon, abbot of Cormery	sale of woods	41
1205	Renaud, dean of Villemaur	*pariage* over his villages	84
1205	abbot of St-Médard of Soissons	pact with knights of Villegruis	**99**

Date	Author	Subject	Number
1205 April	Jean of Brienne	sale of Fontaine-Mâcon	22
1205 May	prior of Cluny	spriritual benefits for Blanche	57
1205 June	Anselm, bishop of Meaux	sale of forest rights	***87**
1205 July	Anselm III of Traînel	Villeneuve is renderable	(*90)**15**
1205 July	Hermesend of Traînel	Villeneuve is renderable	***91**
1205 July	dean of St-Quiriace of Provins	taverners exempted from tax	**76**
1205 September	Hugh IV of Broyes	surety for mother's debt	24
1205 October	Pope Innocent III	prohibits taxing Templars	*89
1205 November	Guy II of Dampierre	exchange of dependent women	3
1205 December	Renier II of Nogent-en-Bassigny	prenuptial agreement	**10**
1205 December	Robert, bishop of Langres	inheritance of Chaumont	55
1205 December	Robert, bishop of Langres	inheritance of Chaumont	96
1206	abbot of St-Remy of Reims	*pariage* over Villiers	**94**
1206/7 March	dean of Châlons-sur-Marne	St-Julien of Courtisols	56
1206 April	Thibaut I, count of Bar-le-Duc	exchange of tenants	2
1206 April	Robert II of Dreux and Braine	La Fère, Torcy fortresses	4
1206 July	abbot of St-Vanne of Verdun	*pariage* over Chaudefontaine	**54**
1206 August	Milo of Pougy	pledge	52
1207 September	Amalvin, abbot of La Sauve-Majeur	*pariage* over La Neuville-aux-Larris	98
1207 December	Iter, dean of St-Etienne	Blanche's dependent man	85
1208 January	Hospitallers	*pariage* over Esnouveaux	**101**
1208 February	Robert, bishop of Langres	sale of house to Blanche	42
1208 May	Simon of Châteauvillain	liege homage	**5**
1208 May	abbot of St-Martin of Epernay	exchange with Blanche	**83**
1208 August	Pierre of Joigny	a 300 *l.* rent	26
1208 August	Renaud of Dammartin	accepts arbiters	33
1208 August	Manasses, abbot of St-Loup	exchange of women	58
1208 October	Geoffroy, bishop of Meaux	minting of coins	110
1208 November	Anselm III of Traînel	sale at Pont-sur-Seine	9
[1209–1210]	archbishop of Canterbury	rights at Chablis	104
1209	Garnier III of Traînel	sale at Pont-sur-Seine	19
1209	Odo III, duke of Burgundy	rights at Chablis	**23**
1209	Guillaume, count of Sancerre	declares liegeance	**47**
1209 March	Robert II of Dreux and Braine	fortress at Lizy	25
1209 April	Isabelle of Châteauvillan	exchange of tenants	20
1209 May	Jean and Helvide of Montmirail	debt of 1,300 *l.*	51
1209 June	Bertrand of Ste-Menehould	sale to Blanche	67
1209 July	Simon of Passavant	Montreuil is renederable	102

Date	Author	Subject	Number
1209 July	King Philip II	treaty with Blanche	App. 2
1209 July	Countess Blanche	treaty with king	**App. 3**
1209 September	Odo III, duke of Burgundy	king's treaty with Blanche	**48**
1210	Guillaume of Nanteuil	sale of a fief	31
1210	Geoffroy, prior of La Charité	sale of dependents	97
1210 January	Guillaume, bishop of Langres	king's treaty with Blanche	65
1210 January	Guillaume, bishop of Langres	king's treaty with Blanche	***120**
1210 January	abbess of Fontevraud	Foissy's debt to Blanche	103
1210 April	Alberic, archbishop of Reims	king's treaty with Blanche	**38**
1210 May	Henri of Sorcy	sale of Dormans	70
1210 June	Guy II of Dampierre	a Jew's debt	7
1210 June	Guy II of Dampierre	castle of Beaufort	53
1210 September	Geoffroy, abbot of Chézy	Blanche's grant	**79**
1210 October	Odo III, duke of Burgundy	agreement on Jews	17
1210 November	Gautier of Vanault	sale of viscounty of Cuis	66
1210 November 22	Pope Innocent III	king's treaty with Blanche	***61**
[1211]	notice	Hermesend of Traînel's debts	*117
1211	Guillaume, provost of Chablis	lease of provostship	71
1211 January	Odo III, duke of Burgundy	sale of Gillancourt	**16**
1211 February	Elizabeth of Châteauvillain	sale of Baudement castle	**21**
1211 April	Milo of Nanteuil, canon	use of a village fief	81
1211 October	dean of St-Pierre of Troyes	exchange of women	75
1212 February	Henri, abbot of St-Denis	exchange of dependent men	*112
1212 February	Henri, abbot of St-Denis	Blanche's rights at Nogent	*113
1212 October 1	Countess Blanche	widow of Grandpré's rights	*116
1212 October	dean of chapter of Reims	La Neuville-au-Pont	***118**
1213 January	abbot of St-Remi of Reims	pariage over Villeneuve	***119**
1213 November	Countess Blanche	15,000 *l.* owed to king	*121
1213 November 21	King Philip II	treaty with Blanche	***62**
1214 July	King Philip II	notice to Templars	*88

BIBLIOGRAPHY

PRIMARY SOURCES

Manuscripts

Archives Départementales de l'Aube (Troyes)
G 6
3 H 9, 3 H 10, Cartulary of Clairvaux (thirteenth century)
3 H 107
4 H 1, Cartulary of Larrivour (thirteenth century)
6 H 13
Archives Départementales de la Haute-Marne (Chaumont)
G 76
7 H 1, 13, 135
Archives Départementales de la Marne (Reims)
56 H 1029, Cartulary B of Saint-Remi of Reims
56 H 1031, Cartulary A of Saint-Remi of Reims
Archives Nationales (Paris)
J 193, 195, 196, 197, 198, 199, 201, 202, 203, 205, 1032, 1035
JJ 31, Cartulary of king Louis IX (ca 1269)
KK 1064, Cartulary-Registers of the counts, 1, 2, 4, 5
Bibliothèque Nationale de France (Paris)
Lat. 2454, copy of the lost *Liber Principum* of 1271 (seventeenth century)
Lat. 5992, Cartulary-Register 6: 'Cartulary of De Thou,' copy of AN, KK 1064 (ca 1232)
Lat. 5993, Cartulary-Register 3: 'Cartulary of Countess Blanche' (ca 1222)
Lat. 5993A, Cartulary-Register 8 (1271)
Lat. 17098, Cartulary of Saint-Etienne of Troyes (ca 1271)

nouv. acq. Lat. 110, Cartulary of Saint-Maclou of Bar-sur-Aube (ca 1273)
Cinq Cents de Colbert, vols. 56, 57, 58, Cartulary-Register 7: copy of the lost *Liber Principum* of 1271 (seventeenth century)
Collection Moreau, vol. 91

Editions and Related Works

Arbois de Jubainville, Henri d'. 'Catalogue d'actes des comtes de Brienne, 950–1356.' *Bibliothèque de l'Ecole des Chartes* 33 (1872): 141–86.

– 'Etudes sur les documents antérieurs à l'année 1285 conservés dans les archives des quatre petits hôpitaux de la ville de Troyes.' *Mémoires de la Société d'agriculture, des sciences, arts et belles-lettres du département de l'Aube* 21 (1857): 49–116.

– *Histoire des ducs et des comtes de Champagne*. 7 vols. Paris, 1859–69.

Aubri of Trois-Fontaines. 'Chronicon.' Ed. P. Scheffer-Boichorst. *Monumenta Germaniae Historica. Scriptores*, 23: 631–930.

Barbiche, Bernard, ed. *Les actes pontificaux originaux des Archives nationales de Paris, 1: 1198–1261*. Vatican City, 1975.

Barthélemy, Edouard de. *Le prieuré de Saint-Laurent de Chaudefontaine*. Paris, 1878.

Beaumanoir, Philippe de. *Coutumes de Beauvaisis*. Ed Amédée Salmon. 2 vols. Paris, 1899–1900.

Brunel, Ghislain, and Elisabeth Lalou, eds. *Sources d'histoire médiévale, IXe-milieu du XIVe siècle. Paris*, 1992.

Brussel, Nicholas. *Nouvel examen de l'usage général des fiefs en France pendant le XI, le XII, le XIII, et le XIVe siècle*. 2 vols. Paris, 1727; 2nd ed. 1750.

Carolus-Barré, Louis, ed. *Les plus anciens chartes en langue française, 1: Problèmes généraux et recueil des pièces originales conservées aux Archives de l'Oise, 1241–1286*. Paris, 1964.

Carrière, Victor, ed. *Histoire et cartulaire des Templiers de Provins*. Provins, 1919.

Chantereau-Lefebvre, Louis. *Traité des fiefs et de leur origine, avec les preuves tirées de diverse auteurs anciens et modernes*. Paris, 1662. Part 2 (*Autres preuves*) contains texts from CR 6 and the lost *Liber Principum* (CR 7).

Chapin, Elizabeth. *Les villes de foires de Champagne des origines au début du XIVe siècle*. Paris, 1937.

Coq, Dominique, ed. *Chartes en langue française antérieures à 1271 conservées dans les départements de l'Aube, de la Seine-et-Marne et de l'Yonne*. Documents linguistiques de la France (série française), vol. 3. Paris, 1988.

Débax, Hélène. 'Le cartulaire des Trencavel (*Liber instrumentorum vicecomitalium*).' In *Les cartulaires*, 291–9.

Delaville le Roulx, J. *Cartulaire général de l'ordre des Hospitaliers de S. Jean de Jérusalem (1100–1310)*. 4 vols. Paris, 1894–1906.

Delisle, Léopold. *Catalogue des actes de Philippe-Auguste*. Paris, 1856.

– *Mémoire sur les opérations financières des Templiers*. Paris, 1889.

– *Le premier registre de Philippe Auguste: reproduction héliotypique du manuscrit du Vatican*. Paris, 1883.

Denaix, Jean, ed. *Chartes des cisterciens de Saint-Benoît-en-Woëvre des origines à 1300*. Verdun, 1959.

Dovetto, Joseph. *Cartulaire des Trencavel: analyse détaillée des 617 actes, 957–1214*. Carcassonne, 1977.

Duchesne, André. *Historiae Francorum Scriptores*. 5 vols. Paris, 1636–49.

– *Histoire généalogique de la maison royale de Dreux et de quelques autres familles illustres*. Paris, 1631.

– *Histoire de la maison de Chastillon sur Marne*. Paris, 1621.

Evergates, Theodore. 'The Chancery Archives of the Counts of Champagne: Codicology and History of the Cartulary-Registers.' *Viator* 16 (1985): 159–79.

– tr. and ed. *Feudal Society in Medieval France: Documents from the County of Champagne*. Philadelphia, 1993.

Gallia Christiana in provincias ecclesiasticas distributa. Paris, 1715–1865.

Gasparri, Françoise. 'Manuscrit monastique ou registre de chancellerie?: à propos d'un recueil épistolaire de l'abbaye de Saint-Victor.' *Journal des Savants* (1976): 131–40.

Gigot, Jean-Gabriel, ed. *Chartes en langue française antérieures à 1271 conservées dans le département de la Haute-Marne*. Documents linguistiques de la France (série française), vol. 1. Paris, 1974.

Grayzel, Solomon. *The Church and the Jews in the XIIIth Century*. 2nd ed. New York, 1966.

Greenway, D.E., ed. *Charters of the Honour of Mowbray, 1107–1191*. Oxford, 1972.

Grosdidier de Matons, Marcel. *Catalogue des actes des comtes de Bar de 1022 à 1239*. Bar-le-Duc, 1922.

Hall, Hubert, ed. *The Red Book of the Exchequer*. 3 vols. London, 1896.

Hérelle, G., and P. Pélicier. 'Chartes en langue vulgaire conservées aux Archives départementales de la Marne (série G), années 1237–1337.' *Bulletin historique et philologique* (1897): 624–717.

Higounet, Charles, and Arlette Higounet-Nadal, eds. *Grand Cartulaire de la Sauve Majeure*. 2 vols. Bordeaux, 1996.

Hugh of Champfleury. 'Epistolorum Regis Ludovici VII et variorum ad eum volumen.' In *RHF*, 16: 2–170.

Lalore, Charles, ed. *Cartulaire de l'abbaye de Basse-Fontaine*. Paris, 1878.

– ed. *Cartulaire de l'abbaye de Chapelle-aux-Planches*. Paris, 1878.

– ed. *Cartulaire de l'abbaye du Paraclet*. Paris, 1878.

– ed. *Cartulaire de Saint-Pierre de Troyes*. Paris, 1880.

– ed. 'Documents pour servir à la généalogie des anciens seigneurs de Traînel.' *Mémoires de la Société académique d'agriculture, des sciences, arts et belles-lettres du département de l'Aube* 34 (1870): 177–271.

– ed. 'Documents sur l'abbaye de Notre-Dame-aux-Nonnains de Troyes.' *Mémoires de la Société académique d'agriculture, des sciences, arts et belles-lettres du département de l'Aube* 88 (1874): 5–148.

– *Les sires et les barons de Chacenay*. Troyes, 1885.

Laplace, Jacqueline, ed. *Actes des princes lorrains (1ère série): princes läiques. 2. Les Comtes. A. Actes des comtes de Bar*, vol. 2: *Thiébaut 1er (1190–1214)*. Préédition. Nancy, 1974.

Laurent, Jacques, ed. *Cartulaires de l'abbaye de Molesme, 916–1250*. 2 vols. Paris, 1907, 1911.

Layettes du Trésor des Chartes. Ed. A. Teulet et al. 5 vols. Paris, 1863–1909.

Lemaire, André. 'Les origines de la communauté de biens entre époux dans le droit coutumier français.' *Revue historique de droit français et étranger*, série 4, 7 (1928): 584–643.

Lesort, André. 'Les chartes de fondation du prieuré de Sermaize (Marne), 1094.' *Bulletin philologique et historique du Comité des Travaux historiques et scientifiques* (1924): 99–110.

Lewis, Andrew W. 'Fourteen Charters of Robert I of Dreux (1152–1188).' *Traditio* 41 (1985): 145–79.

Liber feudorum maior. Ed. Francisco Miguel Rosell. 2 vols. Barcelona, 1945, 1947.

Liber instrumentorum memorialium, cartulaire des Guilhems de Montpellier. Ed. Alexandre C. Germain. 2 vols. Montpellier, 1884, 1886.

Longnon, Auguste, ed. *Documents relatifs au comté de Champagne et de Brie (1172–1361)*. 3 vols. Paris, 1901–14.

Martène, Edmond, and Ursin Durand, eds. *Veterum scriptorum et monumentorum historicorum, dogmaticorum, moralium amplissima collectio*. 9 vols. Paris, 1724–33.

– eds. *Thesaurus novus anecdotorum*. 5 vols. Paris, 1717.

Major, Kathleen, ed. *Acta Stephani Langton Cantuariensis Archiepiscopi, A.D. 1207–1228*. Canterbury and York Series, vol. 50. Oxford, 1950.

Mayer, Hans Eberhard. *Die Kanzlei des lateinischen Könige von Jerusalem*. 2 vols. Monumenta Germaniae Historica. Schriften, Bd. 40. Hannover, 1996.

Mesqui, Jean. *Les routes dans la Brie et la Champgane occidentale: histoire et techniques*. Paris, 1980.

Monicat, Jacques, and Bernard de Fournoux, eds. *Chartes du Bourbonnais, 918–1522*. Moulins, 1952.

Morelle, Laurent. 'Mariage et diplomatique: autour de cinq chartes de douaire dans le laonnois-soissonais, 1163–1181.' *Bibliothèque de l'Ecole des Chartes* 146 (1988): 225–84.

– 'The Metamorphosis of Three Monastic Charter Collections in the Eleventh Century (Saint-Amand, Saint-Riquier, Montier-en-Der).' In *Charters and the Use of the Written Word in Medieval Society*. Ed. Karl Heidecker. Turnhout, 2000. 171–204.

Mortet, Victor, and P. Deschamps, eds. *Recueil de textes relatifs à l'histoire de l'architecture en France au moyen âge, XIe–XIIe siècles*. 2 vols. Paris, 1929.

Newman, William Mendel. *Les seigneurs de Nesle en Picardie (XIIe–XIIIe siècle)*. 2 vols. Philadelphia, 1971.

Nicaise, Auguste. *Epernay et l'abbaye Saint-Martin de cette ville*. 2 vols. Châlons-sur-Marne, 1869.

Nortier, Michel. 'Les actes de Philippe Auguste: notes critiques sur les sources diplomatiques du règne.' In *La France de Philippe Auguste: le temps des mutations*. Ed. Robert-Henri Bautier. Paris, 1982. 429–51.

Obituaires de la province de Sens, 4: Diocèses de Meaux et de Troyes. Ed. Boutellier du Retail and P. Piétresson de Saint-Aubin. Paris, 1923.

Paris, Louis. *Histoire de l'abbaye d'Avenay*. 2 vols. Paris, 1879.

Patrologiae cursus completus ... series ... ecclesiae latinae. Ed. J.P. Migne. 222 vols. Paris, 1844–64.

Pélicier, L. P., ed. *Cartulaire du chapitre de l'église cathédrale de Châlons-sur-Marne, par le chantre Warin*. Paris, 1897.

Petit, Ernest. *Histoire des ducs de Bourgogne de la race capétienne*. 9 vols. Paris, 1885–1905.

Pipon, Brigitte, ed. *Le chartrier de l'Abbaye-aux-Bois (1202–1341)*. Paris, 1996.

Portejoie, Paulette, ed. *L'ancien coutumier de Champagne (XIIIe siècle)*. Poitiers, 1956.

Quantin, Maximilien, ed. *Cartulaire général de l'Yonne*. 2 vols. Auxerre, 1854, 1860.

– ed. *Recueil de pièces pour faire suite au Cartulaire général de l'Yonne*. Auxerre, 1873.

Recueil des actes de Louis VI, roi de France (1108–1137). Ed. Jean Dufour. 4 vols. Paris, 1992–4.

Recueil des actes de Philippe Auguste, roi de France. Ed. H.-François Delaborde et al. 4 vols. Paris, 1916–79.

Recueil des historiens des Gaules et de la France. 24 vols. Paris, 1734–1904.

Les registres de Philippe Auguste, 1: Texte. Ed. John W. Baldwin, in collaboration with Françoise Gasparri, Michel Nortier, and Elisabeth Lalou. Paris, 1992.

Robert of Auxerre. 'Chronicon.' Ed. O. Holder-Egger. *Monumenta Germaniae Historica. Scriptores*, 26: 219–76.

Robert, Gaston. 'La ville neuve de La Neuville-au-Pont.' *Travaux de l'Académie nationale de Reims* 144 (1929–30): 112–85.

Saige, Gustave, Henri Lacaille, and L.H. Lebande, eds. *Trésor des chartes du comté de Rethel [1081–1415]*. 5 vols. Monaco, 1902–16.

Socard, Emile. 'Chartes inédites extraits des cartulaires de Molême intéressant un grand nombre de localités du département de l'Aube.' *Mémoires de la Société académique d'agriculture, des sciences, arts et belles-lettres du département de l'Aube* 28 (1864): 163–364.

Stein, Henri. *Bibliographie générale des cartulaires français*. Paris, 1907.

Suger. 'Epistolae Sugerii Abbatis S. Dionysii.' In *RHF*, 15: 483–532.

Varin, Pierre. *Archives administratives de la ville de Reims*. 5 vols. Paris, 1839–48.

Veissière, Michel. *Une communauté canoniale au moyen âge: Saint-Quiriace de Provins (XIe-XIIIe siècles)*. Provins, 1961.

Waquet, Jean, et. al. *Recueil des chartes de l'abbaye de Clairvaux*. Fascicules 1–2. Troyes, 1950, 1982.

SECONDARY SOURCES

Arbois de Jubainville, Henri d'. *Recherches sur les premières années de Jean de Brienne, roi de Jérusalem, empereur de Constantinople*. Paris, 1868.

– 'Les premiers seigneurs de Ramerupt.' *Bibliothèque de l'Ecole des Chartes* 23 (1861): 440–58

Baldwin, John W. *The Government of Philip Augustus*. Berkeley, 1986.

Barrow, Geoffrey W.S. 'The English Royal Chancery in the Earlier 13th Century.' *Archiv für Diplomatik* 41 (1995): 241–8.

Barthélemy, Anatole de. 'Notice historique sur la maison de Grandpré.' *Revue de Champagne et de Brie* 9 (1880): 97–105.

Baumel, Jean. *Histoire d'une seigneurie du Midi de la France: naissance de Montpellier (985–1213)*. 4 vols. Montpellier, 1969.

Bautier, Robert-Henri. 'L'authentification des actes privés dans la France médiévale: notariat public et juridiction gracieuse.' In *Notariado público y documento privado: de les orígines al siglo XIV*. 2 vols. Valencia, 1989. 701–72. Reprinted in his *Chartes, sceaux et chancelleries: études diplomatiques et de sigillographie médiévale*. 2 vols. Paris, 1990. 1: 269–340.

– 'Cartulaires de chancellerie et recueils d'actes des autorités laïques et ecclésiastiques.' In *Les Cartulaires*. 363–77.

Bedos-Rezak, Brigitte. *Form and Order in Medieval France: Studies in Social and Quantitative Sigillography*. Great Yarmouth, 1993.

Bisson, Thomas N. *Conservation of Coinage: Monetary Exploitation and Its Constraint in France, Catalonia and Aragon, c. 1000–1225 AD*. Oxford, 1997.

Blampignon, Emile-Antoine. *Bar-sur-Aube*. Paris, 1900.

Boitel, Abbé (Alexandre Clement). *Histoire du bienheureux Jean, surnommé l'humble, seigneur de Montmirail-en-Brie*. Paris, 1859.

Bouchard, Constance Brittain. *Sword, Miter, and Cloister: Nobility and the Church in Burgundy, 980–1198*. Ithaca, 1987.

Bresslau, Harry. *Handbuch der Urkundenlehre für Deutschland und Italien*. 2 vols. 2nd. ed. Leipzig, 1912–32.

Bulst-Thiele, Marie Luise. *Sacrae Domus Militiae Templi Hierosolymitani Magistri: Untersuchungen zur Geschichte des Templerordens, 1118/19–1314*. Göttingen, 1974.

Bur, Michel. *Le Château*. Typologie des sources du moyen âge occidental, facsicule 79. Turnhout, 1999.

– 'Le défrichement et le partage de la forêt du Mans près de Meaux (1150–1250).' *Bulletin philologique et historique (jusqu'à 1610) du Comité des Travaux historiques et scientifiques* (1963): 93–127.

– *La formation du comté de Champagne, v.950–v.1150*. Nancy, 1977.

– et al. *Vestiges d'habitat seigneurial fortifié du Bas-Pays Argonnais*. Inventaire des sites archéologiques non monumentaux de Champagne, 1. Reims, 1972.

– et al. *Vestiges d'habitat seigneurial fortifié en Champagne central*. Inventaire des sites archéologiques non monumentaux de Champagne, 3. Reims, 1987.

Cartulaires, Les. Ed. Olivier Guyotjeannin, Laurent Morelle, and Michel Parisse. Paris, 1993.

Chassel, Jean-Luc. 'L'usage du sceau au XIIe siècle.' In *Le XIIe Siècle: mutations et renouveau en France dans la première moitié du XIIe siècle*. Ed. Françoise Gasparri. Paris, 1994. 61–101.

Cheyette, Fredric. 'The Castles of the Trencavels: A Preliminary Aerial Survey.' In *Order and Innovation in the Middle Ages: Essays in Honor of Joseph R. Strayer*. Ed. William C. Jordan, Bruce McNab, and Teofilo F. Ruiz. Princeton, 1976. 255–72.

Clanchy, M.T. *From Memory to Written Record: England, 1066–1307*. 2nd ed. Oxford, 1993.

Constable, Giles. *Letters and Letter Collections*. Typologie des sources du moyen âge occidental, fascicule 17. Turnhout, 1976.

Corbet, Patrick. 'Les collégiales comtales de Champagne (v. 1150–v. 1230).' *Annales de l'Est* 29 (1977): 196–241.

Delaborde, H.-F. *Jean de Joinville et les seigneurs de Joinville, suivi d'un catalogue de leurs actes*. Paris, 1894.

Desportes, Pierre. *Reims et les Rémois aux XIIIe et XIVe siècles*. Paris, 1979.

– *Fasti Ecclesiae Gallicanae*. 3: *Diocèse de Reims*. Répertoire prosopographique des évêques, dignitaires et chanoines des diocèses de France de 1200 à 1500. Turnhout, 1998.

Dessargues, Pierre Médard. 'Notes d'histoire généalogique sur la maison de Marac aux XIIe et XIIIe siècles.' *Les Cahiers Haut-Marnais* 205–6 (1996): 8–13.

Devailly, Guy. *Le Berry du Xe siècle au milieu du XIIIe*. Paris, 1973.

Dufour, Jean. 'Peut-on parler d'une organisation de la chancellerie de Philippe Auguste?' *Archiv für Diplomatik* 41 (1995): 249–68.

Evergates, Theodore. 'Aristocratic Women in the County of Champagne.' In *Aristocratic Women in Medieval France*. Ed. Theodore Evergates. Philadelphia, 1999. 74–110.

Faget de Casteljau, Henri de. 'A la recherche des anciens seigneurs de Nogent-en-Bassigny (XIe-XIIe siècles).' *Les Cahiers Haut-Marnais* 137 (1979): 57–73.

Fontevraud, nuns of. *Histoire de l'Ordre de Fontevrault (1100–1908)*. 3 vols. Auch, 1911–13.

Fromageot, Jean. *Tonnerre et son comté des origines à la révolution de 1789*. Dijon, 1973.

Gaztambide, Jose Goñi. *Historia de los obispos de Pamplona, 1: siglos IV–XIII*. Pamplona, 1979.

Gervers, Michael, ed. *Dating Undated Medieval Charters*. Woodbridge, 2000.

Giry, Arthur. *Manuel de diplomatique*. Paris, 1894.

Grésy, Eugène. *Etude historique et paléographique sur le rouleau mortuaire de Guillaume des Barres, comte de Rochefort, grand sénéschal du roi Philippe-Auguste*. Paris, 1865.

Guyotjeannin, Olivier, Jacques Pycke, and Benoît-Michel Tock. *Diplomatique médiévale*. Turnhout, 1993.

Guyotjeannin, Olivier. *Episcopus et comes: affirmation et déclin de la seigneurie épiscopale au nord du royaume de France (Beauvais-Noyon, Xe-début XIIIe siècle)*. Geneva, 1987.

Hemptinne, Thérèse de, Walter Prevenier, and Maurice Vandermaesen. 'La chancellerie des comtes de Flandre (12e–14e siècle).' In Silagi, *Landesherrliche Kanzleien*. 433–54.

Heslop, T.A. 'The Seals of the Twelfth-Century Earls of Chester.' In Thacker, *The Earldom of Chester*. 179–97.

Higounet, Charles. *Défrichements et villeneuves du bassin parisien (XIe–XIVe siècles)*. Paris, 1990

Hudson, John. 'Diplomatic and Legal Apects of the Charters.' In Thacker, *The Earldom of Chester*, 153–78.

Hulbot, J.-C. 'Guillaume II de Joinville, évêque de Langres, puis archevêque de Reims.' *Revue de Champagne et de Brie* 18 (1893): 486–504.

Jolibois, Emile. *La Haute-Marne ancienne et moderne: dictionnaire géographique, statistique, historique et biographique*. Avallon, 1861.

Katsura, Hideyuki. 'Serments, hommages et fiefs dans la seigneurie des Guilhem de Montpellier (fin XIe–début XIIIe siècle).' *Annales du Midi* 104 (1992): 141–61.

Keefe, Thomas K. *Feudal Assessments and the Political Community under Henry II and His Sons*. Berkeley, 1983.

Kosto, Adam J. 'The *Liber feudorum maior* of the Counts of Barcelona: The Cartulary as an Expression of Power.' *Journal of Medeval History* 27 (2001): 1–22.

Lespinasse, René. *Le Nivernais et les comtes de Nevers*. 3 vols. Paris, 1909–14.

Lombard-Jordan, Anne. *Paris, genèse de la ville: la rive droit de la Seine des origines à 1223*. Paris, 1976.

Longnon, Jean. *Les compagnons de Villehardouin: recherches sur les croisés de la quatrième croisade*. Geneva, 1978.

– *Recherches sur la vie de Geoffroy de Villehardouin*. Paris, 1939.

LoPrete, Kimberly A. 'Adela of Blois: Familial Alliances and Female Rulership.' In Evergates, *Aristocratic Women in Medieval France*. 7–43.

Lusse, Jackie. 'D'Etienne à Jean de Joinville: l'ascension d'une famille seigneuriale champenoise.' In *Jean de Joinville: de la Champagne aux royaumes d'outre-mer*. Ed. Danielle Quéruel. Paris, 1998.

Magnou-Nortier, Elisabeth. 'Fidélité et féodalité méridionales d'après les serments de fidélité.' In *Les structures sociales de l'Aquitaine, du Languedoc et de l'Espagne au premier âge féodale*. Paris, 1969. 119–28.

Maleczeck, Werner. *Papst und Kardinalskolleg von 1191 bis 1216: Die Kardinäle unter Coelestin III. und Innocenz III*. Vienna, 1984.

Malo, Henri. *Un grand feudataire: Renard de Dammartin*. Paris, 1898.

Mathieu, Jean-Noël. 'A propos des châtelains de Châtillon-sur-Marne.' *Mémoires de la Société d'agriculture, commerce, sciences et arts du département de la Marne* 107 (1992): 7–27.

Mathieu, M. R. *Montmirail en Brie: sa seigneurie et son canton*. Paris, 1975.

Nicholas, Karen. 'Countesses as Rulers in Flanders.' In Evergates, *Aristocratic Women in Medieval France*. 111–37.

Parisse, Michel. *Noblesse et chevalerie en Lorraine médiévale: Les familles nobles de XIe au XIIIe siècle*. Nancy, 1982.

– 'Thiébaut, comte de Bar et de Luxembourg.' In *Ermesinde et l'affranchissement de la ville de Luxembourg*. Ed. Michel Margue. Luxemburg, 1994. 161–77.

Patterson, Robert B. *The Scriptorium of Margan Abbey and the Scribes of Early Angevin Glamorgan: Secretarial Administration in a Welch March Barony, c. 1150–c.1225*. Woodbridge, 2002.

Piétresson de Saint-Aubin, P. 'Notes sur le prieuré de Beaumont-lez-Montmirail.' *Nouvelle revue de Champagne et de Brie* 15 (1938): 236–49.

Poull, Georges. *La maison souveraine et ducale de Bar*. Nancy, 1994.

Powicke, F.M. *Stephen Langton*. Oxford, 1928.

Prevenier, Walter. 'La chancellerie des comtes de Flandre dans le cadre européen à la fin du XIIe siècle.' *Bibliothèque de l'Ecole des Chartes* 125 (1967): 34–93.

Richard, Jean. 'La chancellerie des ducs de Bourgogne de la fin du XIIème au début du XVe siècle.' In Silagi, *Landesherrliche Kanzleien*. 381–413.

Roserot, Alphonse. *Dictionnaire historique de la Champagne méridionale (Aube) des origines à 1790*. 3 vols. Langres, 1942–8. Reprint: Marseille, 1983.

Sassier, Yves. *Recherches sur le pouvoir comtal en Auxerrois du Xe au début de XIIIe siècle*. Auxerre, 1980.

Savetiez, Charles. 'Maison de Dampierre-Saint-Dizier.' *Revue de Champagne et de Brie* 17 (1884): 113–25.

Silagi, Gabriel, ed. *Landesherrliche Kanzleien im Spätmittelalter*. Munich. 1984.

Thacker, A.T., ed. *The Earldom of Chester and Its Charters: A Tribute to Geoffrey Barraclough* [*Journal of the Chester Archaeological Society*, 71]. Chester, 1991.

Trindade, Ann. *Berengaria: In Search of Richard the Lionheart's Queen*. Dublin, 1999.

Webber, Teresa. 'The Scribes and Handwriting of the Original Charters.' In Thacker, *The Earldom of Chester*. 137–51.

Weemaes, R. 'Les actes privées en Belgique depuis le Xe jusqu'au commencement du XIIIe siècle: étude diplomatique.' *Analectes pour servir à l'histoire ecclésiastique de la Belgique*, 3 série, t. 4 [34] (1908): 5–45, 305–40, 416–40.

INDEX RERUM

Numbers in roman type refer to items in the edition; numbers in italic refer to pages. Vernacular terms are also in italics.

INDEX NOMINUM

Numbers in roman type refer to items in the edition; numbers in italic type refer to pages. Abbreviations: dép. (département), ar. (arrondissement)

Table 1
The Counts and Countesses of Champagne

Hugh, 1093–1125
Thibaut II, 1125–52
Henry I, 1152–81
Marie, 1181–7 (regent)
Henry II, 1187–90
Marie, 1190–8 (regent)
Thibaut III, 1198–1201
Blanche, 1201–22 (regent)
Thibaut IV, 1222–53
Margaret, 1253–6 (regent)
Thibaut V, 1256–70
Henry III, 1271–4
Blanche of Artois, 1274–84 (regent)
Jeanne, countess and queen, 1285–1305

Table 2
Letters in the Chancery Archive Dated before 1188

Date	Author	Subject	Layettes	CR 1	CR 3,4	CR 7
Count Henry I, 1152–81						
1158	Count Henry I	A. of Sully's fief		46		
1160	Robert I of Dreux	Savignies fortress		1	3,4	
1162	chapter of Senlis	notification to count		64	3,4	
1165	Count Henry I	Jouy forest		32	3,4	7.1
1165	Count Henry I	Sourdun forest	1:185	39		7.1
1167	King Louis VII	Savignies	1:208			7.3
1168	King Louis VII	Giles of Seuil's fief	1:215			
1174	Count Henry I	gift by countess Marie				7.1
1176	King Louis VII	merchants of Brienne	1:270			7.1
1176	Count Henry I	gift to Reclus	1:271			7.1
1177	King Louis VII	Traînel's fortification	1:277			7.3
1177	Count Henry I	a mortgaged fief		82	3,4	
1177	Count Henry I	Robert of Mitoy's men				7.1
1179	Count Henry I	Raoul of Combault		45	3,4	7.1
1179	Count Henry I	commune of Meaux	1:299			7.1
Countess Marie, 1181–87						
1186	Countess Marie	Ferté-Louptière	5:90	37		7.1
Count Henry II, 1187–90						
1187	Count Henry II	dispute over dependents		44		
1187	Abbot of St-Oyand	*pariage* over Sermaize	1:347	74	3	

A bolded date indicates an extant letter in the Archives Nationales.
Layettes (volume, edition number): letters existing in the chancery archive when it was transferred to Paris in the fourteenth century.
CR 1 (edition number here): letters copied into the extant folios of the Cartulary of 1211 (CR 1).
CR 3,4: letters copied into comital cartularies CR 3 and CR 4 (1222–24).
CR 7: letters copied into the comital cartulary CR 7 (1271).

Table 3
State of the Cartulary

In 1211 (Quires)	In ca. 1222 (Folios)	In 1232 (Quires)	In 15th century (KK 1064: folios)	Edition (numbers)
1	[I–VIII]	(30)		
2	[6 folios–] IX–X[1]	23	254–255	54–62
3	[4 folios–] XI–XIIII[2]	33	256–259	63–89
	[XV–XVI]		259bis[3]	90–91
4	XVII–XXIII [XXIIII]	(34)	260–266	92–122
5	XXV–XXXII	31	238–245	1–53

[missing folio]
(missing quire number)
1 The first six folios of this quire were missing at the time of the original foliation (see 54).
2 Folio XIIII is the last folio of a quire.
3 The left half of a single folio.

Table 4
Authors of the Letters

	1158–97	1198–1201	1201–11	1212–14	Total
Lay persons					
King				2	2
Count(ess) of Champagne	7	4	1	2	14
Duke, count	1	3	14		18
Baron, lady		3	22		25
Other			3		3
Subtotal	8	10	40	4	62
Religious persons					
Pope, legate		2	2		4
Archbishop, bishop	1	4	12		17
Abbot, prior	1	4	16	3	24
Dean of chapter	1	1	10	1	13
Military order			1		1
Subtotal	3	11	41	4	59
Total	11	21	81	8	121

Table 5
Subjects of the Letters

Subject	1158–97	1198–1201	1201–11	1212–14	Total
Homage		1	1		2
Castles					
Renderable	1		2		3
M*ouvance*			5		5
Fiefs					
Grant		2	1		3
Mouvance	1				1
Sale, mortgage, exchange	3	2	10		15
Dowry, dower		1	1	1	3
Subtotal	5	6	20	1	32
Lordship					
Pariage	1	4	6	2	13
Dependents, safeconduct	2	1	13	1	17
Property rights	2	3	18	1	24
Debts		4	10	1	15
Over religious persons	1	2	8		11
Subtotal	6	14	55	5	80
Succession of Thibaut IV			5	2	7
Spiritual matters		1	1		2
Total	11	21	81	8	121

Table 7
Transactions Described in the Letters

Type	1158–97	1198–1201	1201–11	1212–14	Total
Grant	1	8	8	1	18
Sale, mortgage, exchange	3	3	23	1	30
Quittance, receipt		3	3		6
Recognition, consent, warranty	3	3	26	1	33
Agreement		2	6	1	9
Dispute resolution	1	1	10	3	15
Notification, directive	3	1	5	1	10
Total	11	21	81	8	121

CHRONOLOGICAL TABLE OF THE LETTERS

Date	Author	Subject	Number[†]
Count Henry I, 1152–81			
1158	Count Henry I	Archambaud of Sully's fief	46
1160	Robert I, count of Dreux	fortress of Savignies	1
1162	dean of chapter at Senlis	notification to Henry I	64
1165	Count Henry I	Jouy forest regulations	32
1165	Count Henry I	Sourdun forest regulations	39
1177	Count Henry I	a mortaged fief	82
1179	Count Henry I	purchase of fiefs	45
Countess Marie, 1181–87			
1186	Countess Marie	*mouvance* of La Ferté-Louptière	37
Count Henry II, 1187–90			
1187	Count Henry II	dispute over dependents	44
1187	Bernard, abbot of St-Oyand	pariage over Sermaise	74
Countess Marie, 1190–98			
[ca. 1194]	Simon, bishop of Meaux	Henry II's gift	107
Count Thibaut III, 1198–1201			
1198 April	Count Thibaut III	homage to the king	App. 1
[1198–1201]	Hugh, abbot of Essômmes	thanks for a grant	59
[1198–1201]	Guillaume, archbishop of Reims	Avenay's license to elect	108
1198	dean of St-Pierre of Troyes	cloister's immunity	92
1198	Count Thibaut III	fief to Raoul Plumquet	*122
[1199–1201]	Guillaume, count of Vienne, Mâcon	payment of fief-rent	49

[†]A bold edition number indicates an extant original document. An asterisk indicates a text added to a completed quire after October 1211.

Date	Author	Subject	Number
[1199–1201]	Octavian, papal legate	Henry II's debts	80
1199 July	Geoffroy V of Joinville	restrictions on tenants	14
1199 July	Guillaume, archbishop of Reims	Queen Adele's wardship	68
1199 November	Michel, archbishop of Sens	Henry II's debt	73
1199 December	Pierre, papal legate	Marie's debts	78
1199 December	Guillaume, archbishop of Reims	exchange of revenues	93
1200	Odo III, Duke of Burgundy	Thibaut III's homage	6
1200 February	Gautier III, Count of Brienne	exchange of villages	18
1200 May	Jean I of Montmirail	wife's new dower	11
1200 October	Milo, abbot of Châtrices	forests to Thibaut III	43
1200 October	Milo, abbot of Châtrices	forests to Thibaut III	100
1200 October	Count Thibaut III	Neuville-au-Pont franchise	*114
1200 October	Count Thibaut III	Neuville-au-Pont pariage	*115
1201 January	Count Thibaut III	grants Gillancourt in fief	12
1201 February	abbot of St-Martin of Troyes	hospital of St-Abraham	69
1201 March	Jean I of Brienne	village of Fontaine-Mâcon	29
Countess Blanche, 1201–22			
[1201–1211]	prior of St-Martin-des-Champs	response to a royal order	60
1201	Pierre, archbishop of Sens	debts owed Blanche's Jews	72
1201 August	Geoffroy V of Joinville	Thibaut III's bequest	8
1202	Archambaud II of Sully	grandfather's fief-rent	34
1202	Odo, bishop of Paris	father's fief-rent	86
1202	Nicholas, dean of Bray	Blanche's prebends	106
1202 December	abbot of St-Martin of Epernay	sale of a woman	40
1203 January	Nicholas, dean of Bray	Blanche's prebends	77
1203 February	abbot of Saint-Jean of Laon	advocacy of Ventelay priory	95
1203 March	bishops of Beauvais and Meaux	Blanche's prebends at Bray	109
1203 June	Countess Blanche	tax rights at Baudement	36
1203 July	abbot of St-Jean-des-Vignes	exchange of revenue	63
1203 September	Henry III of Grandpré	*mouvance* of St-Jean-sur-Tourbe	13
1203 November	dean of St-Pierre of Troyes	exchange of dependent women	111
1204	dean of St-Pierre of Troyes	resolution of dispute	35
1204 January	Hugh, castellan of Vitry	pledge for a debt	50
1204 March	Pierre, count of Auxerre	arbitration of safeconduct	28
1204 November	Odo III, duke of Burgundy	a confiscated fief-rent	27
1204 December	abbot of St-Vanne of Verdun	*pariage* over Chaudefontaine	105
1205	Pierre, count of Auxerre	safeconduct	30
1205	Simon, abbot of Cormery	sale of woods	41
1205	Renaud, dean of Villemaur	pariage over his villages	84
1205	abbot of St-Médard of Soissons	pact with knights of Villegruis	99

Date	Author	Subject	Number
1205 April	Jean of Brienne	sale of Fontaine-Mâcon	22
1205 May	prior of Cluny	spriritual benefits for Blanche	57
1205 June	Anselm, bishop of Meaux	sale of forest rights	*87
1205 July	Anselm III of Traînel	Villeneuve is renderable	(*90)15
1205 July	Hermesend of Traînel	Villeneuve is renderable	*91
1205 July	dean of St-Quiriace of Provins	taverners exempted from tax	76
1205 September	Hugh IV of Broyes	surety for mother's debt	24
1205 October	Pope Innocent III	prohibits taxing Templars	*89
1205 November	Guy II of Dampierre	exchange of dependent women	3
1205 December	Renier II of Nogent-en-Bassigny	prenuptial agreement	10
1205 December	Robert, bishop of Langres	inheritance of Chaumont	55
1205 December	Robert, bishop of Langres	escheat of Chaumont	96
1206	abbot of St-Remy of Reims	pariage over Villiers	94
1206/7 March	dean of Châlons-sur-Marne	St-Julien of Courtisols	56
1206 April	Thibaut I, count of Bar-le-Duc	exchange of tenants	2
1206 April	Robert II of Dreux and Braine	La Fère, Torcy fortresses	4
1206 July	abbot of St-Vanne of Verdun	pariage over Chaudefontaine	54
1206 August	Milo of Pougy	pledge	52
1207 September	Amalvin, abbot of La Sauve-Majeur	pariage over La Neuville	98
1207 December	Iter, dean of St-Etienne	Blanche's dependent man	85
1208 January	Hospitallers	pariage over Esnouveaux	101
1208 February	Robert, bishop of Langres	sale of house to Blanche	42
1208 May	Simon of Châteauvillain	liege homage	5
1208 May	abbot of St-Martin of Epernay	exchange with Blanche	83
1208 August	Pierre of Joigny	a 300 *l.* rent	26
1208 August	Renaud of Dammartin	accepts arbiters	33
1208 August	Manasses, abbot of St-Loup	exchange of women	58
1208 October	Geoffroy, bishop of Meaux	minting of coins	110
1208 November	Anselm III of Traînel	sale at Pont-sur-Seine	9
[1209–1210]	archbishop of Canterbury	rights at Chablis	104
1209	Garnier III of Traînel	sale at Pont-sur-Seine	19
1209	Odo III, duke of Burgundy	rights at Chablis	23
1209	Guillaume, count of Sancerre	declares liegeance	47
1209 March	Robert II of Dreux and Braine	fortress at Lizy	25
1209 April	Isabelle of Châteauvillan	exchange of tenants	20
1209 May	Jean and Helvide of Montmirail	debt of 1,300 *l.*	51
1209 June	Bertrand of Ste-Menehould	sale to Blanche	67
1209 July	Simon of Passavant	Montreuil is renederable	102

Date	Author	Subject	Number
1209 July	King Philip II	treaty with Blanche	App. 2
1209 July	Countess Blanche	treaty with king	App. 3
1209 September	Odo III, duke of Burgundy	king's treaty with Blanche	48
1210	Guillaume of Nanteuil	sale of fief	31
1210	Geoffroy, prior of La Charité	sale of dependents	97
1210 January	Guillaume, bishop of Langres	king's treaty with Blanche	65
1210 January	Guillaume, bishop of Langres	king's treaty with Blanche	*120
1210 January	abbess of Fontevraud	Foissy's debt to Blanche	103
1210 April	Alberic, archbishop of Reims	king's treaty with Blanche	38
1210 May	Henri of Sorcy	sale of Dormans	70
1210 June	Guy II of Dampierre	a Jew's debt	7
1210 June	Guy II of Dampierre	castle of Beaufort	53
1210 September	Geoffroy, abbot of Chézy	Blanche's grant	79
1210 October	Odo III, duke of Burgundy	agreement on Jews	17
1210 November	Gautier of Vanault	sale of viscounty of Cuis	66
1210 November 22	Pope Innocent III	king's treaty with Blanche	*61
[1211]	notice	Hermesend of Traînel's debts	*117
1211	Guillaume, provost of Chablis	sale of provostship	71
1211 January	Odo III, duke of Burgundy	sale of Gillancourt	16
1211 February	Elizabeth of Châteauvillain	sale of Baudement castle	21
1211 April	Milo of Nanteuil, canon	use of a village fief	81
1211 October	dean of St-Pierre of Troyes	exchange of women	75
1212 February	Henri, abbot of St-Denis	exchange of dependent men	*112
1212 February	Henri, abbot of St-Denis	Blanche's rights at Nogent	*113
1212 October 1	Countess Blanche	widow of Grandpré's rights	*116
1212 October	dean of chapter of Reims	La Neuville-au-Pont	*118
1213 January	abbot of St-Remi of Reims	pariage over Villeneuve	*119
1213 November	Countess Blanche	15,000 *l.* owed to king	*121
1213 November 21	King Philip II	treaty with Blanche	*62
1214 July	King Philip II	notice to Templars	*88

www.ingramcontent.com/pod-product-compliance
Lightning Source LLC
Chambersburg PA
CBHW021011120726
47905CB00009B/2966